DEVELOPING READING COMPREHENSION

The Essential Library of PreK–2 Literacy

Sharon Walpole and Michael C. McKenna, *Series Editors*
www.guilford.com/PK2

Supporting the literacy development of our youngest students plays a crucial role in predicting later academic achievement. Grounded in research and theory, this series provides a core collection of practical, accessible resources for every teacher, administrator, and staff developer in the early grades. Books in the series contain a wealth of lesson plans, case examples, assessment guidelines, and links to the Common Core State Standards. Issues specific to each grade—and the essential teaching and learning connections between grades—are discussed. Reproducible materials in each volume are available online for purchasers to download and print in a convenient 8½″ × 11″ size.

Reading Intervention in the Primary Grades:
A Common-Sense Guide to RTI
Heidi Anne E. Mesmer, Eric Mesmer, and Jennifer Jones

Developing Word Recognition
Latisha Hayes and Kevin Flanigan

Developing Vocabulary and Oral Language in Young Children
Rebecca D. Silverman and Anna M. Hartranft

Developing Fluent Readers:
Teaching Fluency as a Foundational Skill
Melanie R. Kuhn and Lorell Levy

Developing Reading Comprehension:
Effective Instruction for All Students in PreK–2
Katherine A. Dougherty Stahl and Georgia Earnest García

Teaching Beginning Writers
David L. Coker Jr. and Kristen D. Ritchey

Developing Reading Comprehension

EFFECTIVE INSTRUCTION FOR ALL STUDENTS IN PreK–2

Katherine A. Dougherty Stahl
Georgia Earnest García

Series Editors' Note by
Sharon Walpole and Michael C. McKenna

THE GUILFORD PRESS
New York   London

© 2015 The Guilford Press
A Division of Guilford Publications, Inc.
370 Seventh Avenue, Suite 1200, New York, NY 10001
www.guilford.com

Printed in the United States of America

This book is printed on acid-free paper.

Last digit is print number: 9   8   7   6   5   4   3   2   1

Library of Congress Cataloging-in-Publication Data
Stahl, Katherine A. Dougherty.
   Developing reading comprehension: effective instruction for all students in preK–2 /
Katherine A. Dougherty Stahl, Georgia Earnest García.
      pages cm—(The Essential Library of PreK-2 Literacy)
   Includes bibliographical references and index.
   ISBN 978-1-4625-1976-7 (paperback)—ISBN 978-1-4625-1977-4 (hardcover)
   1. Reading comprehension—Study and teaching (Elementary)   I. García, Georgia
Earnest.   II. Title.
   LB1573.7.S73 2015
   372.47—dc23
                                                                        2014031145

About the Authors

Katherine A. Dougherty Stahl, EdD, is Clinical Associate Professor of Reading at New York University (NYU), where she serves as Director of the Literacy Program and teaches graduate courses. In addition to teaching in public elementary school classrooms for over 25 years, she has extensive experience working with struggling readers in clinical settings. Her research focuses on reading acquisition, struggling readers, and comprehension. Dr. Stahl is the author or editor of several books, and her articles have appeared in leading journals of research and practice. She is a recipient of the Jeanne S. Chall Visiting Researcher Award from Harvard University and the Teaching Excellence Award from the NYU Steinhardt School of Culture, Education, and Human Development.

Georgia Earnest García, PhD, is Professor Emerita in the Department of Curriculum and Instruction at the University of Illinois at Urbana–Champaign. She served on the National Literacy Panel on Language-Minority Children and Youth and the RAND Reading Study Group on Skillful Reading, and was Associate Editor of the *American Educational Research Journal*. Her work has been published in leading academic journals. Dr. García was previously a bilingual/ESL/English teacher at the elementary, middle school, high school, and community college levels. Although retired, she continues to work with teachers and schools and conduct research on the literacy development, instruction, and assessment of students from diverse cultural and linguistic backgrounds.

Series Editors' Note

No one doubts the importance of fostering reading comprehension in the primary grades. In our experience, however, it is a destination without a clear path. Teachers in the primary grades are challenged by the need to serve students who vary widely in their command of English, their decoding proficiency, and their experiential background. Their development as comprehenders depends on a teacher's ability to recognize these differences and plan instruction that is both flexible and cohesive. Providing teachers with the guidance they need to do so is no easy task. This is why it is rare to discover a book that addresses, thoroughly and well, so many of the essential aspects of comprehension instruction. In this book, Stahl and García do exactly that!

As master teachers themselves, they understand the concerns of the contemporary classroom, and they write in clear, accessible terms that any professional will appreciate. As accomplished researchers, they summarize current thinking about comprehension development and evidence-based instruction. Their writing is punctuated with examples, analogies, and vignettes that make abstract ideas come to life in the form of down-to-earth, practical applications.

The authors begin by laying the conceptual foundation needed to understand when and why some practices are more effective than others. Upon this foundation they then build the know-how that teachers will need to answer a host of pressing questions:

- Which approaches will enable you to meet the text complexity challenges of the Common Core?
- How can you scaffold students while gradually transferring responsibility to them?

- How do you ensure the comprehension development of English learners?
- What are the most effective ways of planning teacher read-alouds and shared reading?
- How can you foster comprehension of informational texts?
- What are the best ways of incorporating multiple texts, including visual sources?
- What is the proper role of strategy instruction?
- How can you plan higher-order discussions that move children beyond the literal level and into the realm of inference and evaluation?
- How can you use text-based writing activities to develop comprehension and writing proficiency simultaneously?
- Which assessments can provide the information you most need to plan instruction and monitor its impact?

Not only do Stahl and García address these issues with care and insight, they do so with the detail necessary to implement new approaches. As you study each chapter, you will be able to contrast your present with your potential practice. And isn't this process at the heart of all professional development?

SHARON WALPOLE, PhD
MICHAEL C. MCKENNA, PhD

Preface

The fundamental goals of reading are making sense of text, using text purposefully, and critically analyzing text. When caregivers read engaging picture books to toddlers, they introduce them to the world of reading by encouraging them to make sense of the books read to them. Unfortunately, instruction in the primary classroom tends to focus on foundational skills, such as sound–symbol correspondence and decoding, making reading less engaging and limiting the emphasis on comprehension. Recent research and the Common Core State Standards (CCSS) for English Language Arts provide the impetus for teachers of young children to give comprehension the instructional attention that it requires and deserves.

However, providing effective comprehension instruction is not easy (Durkin, 1978–1979). Comprehension instruction in the primary grades is complicated by the need to balance time for teaching the foundational skills, using both complex texts and simple texts that children can read independently, and supporting children as they acquire the speaking and writing skills they need to effectively communicate their comprehension. Teachers also have to take into account developmental considerations, such as young children's short attention span, limited world experiences, and minimal ability to self-regulate their behavior.

Our goal in this book is to describe the instruction that children need to help them transition from learning from their own experiences to learning from text, and from developing listening comprehension to reading comprehension. We provide descriptions of research-validated practices that can be implemented in preschool to second-grade classrooms so that children improve their comprehension and can articulate their understanding in both oral and written formats. Additionally, this book provides recommendations to help teachers support emergent bilinguals (children who know one language at home, but who are acquiring English at school, often called English learners), dialect speakers, and children from diverse cultural and linguistic backgrounds. We also focus on children who require something extra to overcome meaning-making hurdles.

This year, as we visited classrooms in multiple states, we heard many similar comments as teachers worked diligently to align their instruction with the CCSS. We heard teachers celebrating the reading accomplishments of their young students. A common exclamation was "I had no idea that they could handle such hard texts, actually enjoy them, and talk about them with true understanding." However, teachers also shared their anxiety and tales of sleepless nights worrying about meeting the needs of young children who often required more time, more individual assistance, and more specialized support than what was delivered. We hope that this book will serve as a guidebook for providing practical, research-based instructional tools that can be used to help *all* children achieve their highest potential.

The book is organized around the essential elements of an inclusive model of comprehension that we introduce in Chapter 1. Consistent with the RAND Reading Study Group's (2002) definition of reading comprehension, the reader plays an active role and is at the center of the comprehension process. The reader is the meaning maker and the communicator of what he or she has comprehended. The outer circle of the model constitutes the contextual factors that contribute to the comprehension process. The contextual factors include the content of instruction, the texts, and how the experience is scaffolded. The middle circle denotes the instructional components needed to enable students to achieve their highest potential in understanding text and in communicating their understanding to others.

Our book begins with a broad discussion of the most important theoretical underpinnings of reading comprehension. The role of development and its influence on the comprehension of young children is explored. Chapter 1 summarizes the research findings related to comprehension instruction in the primary grades. We hope that you will take a few moments to complete the Teacher Self-Assessment and Goal Setting form on page 9 to make your reading of this book more personalized.

Chapter 2 takes an in-depth look at the unique needs of emergent bilinguals, dialect speakers, and other students from diverse cultural and linguistic backgrounds. This chapter reviews the research that can help teachers distinguish between instructional practices that are likely to meet the needs of all students and alternative practices that will bolster the comprehension of students from diverse cultural and linguistic backgrounds.

Chapters 3 and 4 address the elements in the outer circle of our essential elements model that create the learning context to support comprehension instruction. In Chapter 3, we address the four instructional reading contexts (read-aloud, shared reading, guided reading, and independent reading) that constitute the structural framework for an effective literacy schedule regardless of the specific literacy program being used. This framework provides the scaffolding that children need to interact successfully with texts that vary in content, genre, and readability. Chapter 4 describes the processes that you can employ to create concept-rich, engaging curriculum units that support the development of world knowledge and vocabulary. These disciplinary units need to be taught in sustained ways that lend themselves to student engagement. Chapters 3 and 4 identify the essential elements that promote high levels of comprehension for all students.

In Chapters 5, 6, and 7, we provide detailed descriptions of instructional processes and classroom examples that will enable you to help students make sense of text and to clearly communicate their invisible, in-head thinking to others. These three chapters provide the nuts and bolts of what good comprehension instruction should consist of, look like, and sound like. We provide information on how to conduct effective strategy instruction, support children's engagement in productive discussions, and help children create strong written compositions and projects that reflect high levels of comprehension. These chapters include vignettes drawn from the classrooms that we have visited to give you a clear picture of how these research-validated techniques look in practice. In each chapter, considerations for English learners are also described.

Assessing the reading comprehension of young children is often done holistically without providing the specific information that teachers need to inform their instruction. In Chapter 8, we provide a range of developmental assessments that you can use with children before they are formally reading, as they learn to read, and when they become fluent readers. We include recommendations and forms to improve the reliability of common comprehension assessments like retelling. Mindful of the CCSS, we identify tools that teachers can use to assess children's comprehension of stories, informational texts, and videos. With an eye to the future, we discuss the development of common formative assessments and the role of Lexiles. As in the other chapters, we delineate considerations for using assessments with English learners and with other students from diverse cultural and linguistic backgrounds. We include several reproducible forms at the end of this chapter so that you can conveniently put these practices to immediate use.

In Chapter 9, we discuss how to identify children who are likely to need support beyond what the typical classroom teacher can provide. We describe several research-validated instructional protocols that may be used with young children in preschool to second grade. We provide research-based recommendations that have the potential to change the reading comprehension trajectory of some children even before they receive formal reading instruction.

   We have tried to create a practical guidebook for teaching young children who are transitioning from listening comprehension to reading comprehension. In writing the book, we wanted to be sensitive to the realities of a teacher's life in a busy classroom while also being sensitive to the range of experiences and knowledge that young children from diverse backgrounds bring with them. We hope that our book will help you to increase your children's level of thinking, engagement, and comprehension. We welcome your feedback, and hope to hear from you as you begin to implement the practices we recommend.

Contents

Purchasers can download and print
larger versions of the forms
from *www.guilford.com/stahl3-forms*.

CHAPTER 1

Unifying Theory, Research, and Practice

GUIDING QUESTIONS

- How does the development of comprehension differ from the development of constrained skills such as letter recognition and phonics?
- How do pressure points (decoding, reading fluency, vocabulary, self-regulation, memory, and world knowledge) interact to influence a reader's comprehension?
- What essential elements must receive deliberate attention in the creation of an all-inclusive comprehension curriculum for young children?

A principal task of formal education is to train a nation's citizens to make sense of text and effectively communicate that understanding to others. The RAND Reading Study Group (2002) defines comprehension as the "process of simultaneously extracting and constructing meaning through interaction and involvement with written language" (p. 11). As classroom teachers in the primary grades, our role is crucial in both setting the course for comprehension instruction and ensuring that children have opportunities to think literally, inferentially, and critically about many different types of text, and to express that thinking through verbal and written formats.

Today we know that comprehension instruction must occur from the very beginning, even well before the child begins to read. The youngest children need opportunities to be "code breakers, meaning makers, text users and text critics" (Muspratt, Luke, & Freebody, 1997, p. 95). However, we must acknowledge that developmental considerations need to dictate our instructional choices and our allocation of time during the instructional day. These considerations are the focus of this book.

What's Development Got to Do with It?

Constrained Skills Theory

The abilities that contribute to reading comprehension begin to develop long before a child accurately reads his or her first word on a page. The development of narrative, the understanding and expression of temporal relationships, concept categorization, and the ever-increasing collection of world experiences all influence the dynamic and ongoing growth in one's ability to comprehend text (Kintsch, 1998; Nelson, 1996). Unlike foundational skills (such as letter identification and phonics), which are acquired to mastery levels over a relatively short time period, comprehension and vocabulary development occur across a lifetime.

Constrained skills theory (Paris, 2005) proposes a continuum of skills ranging from high to low levels of constraint (see Figure 1.1). These levels are reflected developmentally, conceptually, and by measurement. Letter identification and phonics are highly constrained because they are mastered quickly, as they consist of a relatively small number of items that are fairly stable once mastered. For example, the letter v has a consistent sound whether in a nursery rhyme or in a medical journal. This consistency and the limited size of the set of items make constrained skills easy to assess.

Phonological awareness and fluency are considered moderately constrained. Fluency tends to develop rapidly across several years, typically reaching a plateau somewhere between third and fifth grade. Before then, factors such as text difficulty and content may greatly influence the rate and expressiveness of reading. Individual differences in highly constrained and moderately constrained skills only exist for a short developmental span and they tend to be codependent. For example, letter recognition differences exist among children in kindergarten, but not by the middle of first grade. Knowledge of letter recognition tends to be related to particular measures of phonological awareness and early phonics skills. However, these abilities have little to do with wider curricular and subject-area knowledge bases. Knowledge of the world has little influence on children's knowledge of the

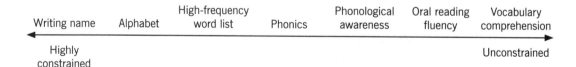

FIGURE 1.1. Continuum of constraint.

letters of the alphabet, nor does their knowledge of the alphabet relate to their ability to explore information about the world around them.

However, unconstrained abilities like comprehension and vocabulary are more difficult to quantify because improvement happens over time and does not reach clear, consistent levels of mastery. There are always new words to learn, more challenging texts to comprehend. Acquired across a lifetime, proficiency varies by text difficulty, genre, task, and instructional context. The differences between constrained and unconstrained skills result in implications for instruction, curricula, and assessment. Reading comprehension instruction must incorporate different types of text across the curriculum for a range of purposes and within a variety of contexts. Unlike constrained skills, comprehension and vocabulary knowledge do have broad transfer to world experiences and curriculum. What readers know about the world influences their ability to comprehend, and in a reciprocal way, how much and how well a person reads increases his or her knowledge of the world. As with constrained skills, explicit instruction is called for, but it is not enough due to the different demands of each task. Scaffolding must be employed over time as a teacher gradually releases responsibility to the child (Pearson & Gallagher, 1983).

Assessment of unconstrained skills is more complicated than assessment of constrained skills and must incorporate multiple sources of evidence. Both oral and written representations must be collected to provide measurable evidence of in-head processes. To gain a comprehensive picture, comprehension assessment also needs to incorporate different types of text. And as children transition from the early grades to intermediate grades, it is important to determine whether differences in comprehension exist between oral and silent reading.

The Role of Thresholds: A Multiple-Component Model

One of the challenges of early reading instruction is dedicating time during a school day to the foundational skills in an explicit, systematic way while still allocating the time needed for rich comprehension instruction. We cannot deny the importance of the foundational skills such as word recognition, phonological awareness, and reading fluency. However, we believe that foundational skills and fluency are necessary but not sufficient for high levels of reading comprehension.

Instead, we adhere to something closer to the notion that skill thresholds among multiple components interact in nonlinear, unequal ways according to the proficiency of the reader and the demands of the text. "In the multiple component model of comprehension, each component must meet a threshold value for minimal comprehension to occur. However, various components, such as decoding, vocabulary and fluency, do not have to be 100% accurate for some comprehension to occur" (Paris & Hamilton, 2009, p. 46). We believe that this theory is crucial in considering the comprehension of a developing reader. It takes into consideration the component skills that are still developing, compensatory techniques that novices may use to fill gaps or support weaknesses, and gradations in the possible level of understanding. Perfetti and Adlof (2012) refer to these components as pressure points. Even when children demonstrate mastery in basic word-recognition skills, there are likely to be individual variations in the depth of comprehension that can be enhanced by scaffolding and instructional context. For example, children who have a great deal of prior knowledge and interest in a topic may be successful in comprehending a text that is written about that topic even though it is a *stretch text* that is slightly beyond their identified reading level. Engaging with complex text requires that children monitor their reading and engage in a range of strategic practices that are likely to require explicit instructional attention and guided practice to enable comprehension at the highest levels of interpretation, inference, and critique.

The Common Core State Standards (CCSS) for English Language Arts (National Governors Association [NGA] Center for Best Practices & Council of Chief State School Officers [CCSSO], 2010) call for children at all grade levels to be reading a wide range of texts, many of which would be too difficult for many children to read on their own. However, your knowledge of your students' abilities allows you to introduce stretch texts to readers while providing the right level of support to maximize both comprehension and continuing development of particular pressure points. Sensitive, knowledgeable teachers know when to use shared reading as opposed to the read-aloud to accelerate student development. Just the right book introduction, a timely prompt, and carefully crafted questioning can transform a frustration-level text to a manageable reading experience for a novice reader.

Using What We Know: Basing Practice on Existing Research

A deliberate approach to comprehension should not be delayed until foundational skills are in place. At this point we want to reiterate that accurate, fluent word-identification skills make a crucial contribution to reading comprehension. We do believe that each primary classroom needs to devote a portion (30 minutes) of the literacy block to explicit, systematic word study instruction. Dedication to an effective method of word-identification instruction ensures that the majority of children master these skills quickly and that the dominant literacy block time allocation is devoted to the difficult task of teaching unconstrained skills: vocabulary, comprehension, and process writing of literary and informational texts. However, the best way to nurture the high-level thinking that is required in later years is to hold children accountable for thinking deeply about rich text in the early years.

The listening comprehension and the comprehension of video presentations by preschool children predicts their reading comprehension in elementary school (Kendeou et al., 2006; Lynch et al., 2008). Before children begin reading on their own, it is beneficial to prompt them to recall and verbally recount the narrative flow of experiences, video presentations, and stories heard. Recognizing the temporal, causal structure of events is an important prerequisite to reading comprehension and can easily be taught and practiced before children are reading formally on their own. Preschool settings and homes can adopt these practices in deliberate, yet naturalistic and developmentally appropriate ways.

Historically, much of the research on reading comprehension was conducted in the intermediate grades, once students' reading abilities were firmly established. For many years, Chall's (1996; Chall & Jacobs, 1983) stage theory influenced the instructional emphasis across the school years. Stage theory was fairly exact in demarcating linear reading stages. Instruction was focused on learning to read in the early grades, followed by the development of fluency that led to reading to learn content material in the intermediate grades. However, a theoretical transition to the concept of emergent literacy and research on comprehension in the primary grades has expanded our knowledge of the capabilities of young readers and what constitutes developmentally appropriate practice. Most recently, the policy implications of the CCSS (NGA & CCSSO, 2010) include an increased emphasis on reading a wide range of texts for meaning, knowledge acquisition, and evaluation in the primary grades. By combining insights gleaned from recent research with the content standards presented in CCSS, we discuss instructional practices that can be used to support the developing reading comprehension of our youngest readers.

Essential Elements

We have created a model that represents the essential elements that should be considered in the design of an all-inclusive comprehension curriculum for young children (see Figure 1.2). Although the circles are displayed as separate layers, they are likely to overlap and influence each other.

Context

In the outer circle, we have contextual factors that influence all comprehension instruction. We present only a brief overview here of how these elements work together, as each of the topics will be covered thoroughly in its own chapter.

In a reading clinic setting, tutors have the luxury of matching student interests with text reading and activities. However, in a classroom it is neither possible

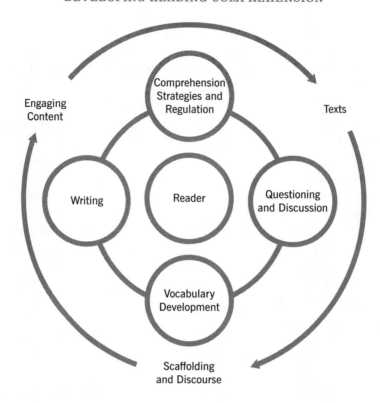

FIGURE 1.2. Model of an all-inclusive comprehension curriculum for young children.

nor desirable to teach each child his or her own self-selected content curriculum. Nevertheless, it is easy to generate student enthusiasm through our own attitudes as teachers and through our approaches to teaching mandated content. In order to expand children's knowledge of the world and to stretch their reading and writing abilities, it is best to build literacy experiences around sustained units of themed disciplinary study whenever possible. By disciplinary study, we are referring to units that combine reading and writing objectives with those in literary forms, social studies, and science. In these ways, we can generate interest in a topic through classroom community activities and read-alouds. Additionally, the vocabulary becomes familiar through repetition, and sustained exposure to specific prose styles supports fluent reading, expanded writing, and oral language development.

It is appropriate and important for even young children to begin to belong to multiple Discourse communities. Gee (1990) distinguishes between discourse (language in use) and Discourse (with a capital *D*). According to Gee, Discourse is a particular way of using language that is representative of a way of thinking, feeling, and valuing, and that identifies one as being an insider within a specific social network. At the most basic level, there are differences between children's primary Discourse, that conversational register learned at home from families, and the Discourse used in storybooks and in classroom discussions of storybooks. The Discourse employed when one reads, writes, evaluates, or discusses literary texts differs from the Discourse of science texts and social studies texts. For example, when we evaluate literary texts, we consider author craft, themes, and the expression of the universal human experience. A small-group discussion of a scientific experiment contains different linguistic elements and analyses than a discussion of a literary text. Instructional contexts that teach literacy through disciplinary units allow for immersion into each disciplinary Discourse style.

There is time across a sustained unit to provide explicit instruction, engage in teacher and student modeling of complex reading and writing processes within a particular genre or text category, and guide and refine student practice. Finally, children engage in their own reading and writing to create independently produced products that enable them to share extended knowledge of a subtopic as an expert in both the content and the literacy processes.

Processes Requiring Instructional Attention

The reader is at the center of our comprehension model. He or she brings existing prior knowledge, mental processing, vocabulary, oral language, and writing abilities to the instructional setting. All of these factors influence the degree to which a reader is able to comprehend text. Attending to these components strengthens the comprehension process. Additionally, since comprehension is an in-head process, we are reliant on a child's ability to create oral and written responses as gauges of comprehension.

There are several instructional practices that do have a strong research foundation in formal school settings for the emergent and novice reader (Shanahan et al., 2010; Stahl, 2004). Shanahan and colleagues (2010) reviewed over 800 studies conducted in the primary grades and selected 27 that met rigorous research standards. Based on an analysis of these studies, they offered five recommendations for teaching comprehension in the primary grades (see Table 1.1). Some practices were included despite minimal evidence because of their potential for developing critical literacy and high levels of thinking. Consistent with our model, this set of practices is most effective when used collectively.

Conclusion

Comprehension develops across a lifetime. Changes over time in children's biosociocultural development and ever-increasing bank of experiences result in changes in reading comprehension capabilities. Capable decoding, language processes, vocabulary, and prior knowledge are pressure points that contribute to

TABLE 1.1. Evidence-Based Practices for Comprehension Instruction in the Early Grades

Recommendation	Evidence
Teach students how to use comprehension strategies.	Strong
Teach students to identify and use the text's structure to comprehend, learn, and remember content.	Moderate
Guide students through focused, high-quality discussion on the meaning of text.	Minimal
Select texts purposefully to support comprehension.	Minimal
Establish an engaging and motivating context in which to teach comprehension.	Moderate

Note. Based on Shanahan et al. (2010, p. 9).

comprehension thresholds. There is evidence that instruction that supports the development of these pressure points improves reading comprehension. Effective comprehension instruction calls for attention to strategy development, high-level discussion, vocabulary development, and writing within an engaging context that includes exposure to a wide variety of texts.

Self-Assessment

Before reading this guidebook, we encourage you to self-assess your comprehension instructional practices by completing Form 1.1 (at the end of the chapter). This is an opportunity to think about how you currently teach comprehension in your primary classroom. It is a means to assess strengths, identify components that are in place, recognize curriculum voids, and highlight urgent needs. You may identify some changes that you want to make immediately, such as a few minor adjustments that will increase your instructional effectiveness. Other changes may require a long-term plan and professional development support. We encourage you to work with your school and your district to recruit additional support.

Teacher Self-Assessment and Goal Setting

	No	To some extent	Yes	Rank top three goals
Comprehension instruction dominates my literacy block.				
Comprehension instruction occurs within a content-driven, engaging context.				
I use a wide variety of texts that are chosen deliberately to support instructional themes and stretch student thinking.				
I implement large-group and small-group discussions about text every day.				
I provide explicit, sustained strategy instruction.				
I explicitly facilitate children's use of verbal and written expression to reflect their thinking about texts.				
My instruction with diverse learners is informed by research on these populations.				

CHAPTER 2

Comprehension Considerations for Students from Diverse Linguistic and Cultural Backgrounds

GUIDING QUESTIONS

- What are the general theoretical assumptions and reading comprehension findings that apply to students from diverse backgrounds?
- What do we specifically need to know about the reading comprehension development and instruction of English learners?
- What do we specifically need to know about the reading comprehension development and instruction of dialect speakers?
- What else do we need to know about the reading comprehension development and instruction of students who attend high-poverty schools and whose cultural and economic backgrounds differ from the general population?

If you have noticed that your school and classroom are becoming increasingly diverse in terms of ethnicity/race, home language or dialect, and socioeconomic status (SES), then you are not alone. According to the *Condition of Education* (Aud et al., 2013), the percentage of Anglo (non-Latina/o white) students between 2000 and 2010 declined from 61 to 52%, while the percentage of Latina/o students increased from 16 to 23%. The African American population declined slightly from 17 to 16%. Projections indicate that sometime between 2016 and 2021 the percentage of Anglo students will be less than 50% due to the increase in Latina/o and Asian students. Although not all English learners (students who know a language other than English at home, but who acquire English at school) are served in bilingual or English as a second language (ESL) classrooms, the percentage of students who received specific instruction due to their status as English learners increased from 9 to 10% between 2002 and 2011, with the majority identified as Spanish speakers. In 2011, approximately 21% of all school-age students (ages 5–17) lived in poverty, compared with 15% in 2000.

Our purpose in this chapter is to discuss what the changes in U.S. student demographics mean for classroom teachers who want their students to excel in reading comprehension. Before we begin our discussion, however, it is important to acknowledge that most of the reading research that influences U.S. reading practices is based on investigations of middle-class, native English-speaking, Anglo students, who we refer to as the general student population. While much of this research is applicable to the reading comprehension development and instruction of students from diverse backgrounds, some of it is not. We have organized our discussion so that we first address the theoretical assumptions and findings derived from research with the general population that apply to the reading comprehension development and instruction of students from diverse backgrounds. Next, we discuss the theoretical assumptions and instructional findings specific first to English learners and then to dialect speakers. We conclude the chapter by focusing on what else we think classroom teachers need to know about the reading development and instruction of students who attend high-poverty schools and who are from cultural and economic backgrounds distinct from the general population.

Common Reading Comprehension Assumptions and Findings

Students from diverse backgrounds appear to use many of the same processes as the general student population to decode and comprehend English text (Adger, Wolfram, & Christian, 2007; García, 2003). For example, both types of students use graphophonic (sound–symbol), lexical (vocabulary), semantic (meaning), syntactic (language structure), and textual and background knowledge (schemata) to decode and comprehend English text. Students who use an interactive approach, in which they integrate textual clues with background knowledge about the text, topic, activity, and themselves as readers, usually comprehend better than students who overrely on a bottom-up approach (driven largely by textual clues) or a top-down approach (guided largely by background and context). Students' comprehension of English text also appears to be enhanced when they are taught to use metacognitive strategies (e.g., talking about what they plan to do next while reading) and cognitive strategies (e.g., predicting, summarizing, visualizing, asking and answering inferential questions, and seeking clarification) during the act of reading according to the demands of the text, the task or activity, and what they know about themselves as readers. We know that teachers' use of high-level talk or high-level questions about text (e.g., open-ended and collaborative discussions about a theme or universal issue) can lead to the increased reading comprehension performance of low-income students from a range of backgrounds (Taylor, Pearson, Clark, & Walpole, 2000; Taylor, Pearson, Peterson, & Rodriguez, 2003). Last, the sociocultural context in which reading and its instruction takes place is a major influence on students' reading comprehension in terms of their motivation to read, engagement, perseverance, and identity as readers (Snow & Sweet, 2003). Yet, in spite of the similarities in processes and instruction, students from diverse backgrounds generally perform less well on standards-based or standardized assessments of their English reading comprehension compared with the general population (Aud et al., 2013).

Issues Specific to English Learners

As we pointed out previously, English learners are children who know one language at home and who are in the process of acquiring another language, English, at school. It is highly likely that English learners are thinking in two languages and interacting with text in two languages across home and school, even when the instruction they receive at school is only in English. For this reason, we use the term *bilingual children* interchangeably with *English learners* throughout this chapter. In fact, English learners who take advantage of their emerging bilingualism while reading English text often offset comprehension problems that they may encounter due to their second-language status. Several researchers have reported that bilingual children younger than age 6 display heightened metalinguistic awareness about literacy tasks that could enhance their reading development (García, 2000).

The Role of Reading in the Home Language

When English learners develop reading skills in their home or native language (L1), they can often use these skills to effectively comprehend English text. In a review of research focused on the reading development of bilingual learners in grades K–2, García (2000) reported that reading in the home language was a stronger predictor of students' second-language literacy than their second-language oral proficiency. Although bilingual children can learn to read and write in two languages at the same time, initial reading instruction in the language students know best (usually their home language or L1) can prevent any type of cognitive confusion that might occur when young students do not understand their teachers' English reading instruction.

Continued instruction through the L1 at school also helps English learners to develop grade-level academic and cognitive knowledge as they acquire English. With the L1 instruction, they do not fall behind in their academic work as they wait for their oral English proficiency to develop. In fact, authors of a recent meta-analysis found that Spanish speakers (the largest group of English learners) who received reading instruction in both Spanish *and* English had significantly higher English reading test scores than other Spanish speakers who only received reading instruction in English (Francis, Lesaux, & August, 2006). Program evaluations of different types of bilingual education and ESL programs also have confirmed these findings. For example, Rolstad, Mahoney, and Glass (2005) reported that English learners enrolled in all types of bilingual education programs outperformed those enrolled in ESL programs or all-English classrooms on English academic measures. English learners enrolled in developmental bilingual education programs, in which students were taught literacy in the home language and English throughout elementary school, outperformed English learners enrolled in transitional bilingual education, in which students initially were taught in their L1, but moved to all-English instruction as quickly as possible, usually by the end of second or third grade.

Although current findings indicate that English learners do best in U.S. schools when their bilingualism and biliteracy development are supported at school (Francis et al., 2006; Rolstad et al., 2005), we understand that not all English learners are provided with these opportunities. States such as Arizona, California, and Massachusetts have approved state legislation that limits or opposes bilingual education. Many of you may be working with English learners in less than ideal situations. Our aims in this chapter and book are to provide those of you who work with English learners in a range of classroom contexts—all English, ESL, bilingual—with the theoretical and applied knowledge you need to promote the students' English reading comprehension.

Academic Language versus Social Language

One reason why English learners may perform better on academic measures in English when they continue to receive instruction in their L1, along with ESL instruction, compared with English learners in English-only settings, is that the former students have been given the time and content knowledge they need to develop cognitive academic language proficiency (CALP) in English. According to Cummins (1981), CALP is the academic language skills that English learners need in order to learn new content material taught in English. In contrast, basic interpersonal communication skills (BICS) are the social language skills that English learners need to communicate with others in daily life (e.g., on the playground, at school, to shop). Cummins and other researchers explain that English learners generally need 4–7 years of quality bilingual instruction to develop their CALP in English, but only 1–3 years of school instruction in an English setting to develop their BICS. CALP includes the type of academic language development emphasized by the CCSS for all students.

Cross-Linguistic Transfer

Another reason why English learners benefit from reading and content instruction in the home language is cross-linguistic transfer. Cross-linguistic transfer refers to the use of skills, strategies, or knowledge acquired in one language in another language. Unfortunately, not all English learners demonstrate cross-linguistic transfer. Cummins (1986) proposed that students who acquired a high level of cognitive expertise in one language (usually the L1), and who were adequately exposed to the other language, would be able to make use of the expertise acquired in one language to approach the other language.

A number of researchers have found evidence for bilingual children's cross-linguistic transfer in several areas related to literacy. For example, several researchers have found that the phonological awareness and word-recognition skills of young bilinguals in Spanish or French are strong predictors of their phonological and word recognition performance in English (Comeau, Cormier, Grandmaison, & Lacroix, 1999; Durgunoğlu, Nagy, & Hancin-Bhatt, 1993). Others have reported that bilingual children who have text-structure knowledge in one language, such as understanding how a fable is organized (Goldman, Reyes, & Varnhagen, 1984), can use this knowledge in the other language without any formal instruction. One of us (Georgia) and her colleagues (García, 1998; Jiménez, García, & Pearson, 1996) found that bilingual children who used cognitive strategies in one language while reading also used them in the other language, indicating cross-linguistic transfer.

Bilingual Strategies

English learners often use strategies unique to their bilingual status to interact with and respond to English text. For example, if young children (PreK–2) are in a context where they know that the teacher or other classroom participants know their L1, then they are likely to use it to answer questions about English text or to discuss it with each other. When they use their L1, they typically give a more complete accounting of what they have understood or have learned about English text because they are not limited by their developing oral English proficiency. They also may code mix (use a word from one language while speaking in the other language) or code switch (alternate sentences in the two languages) while speaking to each other or while responding to English text. Georgia discovered that when bilingual students code mixed or code switched, they often demonstrated greater comprehension of English text (García, 1998, 2003). In light of these findings, we do not want to discourage students' use of code mixing or code switching.

Another bilingual strategy that young English learners, beginning in grade 2, may be able to use involves cognates (García, 1998). Cognates are words in two languages with an ancestral history (e.g., Spanish and English, German and English), and that look similar and have similar meanings. Sometimes the cognates are identical in appearance and meaning, but different in pronunciation, such as *animal* in English and Spanish. Other times they vary in both appearance and pronunciation, such as *lamp* and *lámpara* in English and Spanish, respectively. When children recognize the cognate relationship, they can often use the known word to figure out the unknown word in the other language.

However, the use of cognates by English learners is not automatic, and as classroom teachers we need to encourage English learners to use them. Even when we do not know the L1, we can ask English learners to identify cognates when they hear or see them. We also can work with bilingual adults and students to list cognate pairs relevant to our classroom readings and curriculum on bulletin boards or white boards.

Differences in Word Recognition of Decoded Words

Although English learners can be just as successful as native English speakers in decoding English text (Lesaux & Geva, 2006), they generally do not comprehend English text as effectively as native English speakers (Snow, 2006). An underlying assumption of beginning decoding instruction for native English speakers is that the vocabulary items the children decode in text are part of their oral vocabulary and already known to them. When native English speakers sound out a word, they automatically recognize the word's meaning, enhancing their comprehension of the text. However, English learners typically do not recognize or know the meanings of all the English words they can decode because not all the words are in their oral English vocabulary (García, 2003).

As classroom teachers, we need to make sure that we do not separate decoding instruction from comprehension instruction because when we do so, English learners may not realize that the goal of decoding is to comprehend text. To offset this problem, we need to make sure that English learners know the meanings of the English words they are learning to decode. We can do this by combining vocabulary instruction with decoding instruction for key words unfamiliar to English learners as well as by providing decoding instruction for words that they already know.

Differences in Syntactical and Grammatical Knowledge

Because English learners are not native English speakers, they may have difficulty with syntactical structures in English that are not present in their home language. For example, Asian speakers often have problems saying or orally reading gender designations (such as *he* and *she*) and verb tenses or endings (such as past tense *-ed* and the gerund *-ing*) in English (García, 2003). The structures need to be taught, but as classroom teachers, we should accept the fact that even accomplished adults who once were English learners may have difficulty producing these structures in their speech, oral reading, or writing. English learners often understand English at a much higher level than they can say or write it. Instead of insisting that children use the appropriate structure while speaking or reading English text, it would be better to find out if they understand that the character is male or female or that the action occurred in the past rather than in the present.

Grammatical items may be marked differently in the L1 and English. For example, quotations in Spanish are indicated with dashes rather than quotation marks. Questions are indicated with an inverted question mark at the beginning of the sentence, along with the same question mark that we use in English at the end. When we, as classroom teachers, know the differences in syntactical and grammatical structures in the L1 and English, then we can better help our students focus on comprehension by knowing how and when to teach and correct the differences. ¿Do you not agree?

Cultural Differences in Background and Vocabulary Knowledge

In a study with older Spanish-speaking and English-speaking students (fourth and fifth graders), Georgia reported that the Spanish-speaking students were less familiar with the topics and vocabulary in English standardized reading test passages even though the two groups of students had been instructed together in the same classrooms for the past 2 years (García, 1991). She found that when the Spanish-speaking students read passages for which they had the appropriate background knowledge, there was no significant difference in their test passage performance. Georgia also reported that the Spanish-speaking average and low readers answered fewer inferential questions correctly compared with the English-speaking average and low readers. When the Spanish speakers knew the vocabulary items in the test questions, they often applied a different interpretation to the vocabulary item than what the author of the test passage had expected. For example, the Spanish speakers knew the meaning of *handicapped* as an adjective, such as "handicapped" children, but did not understand the term when it was used as a noun or as a trade limitation, as illustrated in the following test question (García, 1991, p. 383):

22. A serious handicap for growth in trade is
    a. a lack of streams
    b. few harbors
    c. icebound harbors
    d. overproduction

When Georgia interviewed one of the Spanish speakers about her interpretation of the term *handicap* in terms of the correct answer (c: icebound harbors), the student replied [English translation in brackets], "Porque los handicapped no pueden pasar por allá. ¿Cómo pasear un niño por allá? Tendrá que balancearse" [Because the handicapped can't go through there. How could a child walk through there? He would have to balance himself] (García, 1991, p. 383).

To make sure that Georgia's findings are not duplicated in grades K–2, as classroom teachers we should give English learners opportunities to read and discuss texts for which they have and do not have appropriate background knowledge. By doing so, we are giving English learners the opportunity to read and discuss stretch texts, as recommended in the CCSS. However, to scaffold English learners' comprehension of these stretch texts, we need to show students how to tap into their background knowledge; at other times, we will need to spend time building the appropriate background knowledge for our students. We also need to provide English learners practice on how to answer a range of comprehension questions that involve identifying the answer in the text, making an inference across several paragraphs of the text, and combining appropriate background knowledge with knowledge in the text. It would also help to open our instruction to find out how our English learners are interpreting key vocabulary and the author's intention. This will clarify any misinterpretations and show students how to implement an interactive approach to English reading by using both top-down and bottom-up strategies.

Making Instruction Comprehensible

When English learners are taught literacy in an English-speaking setting, it is important for teachers to shelter or scaffold their literacy instruction so that the children understand what is being taught. We don't have the space to review the various instructional programs that have been developed to help teachers of English learners make their instruction comprehensible (such as specially designed academic instruction in English [SDAIE] and the Sheltered Instruction Observation Protocol [SIOP]; Echevarría, Vogt, & Short, 2010). However, there are several principles (see the text box on the next page) that classroom teachers can remember and implement so that English learners understand the purpose behind instruction and how to follow directions. These principles can be implemented in a range of PreK–2 classrooms: general classrooms with only a few English learners enrolled along with native English speakers, ESL classrooms that serve only English learners, in the English component of bilingual classrooms, or in dual-language classrooms that serve both native English speakers and English learners.

When presenting new material, giving instructions, or reading a book aloud in English to beginning English learners, you should slow down the pace of your speech, clearly enunciate, and use controlled vocabulary, checking to see whether

PRINCIPLES FOR MAKING INSTRUCTION COMPREHENSIBLE

- For beginning English learners, slow the pace of speech, clearly enunciate, use controlled vocabulary, and check for understanding.
- Post and review literacy objectives in child-friendly language (Echevarría et al., 2010).
- Accompany verbal talk, instruction, and teacher read-alouds with gestures, illustrations, realia, physical demonstrations, hands-on activities, and modeling.
- Integrate reading, writing, listening, and speaking.
- Encourage students to work together in English and the L1 to figure out and complete instructional activities.

all your students understand what you are saying. You can facilitate students' comprehension of your oral speech or teacher read-alouds when you illustrate and act out what you are saying or reading by using gestures, photos, or illustrations; realia (actual objects); physical demonstration; and hands-on activities. For example, if you want your K–2 students to read to each other in pairs, we recommend that you post step-by-step instructions on the white board, then bring two children to the front of the room and model the instruction with the children as you explain to the class what you want them to do by pointing to the step-by-step instructions.

Posting and reviewing with K–2 students specific literacy objectives for the lesson or unit being taught will benefit English learners at all levels of oral English proficiency. When you post and review the literacy objectives in child-friendly language, you are clearly identifying the point or purpose of the lesson. For example, if you are teaching students how to identify the settings in picture storybooks, and asking them to work together to complete a graphic organizer to identify the timing of the story, the locale, and the season, you could post and review the following literacy objectives with the students before and after the lesson:

Literacy Objectives

1. Work with your partner to answer the questions about the setting in *The Polar Express*.
2. Choose the correct words to complete the sentences about when and where the story took place (e.g., seasons: fall, winter, spring, summer).

Because English learners are acquiring English at the same time that they are developing their literacy in English, it is helpful when classroom teachers identify the specific English language features or academic language demands, as indicated in objective 2 above, that are involved in students meeting the literacy objective. The process of identifying English language features or demands makes us aware of the specific features of English that we need to emphasize and teach to English learners so that they can complete our instruction and further develop their English (Echevarría et al., 2010). If you decide to take an ESL course, you will discover that within the ESL field, the second objective is called an English language objective, and often posted separately from the literacy objective.

Teachers in grades K–2 also should list what they say in writing as much as possible on a white board or blackboard, read it to the children, and have the children chorally repeat it or read it to you. For example, in kindergarten, if you are teaching about the community and key community locales, such as the hospital, post office, fire station, police station, and so on, you would post these words as you say them, and put a laminated magnetized illustration or photo of each locale by the respective word. Then, you would ask the children to use the posted words to respond to questions that you ask about the community locales. When you ask the children to copy what is posted or to use the posted words in their own writing, then you have provided them with multiple language cues and integrated listening, speaking, reading, and writing in the new language.

English learners may not understand everything that is said in the classroom, but by encouraging them to work together, they have more opportunities to figure out what is being said. Working together also means that they have more opportunities to use English and practice literacy with each other than sitting in the classroom watching you, the teacher, read, speak, or write, or waiting for you to work with them individually. Georgia found that when she allowed English learners to use their L1 to discuss English text, then they demonstrated much more understanding of what they had read (García, 1991, 1998, 2003).

Collaborative and Themed Disciplinary Content Instruction

Because English learners in grades K–2 often are in multiple instructional settings, it is important for teachers to collaborate across those settings. With this type of collaboration, you can discover what students understand and do not understand. If students are in three types of instructional settings (L1, ESL, all-English classroom), new content topics or concepts can be introduced in the L1 classroom so that English learners understand the new material. The ESL teacher can teach the students the key English words and syntactic structures for the new topic or concept introduced in the L1 classroom, and you, the general classroom teacher, can use the English words and syntactic structures taught by the ESL teacher to expand on the initial L1 instruction.

Themed disciplinary content instruction (as described in Chapter 4) that cuts across the different settings is one way to accomplish this type of collaboration. For example, a common theme taught in grades 1 and 2 is community. This theme would be the instructional focus across the varied language settings, so that the English learners would acquire the needed academic vocabulary and background knowledge in both the L1 and English. A typical cycle of instruction would involve introducing the community topic and key vocabulary in the L1 setting (or, if the L1 setting is not available, in the ESL setting), with the teacher in the next setting (ESL or general classroom) teaching the students how to use English to interact with the topic. If all three settings are available, then you, as the classroom teacher, would use English to expand on what the students already have learned, and the L1 teacher would make sure to use the L1 to review the new information presented in English before adding new content information.

Issues Specific to Dialect Speakers

According to linguists, no one in the United States speaks a "standard" or officially approved version of English because we do not have a national language or an official national language academy that promotes standardization (Adger et al., 2007). Although there is a version of academic English that is promoted in textbooks and in English classrooms, all of us speak a regional or social dialect of English, with phonological, syntactical, and lexical variations. Dialects, unlike slang, are fully formed, rule-governed systems that are fully adequate and effective for social communication and thinking (Adger et al., 2007; Lindfors, 1987). No one dialect is more viable than any other dialect. Nonetheless, some dialects of English are more respected than others, especially in U.S. schools, and the discrimination that dialect speakers face in school can impede their literacy development.

In this section, we deal with two dialect groups that, due to their regional and social origins and low SES, often do not receive the respect that they deserve in U.S. schools: speakers of African American Vernacular English (AAVE), often referred to as black dialect, and speakers of an Appalachian dialect. Much of what we say about these groups and their reading comprehension instruction also is applicable to other dialect groups in the United States, such as speakers of Cajun dialect, Hawaiian dialect, American Indian tribal dialects, and so on.

Linguists and educational researchers have investigated the low reading performance of dialect speakers in the United States and have concluded that the use of a dialect of English does not cause cognitive problems when students learn to read (Adger et al., 2007). Rather, the origins of the low reading performance of dialect speakers tend to be rooted in issues involving self-esteem, attitude, and instruction.

When teachers are unfamiliar with the dialect spoken by their students, they sometimes treat it as a deviant form of English. Yet, when children use their home dialect to read in English, it does not mean that the children have misunderstood what they are reading. In fact, accurate translation of the written English text into their own dialect actually demonstrates that they have comprehended the text, as indicated below (underlining indicates use of the AAVE dialect):

Text: *The cat eats. The dog eats. The man eats. They all eat.*

Deron reads: <u>Da</u> cat <u>eat</u>. <u>Da</u> dog <u>eat</u>. <u>Da</u> man <u>eat</u>. <u>Dey</u> all eat.

In the above example, Deron, in accordance with his use of AAVE, has pronounced *the* as "da"; dropped the third-person, present-tense marker on *eats*; and pronounced *they* as "dey." His correct use of AAVE to read the short passage shows that he understands what he has read.

Unfortunately, many teachers do not understand the importance of not correcting students' use of the home dialect when they are using it to read aloud. In the example below, Jason, a speaker of Appalachian dialect, does not understand what the teacher wants him to say when she corrects his pronunciation of the word *it*. The teacher, in turn, does not understand that Jason is reading the sentence correctly ("It will not go"), but in his dialect (*italics* show emphasis):

JASON: Hee-it wee-ll nat go.

TEACHER: No, *it* will not go.

JASON: Hee-it wee-ill nat go.

TEACHER: That word is *it*.

At the end of Jason's turn to read aloud, the teacher "turns to the researcher in the room, shrugs, and says, 'He can't get it'" (McIntyre & Turner, 2013, p. 137).

In the example below (Collins, unpublished manuscript, excerpted from Cazden, 1988, p. 87), Monica, an AAVE speaker, is focused on her oral reading and does not understand why the teacher is correcting her pronunciation of *garbage*. The constant interruptions make it difficult for her and the other students in the class to comprehend what is being read:

MONICA: And then he [TEACHER: Sound it out, *threw*] threw his bu, boat . . . into the [TEACHER: guh] gahbage can.

TEACHER: Garbage. Say *garbage*.

MONICA: Gahbage.

TEACHER: Don't say *gahbage*. Look at me. Say *garbage*. Gar. Say it. Everybody say it.

CLASS: Garbage.

TEACHER: Celena, say it.

CELENA: Garbage.

MONICA: (Continues reading, with teacher interrupting.)

TEACHER: She saw what he did. Now what did he do?

MONICA: He threw his things in the gahbage.

TEACHER: Garbage. Right. Go on.

Similar types of overcorrection occur when children use their home dialect to authentically communicate with their teacher and classmates. Most children do not incorporate their teacher's corrections into their speech, but withdraw and often internalize their teacher's view of them as incompetent. In the example below (Smitherman, 1986, pp. 217–218), Bernadette, an AAVE speaker, is trying to tell her teacher about a movie she and her mother saw, but gets frustrated with the teacher's constant corrections, and eventually stops talking:

BERNADETTE: Miz Jones, you remember that show you tole us bout? Well, me and my momma.

TEACHER: Bernadette, start again, I'm sorry, but I can't understand you.

BERNADETTE: (*confused*) Well, it was that show, me and my momma.

TEACHER: Sorry, I still can't understand you.

BERNADETTE: (Is silent and looking at the floor)

TEACHER: Now, Bernadette, first of all, it's Mrs. Jones, not Miz Jones. And you know it was an exhibit, not a show. Now, haven't I explained to the class over and over again that you always put yourself last when you are talking about a group of people and yourself doing something? So, therefore, you should say what?

BERNADETTE: My momma and me.

TEACHER: (*exasperated*) No! My mother and I. Now, start again, this time right.

BERNADETTE: Aw, that's okay, it wasn't nothin'.

We aren't saying that it isn't important for dialect speakers to learn the version of English being spoken and written in school. However, young children's dialect is part of their identity. The best way to work with young dialect speakers is to validate their use of the home dialect at the same time that we expose them to the school version of English (Adger et al., 2007; Perry & Delpit, 1998). This approach enables dialect speakers to develop strong self-esteem and to acquire a strong student identity as a reader. For example, as classroom teachers, we can make sure to include children's literature that uses dialect in the classroom library, make it available for children's independent reading, use it in a listening center, and allow dialect speakers to use their home dialect to share information and to write letters to family and friends and in journals. When we learn some of the features of the home dialect, then we can do teacher read-alouds of dialect literature, and include it for shared reading instruction.

With older children (beginning in second grade), you can provide authentic opportunities for dialect speakers to use the school version of English by using Readers' Theater or putting on plays with characters that speak the school version of English. Because actors are supposed to use the language and pronunciation of the characters, it is appropriate for you to help your students to speak like the characters. You also can specifically compare and contrast features of the home dialect and school dialect through the daily oral message, mini-lessons on writing, role playing, the analysis of different music genres (such as classical music vs. rap or hip-hop), a comparative analysis of the language used in letters to the editor versus letters to friends, and characters' use of dialects in television shows or the use of varied dialects by popular television and radio personalities (see Perry & Delpit, 1988). Because some of the syntactic structures in AAVE and in the written version of English at school are quite different, we suspect that explicit instruction on some of the structural differences might help AAVE speakers' reading comprehension (e.g., the use of *s* to show possession, the use of the third-person *s* to show present tense; Lindfors, 1987).

Other Issues Specific to Students in High-Poverty Schools and from Diverse Backgrounds

Students in high-poverty schools generally receive whole-class, teacher-directed, passive instruction, with a limited focus on reading comprehension (García, Bray, et al., 2006). Many times, there are too many students in the classroom for the teacher to easily implement small-group instruction. Other times, there are limited materials. However, as classroom teachers, we need to remember that it is important for children to spend considerable time reading, writing, and discussing texts rather than watching others do so, whether it is the teacher or other children. Similarly, students in high-poverty schools need access to high-quality instruction that teaches them how to improve their reading comprehension.

In a study with bilingual students in a high-poverty school district, Georgia and her colleagues (García, Bray, et al., 2006) described how a second-grade teacher succeeded in getting her students to use student-led small groups to discuss the flexible use of cognitive strategies while reading. The teacher first used teacher read-alouds of children's literature to introduce the students to the use of each strategy. Then, she gave them opportunities to identify and discuss the flexible use of strategies while working in the whole-class setting and in pairs. Later, she had them identify and discuss the use of strategies while reading guided reading books in student-led small groups. The small groups worked best when the teacher assigned students to serve as leaders for the groups, had students decide on rules for the small groups, and watched and discussed videos of other second graders working in small groups to discuss texts. For more information on how to implement strategy instruction, see Chapter 5.

It is also important to remember that all children acquire cultural practices, values, and knowledge from their families, and that schools in the United States tend to reflect the cultural practices, values, and knowledge that middle-class, European American teachers learned from their families (Diaz-Rico & Weed, 2010; Hernández, 1989; Lindfors, 1987). Differences in cultural practices include how questions are used, stories are told, children are taught to participate in conversations (e.g., interrupt, stay on topic, get a turn, gaze, request clarification), collaborate or compete, be punished and praised, obtain authority or respect, and so on (Hernández, 1989; Lindfors, 1987). When there is greater distance between home and school cultural practices, values, and knowledge, then "hidden" conflicts are likely to occur. Hernández (1989) uses the term *hidden curriculum* to highlight the fact that, as classroom teachers, we frequently are unaware of the cultural conflicts inherent in the practices, values, and knowledge that we expect all our students to display. We often do not realize that such practices, values, and knowledge are an ingrained part of our own cultural upbringing, and not always essential for effective teaching and student learning.

For example, Heath (1982) discovered that African American elementary-age children in the Carolina Piedmonts were not used to answering nonauthentic questions, questions for which teachers already knew the answers (e.g., "Who is the main character in the story?"), or questions that required students to analyze the attributes of objects and events (e.g., "What type of car did John want to buy?"). Yet, these were the very types of questions that the students' teachers used to shape their reading instruction. In contrast, the African American children were accustomed to using questions, such as requests for analogies (e.g., "What's that like?") and story-starter questions. These were high on Bloom's (1956) question taxonomy but were question types that the teachers rarely used. Heath worked with the teachers to create an intervention that provided the African American children with more opportunities to respond to the types of questions that they were accustomed to in their homes at the same time that the teachers created non-threatening opportunities for the children to learn how to respond to the questions that the teachers considered imperative for their instruction.

Au and Jordan (1981) shared an example from Hawaii that revealed that the teachers' practice of calling on individual students to answer set comprehension questions about basal reading selections did not lead to the high reading engagement and performance of native-Hawaiian students. A comparison of how the Hawaiian students effectively participated in their homes and community with what their teachers expected showed that there was a hidden conflict in the teachers' expectations for classroom participation. For example, in the Hawaiian community, the children were accustomed to working together to complete tasks without relying on adults' specification of rules or instruction for task accomplishment.

As teachers, we can begin to rectify the "hidden curriculum" problem (Hernández, 1989) by becoming informed about the cultural and linguistic practices and histories of the various groups of students who are in our classrooms and schools. We can read books and articles about the diverse groups; visit the communities in which our students live; and invite parents, family members, and community members into our classrooms to share their talents and knowledge. To avoid stereotyping, we recommend that teachers develop an "I wonder" stance, so that when students or parents from a specific group do not respond positively to a classroom practice or expectation, teachers reflect on what they personally expected, and compare their expected response with what they are learning about the specific group of students in their classroom. Then, we recommend that teachers address three questions before deciding on a course of action for addressing conflicts in cultural and linguistic practices:

1. "What can I change or how can I accommodate my instruction so that it is more culturally and linguistically appropriate for my students?"
2. "What do I need to do to build a bridge between what I expect and what the students expect?"
3. "What parts of my instruction need to stay but should be explicitly taught?"

The Heath case (Heath, 1982) and the Hawaiian case (Au & Jordan, 1981) illustrate how teachers can apply the above questions. For example, when the teachers in the two settings changed key parts of their reading instruction so that it was more culturally and linguistically appropriate for the students from diverse backgrounds, they were addressing the first question. When the teachers in the Hawaiian example purposefully chose to focus their reading instruction on basal reading selections with which their students could personally connect, then they were addressing the second question. Last, when the teachers in the Heath example created an intervention in which they gave their African American students nonthreatening practice in answering nonauthentic questions and explicitly told their African American students the purpose of these questions (e.g., they used them to assess how well the students understood what they were reading), they were addressing the third question.

Finally, Moll (2001) warns that if educators are serious about improving the instruction and performance of students from diverse backgrounds, then it is imperative for us to recognize that the cultural experiences of students from diverse backgrounds and those of their families historically have not been acknowledged and recognized in U.S. schools, making it difficult for the students and their parents to identify with the schools and their mission. One way to acknowledge the diverse experiences and knowledge of culturally and linguistically diverse students is to incorporate culturally specific literature into our reading instruction (Bishop, 1997; Harris, 2003). Using culturally specific literature (literature written by and about people from diverse backgrounds) would help students from diverse backgrounds see themselves, their families, and their communities reflected in the school curriculum. Its use also would give students from diverse backgrounds the opportunity to integrate their background knowledge with textual content, providing them with opportunities to make accurate inferences and to use an interactive approach for textual comprehension.

Conclusion

There are similarities and differences in how students from diverse linguistic and cultural backgrounds (such as English learners, dialect speakers, students who attend high-poverty schools) and the general population approach, process, and interact with English text. There also are similarities and differences in the recommended instructional practices. For example, English learners often think about text in both their L1 and English even when their school instruction only is in English. English learners who learn to read in their two languages and who continue to develop their L1 content knowledge throughout elementary school outperform those who only learn to read in English. One reason for this is that it takes English learners much longer to develop their CALP than their social language, and they need CALP to learn new content through the medium of English. Also, many English learners are able to use cross-linguistic transfer, along with bilingual strategies, to facilitate their academic development and reading comprehension in English.

To help English learners understand your instruction in English, you should use ESL sheltering techniques to make your instruction comprehensible, collaborate with their ESL and L1 teachers, and use thematic disciplinary content instruction. Because English learners don't always know the meanings of the English words they can decode, you need to combine vocabulary instruction with decoding instruction so that they understand that the purpose of decoding is comprehension. To promote their English reading comprehension, you should give them experience reading both familiar and unfamiliar topics, discover how they are interpreting vocabulary, and ask them a range of comprehension questions. Learning the structural differences between English and your students' home languages is helpful because then you are better prepared to teach and correct their use of syntactical structures in English.

Linguists have shown that no one dialect is better than any other dialect for communication and thinking, although the dialect spoken and written in school has the most prestige. When young dialect speakers (such as speakers of AAVE or an Appalachian dialect) use their home dialect to read English text aloud, they are demonstrating that they understand the English text and should not be corrected. Similarly, young dialect speakers should not be corrected when they use their home dialect for authentic oral communication. Constant correction of dialect speakers' oral reading or speech makes it difficult for the participating students to comprehend what is being read or said, and often leads to negative identity and self-esteem issues. Teachers can help their dialect speakers to learn the version of English used in school by validating their use of the home dialect through the incorporation of dialect reading materials into their classroom instructional activities, providing dialect speakers with positive opportunities for using the school version of English, and encouraging dialect speakers in second grade and above to compare and contrast the structure and use of the two dialects.

Students enrolled in high-poverty schools often receive whole-class, teacher-directed, passive instruction, which adversely impacts their reading comprehension. They need opportunities to read, write, and discuss texts rather than watch the teacher or other students do these tasks. Providing students with culturally specific literature is one way to motivate and engage them. There may be "hidden" conflicts among the cultural practices, values, and knowledge that teachers expect from their students, and those acquired by students from diverse backgrounds. Because many of the conflicts are not necessary for instruction or learning, we recommended that teachers take an "I wonder" stance, and find out what is appropriate within the respective cultural group. Once you understand the source of the conflict, then you need to take action by asking yourself: What can I change or accommodate in my reading instruction? What do I need to bridge? and What do I need to explicitly teach? In Chapter 3, we present instructional guidance on how you can support young children so that they develop their literate identities and comprehend a range of texts.

CHAPTER 3
. . . .
It's All About Scaffolding

GUIDING QUESTIONS
. . . .

- Why is the gradual release of responsibility an important pedagogical understanding for teaching reading comprehension?
- How does each instructional context allow for the gradual release of responsibility to students?
- How does utilizing the four instructional contexts provide students with the opportunities to read texts along a wide band of complexity every day?
- What are the functions of each instructional context?

Reading comprehension is never really mastered. There is always a text that stretches our meaning-making capabilities. As adults, our comprehension is often taxed when reading material is conceptually dense or addresses a topic that we know little about. A narrative might be difficult to understand if it doesn't follow a linear time sequence and jumps between different time periods. As adults, we often choose to join a study group or a book club to stretch our comprehension of texts or to expand our reading diet and perspectives. For example, many people who wish to gain a deeper understanding of their religion join a Koran, Talmud, or Bible study group. Participating in a teacher book club to discuss this book with your peers will yield more professional transformation than reading it alone on the beach, although that method is not without merit. Reading one of Oprah's popular book club selections guarantees that you will have opportunities for social interaction on compelling social issues.

The CCSS (NGA & CCSSO, 2010) call for students of all ages to read a wide range of complex texts. Often these challenging texts are beyond the reading abilities of many children in the classroom. Due to both the variety of text types and the range of text readability, the role of instructional support is important in developing increasingly sophisticated reading comprehension. Often as we work in schools, we hear teachers discussing the challenge of navigating the tension between providing children with opportunities to be independent problem solvers as opposed to exposing children to the complex texts that require a great deal of teacher support. These two seemingly contradictory positions leave teachers feeling torn and unsure of how to do what is best for their students. Finally, teachers struggle with doing it all within the time constraints of a school day.

Applying the Gradual Release of Responsibility

The gradual release of responsibility (GRR; Pearson & Gallagher, 1983) is an instructional tool that provides a continuum of support, with the teachers assuming responsibility for the task on one side and the students assuming the responsibility on the other side of the continuum (see Figure 3.1). There is evidence that this tool works well for comprehension instruction due to the complexity and multidimensional nature of comprehension processes. The GRR is related to the Vygotskian (1978) concept of the zone of proximal development (ZPD), defined as the distance between what a learner can do alone and what the learner can do with assistance. Initially, high levels of support are provided by a more knowledgeable other and over time the learner assumes increased responsibility for the task as he or she internalizes the language and behaviors associated with the task.

Task	Share of Responsibility for the Task				
Explicit Instruction					
Modeling					
Collaborative Use					
Guided Practice					
Independent Application					

[■] Students   [ ] Teachers

FIGURE 3.1. The gradual release of responsibility. Based on Duke and Pearson (2002), Pearson and Gallagher (1983), and Shanahan et al. (2010, p. 15).

The term *scaffolding* has been used to describe the instruction because it provides a temporary support system during the child's construction of knowledge. The GRR typically addresses four broad task categories that occur during this construction process: (1) I do it, (2) We do it together, (3) You (multiple students) do it together, and (4) You (single student) do it independently. In something as complex as comprehension, it is likely that children might be in different stages of this process depending on the type of text or task. By incorporating a range of instructional contexts that vary by level of teacher support throughout a school day, it is possible for children to successfully read texts that span a wide range of readability (see Table 3.1).

The Role of Scaffolding in Instructional Organization

When planning instruction, we need to intentionally balance the type and amount of teacher support provided during literacy instruction. This balance can be built into the daily schedule of activities (see Figure 3.2 and Appendices 3.1–3.3 at the end of the chapter). The schedule enables children to have opportunities each day for reading easy texts of their choosing, being held accountable for precise reading of books at their instructional level, and exposure to texts that stretch their minds. In this chapter we provide a detailed description of the different levels of scaffolding that occur in reading during the course of a literacy block. How to support children's written responses to reading are described in Chapter 7.

It is important to notice that the schedule in Figure 3.2 allocates a distinct 30 minutes of explicit instruction in phonological awareness, phonics, spelling, and high-frequency words that we refer to collectively as foundational skills (CCSS), phonics, or word study. Ideally, differentiation by developmental level as identified by a spelling inventory or phonics inventory occurs during the word study time

TABLE 3.1. Literacy Instructional Contexts Providing Most to Least Support

Reading	Responsibility	Writing
Teacher read-aloud	Teacher assumes responsibility with student participation.	Collaborative writing language experience (teacher holds the pen)
Shared reading	Responsibility is shared.	Interactive writing (teacher and child share the pen)
Guided reading	Child assumes responsibility with teacher support.	Guided writing (child holds the pen)
Individual reading	Child assumes responsibility and accountability.	Individual writing (child holds the pen)

	Time	Grouping	Text
Teacher read-aloud	15–30 minutes	Whole-class, heterogeneous	Complex text
Shared reading and writing	45 minutes	Whole-class, heterogeneous	Complex text
Guided reading and independent reading/writing	60 minutes	Small-group, differentiated	Instructional-level text
Word study—spelling/phonics	15–30 minutes	Differentiated	Ability-level activities

FIGURE 3.2. A primary classroom schedule.

block. It is imperative that children at this developmental stage receive explicit, systematic instruction in these skills (National Institute of Child Health and Human Development [NICHD], 2000). While these foundational skills must be mastered, they should not dominate the literacy block. Reading comprehension skills (and written and spoken responses to reflect comprehension) are more complex and require more time for instruction and practice than constrained skills. The CCSS K–2 standards reflect this comprehension emphasis. During word study children might read decodable texts that provide concentrated practice in specific words and patterns that have been taught. However, decodable texts are not appropriate for the instructional time blocks described below, including guided reading where children are expected to transfer decoding skills and orchestrate all reading processes with more natural, authentic text.

The Teacher Read-Aloud

The teacher read-aloud serves multiple key instructional functions in the early childhood classroom. Particularly for young children with limited word-recognition abilities, the teacher read-aloud is among the most important instructional time periods of the school day. In years gone by, some of us may remember being in darkened classrooms with children's heads on desks and many eyes closed during the teacher read-aloud. Teachers may have viewed it as a time of the day for "relaxing" with a good book or as a classroom management technique, useful for calming children after recess or lunch. Hopefully, teachers now recognize that read-aloud time is one of the best opportunities for nurturing comprehension skills in developmentally appropriate ways. The questions in the text box on the next page will enable you to do a self-check on the status of your current read-aloud practices and provide some ideas for setting goals for enhancing your current read-aloud procedures.

The teacher read-aloud is at the top of the GRR staircase because the teacher assumes the greatest share of responsibility for the activity. It is most commonly

READ-ALOUD TEACHER CHECK

- Are read-alouds supporting instructional themes?
- Are the books being read and reread in large- and small-group settings?
- Are the books later accessible to the students for personal reading?
- Do children have choice reading time daily?
- Do discussions include open-ended questions and questions that address characters' motivations, the relationship of plot sequences, and vocabulary development?
- Are strings of follow-up questions asked that provide the bridges that young children need to arrive at high levels of thinking?
- Is an implicit management style being used to increase time on task?

Note. Based on Dickinson, McCabe, and Anastasopoulos (2003).

conducted in a whole-class setting with challenging texts. However, in prekindergarten and kindergarten, time should also be allocated for small-group teacher read-alouds to support language development.

Building a Literacy Community

Bringing the whole class together around a common read-aloud text creates a literacy community. Many books are literary classics that all children at a particular developmental stage should be exposed to with discussion. Some books serve as anchors for literary or disciplinary units. These books should be read and discussed as a whole class during the read-aloud, so they might be referenced throughout the unit in classroom discussions. This is a setting for building engagement, excitement, and common knowledge surrounding the disciplinary content units. As classroom teachers we have an obligation to teach certain topics and to expand students' interests, knowledge, tastes, and beliefs. These texts often serve as introductions to well-known authors and book series, or as springboards for students to pursue further individual study or reading. The heterogeneity of the group is an asset as children share wide-ranging responses in the teacher-led instruction and discussion.

Introducing Challenging Texts

The teacher read-aloud is an ideal setting for introducing texts that may pose challenges for young children either in readability level, conceptual difficulty, or both. It is also the setting for introducing compelling, controversial, and sensitive topics that yield high-level discussion and critical thinking.

Young children are able to discuss and learn from texts that may be far too difficult for them to read independently. Books that have rich themes, sophisticated vocabulary, and new concepts are best introduced in a setting that provides strong teacher support. Books with enough grist for building new knowledge or exploring the depth of the human experience are often beyond the readability of the emergent or novice reader. Therefore, high-level comprehension instruction needs to occur during the teacher read-aloud.

Beautiful informational texts open the doors to building knowledge from text at a young age. Contemporary children's literature addresses the common human experiences of divorce, death, bullying, and physical disabilities. Children should be exposed to these topics under the guidance of a teacher who is able to serve as expert discussion leader, sensitive to the nuances of the children's responses. Children need to begin thinking critically about text and relating to the human experience in literary text at a young age so they know that those are among the purposes and the gifts of reading.

Instruction of Complex Thinking Processes

In order for children to apply higher-level thought processes such as inference, evaluation, and critique, texts must have compelling ideas. Children's initial responses to text may be at explicit levels. Or they may not even understand the explicit information stated in a text and be unaware that they missed key ideas. The read-aloud is the context for gathering all children together to present the explicit introductory strategy lessons. Teaching children to monitor their own comprehension, overcome meaning-making hurdles, and to analyze, synthesize, evaluate, and think critically about text requires repeated exposures of explicit instruction, teacher modeling, deep questioning, and sensitive prompting. The extensiveness of this process means that there are not enough hours in the school day to do this repetitively during individual conferences or small-group instruction. It must initially occur with rich text in a whole-class setting. Then follow-up of student application occurs in *both* small-group and individual settings.

Types of Read-Alouds

Not all teacher read-alouds are created equal. Research has determined that certain styles of reading or reader characteristics have been more or less effective in accomplishing particular aims. Additionally, some researchers have developed, studied, and refined particular read-aloud protocols to yield particular outcomes such as conceptual vocabulary development, language development, comprehension, or content knowledge acquisition. These protocols are particularly useful since the new CCSS bring high-level thinking and complex text to the forefront in the primary grades.

Dialogic Reading

Dialogic reading (Zevenbergen & Whitehurst, 2003) is a form of picture book read-aloud that is similar to a conversational read-aloud conducted by many parents of young children.

Protocols have been developed for reading to children as young as 2–3 years old, and more sophisticated protocols have been designed for children from 4 to 5 years of age. Our discussion will be limited to the latter. These protocols are based on the premise that guided practice in using language, specific feedback regarding language use, and scaffolded adult–child interactions around picture book read-alouds facilitate the language development of young children. Using these protocols results in greater language development than when adults simply read a book aloud to young children. Research has demonstrated that these techniques enhance language development for upper- and middle-SES children, but that they most strongly influence the language skills of low-SES children. Dialogic reading increases expressive and receptive vocabulary, the length of utterances, linguistic complexity of spontaneous child verbalizations, and print concept awareness.

It is important to note that, as with any protocol, the degree of effectiveness is directly related to fidelity to the protocol. Dialogic reading should be conducted for 10–15 minutes daily in small groups of no more than five children so that engagement can be maximized. Children of linguistic diversity are likely to get greater benefits if there are opportunities for them to engage with an adult in a one-on-one setting. Whitehurst and colleagues (1994) found that the strongest results can be achieved when parents are also trained using videos to conduct dialogic reading at home, so that children are participating in dialogic reading both at home and at school. Video training was more effective than asking parents to attend a single training session conducted by a teacher or some other form of "live" training. Providing parents with videos (or DVDs) enabled them to repeatedly view many models of adults and children engaging in the read-aloud procedure.

The dialogic reading protocol for children ages 4 and 5 years old centers on asking particular types of questions, evaluating student responses, supporting the children in expanding and refining their responses, and then having the children repeat those refinements or elaborations. Its purposes and procedures are highlighted in the text box on the next page. PEER is an acronym that provides a reminder of the goals of the read-aloud (prompt, evaluate, expand, and repeat). CROWD is an acronym used to help adults remember the types of questioning prompts that should be used during the read-aloud (completion, recall, open-ended, Wh-, and distancing).

Neuman (1996) determined that different types of texts yielded different types and amounts of talk. So you should strive for a balance of predictable text, narratives, and informational texts to provide variety and to stretch children's responses.

As with all read-alouds, it is important to remember that the dialogic read-aloud should be enjoyable and well paced, and that every page need not be

DIALOGIC READING PROTOCOL

Dialogic reading is an adult read-aloud protocol that was designed to promote language development for children between the ages of 3 and 5 years old. It is most effective when conducted individually or in small groups.

Purposes

Increase expressive and receptive vocabulary, expand the length and linguistic complexity of children's responses to texts.

Overview: PEER

- *Prompt* the child to discuss the story, ask questions to encourage further discussion.
- *Evaluate* the child's responses. Use praise generously and reference specific behaviors. Use discussion to refine labels or to scaffold misunderstandings or misrepresentations of the text.
- *Expand* the child's comments through repetition and elaboration.
- *Repeat* by shaping the conversation so that the child has the opportunity to repeat the refinements and elaborations without making the dialogue slow or forced.

Prompts to Facilitate Rich Dialogue: CROWD

- *Completion* prompts: fill-in-the-blank statements or questions (e.g., "The three fruits on this page are _____").
- *Recall* prompts: recalling what has been read (e.g., "Can you remember some places where Spot's mother looked for him?").
- *Open-ended* prompts: require the child to generate his or her own words and structure to tell something about the book (e.g., "Tell me what has happened so far in the story").
- *Wh-* prompts: *what, where*, and *why* questions (e.g., "What is the name for this animal?" "Why do you think Sally is hiding?").
- *Distancing* prompts: questions that require the child to connect the events of the book to life outside the book ("Tell me about a snowy day that you remember").

Note. Based on Whitehurst et al. (1994).

discussed. Your purpose should be to enrich the children's experience with the book, not exhaust all possibilities. Comprehension and vocabulary development can only happen if the children are engaged. If they have tuned out because the discussion has dragged on too long and the dialogue has become a teacher monologue, the lesson is over. Monitor the energy and engagement of the children and adjust accordingly.

Performance Reading

In a study of preschools, Tabors, Snow, and Dickinson (2001) found that one of the most effective styles of teacher read-aloud was what they referred to as the *performance approach*. Unlike the dialogic approach, these teachers did minimal talking during their animated, energetic reading of the text. Teachers applying the performance approach made the picture books come to life through the use of pitch, volume, pacing, characters' voices, and facial expressions. Some unfamiliar vocabulary was briefly defined and children might be asked to predict what would come next during reading. However, extensive discussion occurred after reading, when the children were asked to recall, analyze, and evaluate the text. These effective teachers used an *implicit management* style. Rather than constant reminders to pay attention, raise hands, and follow class rules, these teachers used eye contact, dramatic reading, questioning, and conversational devices to hold the students' attention. As a result, these preschool children sustained their focus on the story and successfully participated in thoughtful discussions. Such discussions address characters' motivations, describe how story events are linked, and analyze the meanings of words. Another important characteristic of effective discussions is the use of follow-up questions in response to the children—questions that yield multiple, connected conversational turns that progress to higher levels of thinking. These features of the performance, along with using the sheltered ESL techniques described in Chapter 2, make this style of read-aloud a good fit for English learners.

Text Talk

Text Talk (Beck & McKeown, 2001) is a teacher read-aloud procedure with a strong research validation for English-speaking children in kindergarten through second grade. The protocol ensures that children are making sense of the language of texts and expanding their vocabulary. Due to the reliance on using language to construct the meaning, we do not recommend using this complete protocol for English learners who may not have the language skills necessary to understand the text.

Text Talk calls for you to ask high-level questions and to explicitly teach sophisticated vocabulary. The text box on the next page describes the procedure for planning a Text Talk lesson. One of the unique features of this read-aloud is the

TEXT TALK READ-ALOUD

Text Talk (Beck & McKeown, 2001) is a structured teacher read-aloud that was designed to promote comprehension and language development for students in kindergarten through second grade. It is used with texts that are rich in language and content.

Purposes

Enhance comprehension; develop vocabulary and language; provide a bridge to decontextualized language.

Procedure

1. Select an intellectually challenging text.
2. Provide a *targeted* prereading discussion to activate prior knowledge.
3. Ask open-ended questions during text reading. Provide follow-up questions to the children's responses to achieve deeper processing and higher levels of thinking. Ask a few open-ended general questions at the conclusion of the book.
4. Pictures. In general, pictures are presented after the children have heard and responded to the particular page of text. Children need to be prepared for this change in procedure.
5. Vocabulary is explicitly taught after reading. Three to eight vocabulary words are selected from the text. Children should know the concept or meaning of the word, but not this particular word as typically used by a sophisticated language user (e.g., *amber, bellow, stroll*). Words should be high-utility words so that multiple exposures are possible during the upcoming weeks. Words chosen are *not* disciplinary-specific words that require conceptual development. Children repeat the word. The teacher rereads or discusses the word's use in the book. The word is defined for the children. The teacher provides a few examples of word use in other contexts. The children are invited to use the word in a sentence. The vocabulary is put on an incentive chart that records the use of the words by the children in speaking or writing during the next week (Word Wizard).
6. This type of read-aloud is likely to be used two or three times a week.

display of illustrations following the reading or discussion of each page rather than while the page is being read. This format requires the listeners to pay attention to decontextualized language. Decontextualized language describes things that can't presently be seen, heard, or experienced. Many children will develop this ability through language experiences in the home when families share personal narratives around the dinner table, recount the events of their day, or exchange family stories. However, research evidence indicates that there are differences by income group in the amount of decontextualized talk that occurs in homes (Hart & Risley, 1995). Children in advantaged homes (in this case, children of college professors) had greater opportunities, with parental scaffolding, to develop extended narratives. Children in low-income families heard fewer words spoken to them and fewer elaborative sentences. Most of the talk was essential talk around the daily functions of life as they were happening. Therefore, read-aloud experiences that provide opportunities for interpreting and applying decontextualized language are essential in the early childhood classroom as a prerequisite to reading comprehension.

Elaborated vocabulary instruction occurs after reading. Beck and McKeown (2001) recommend that you select between three to eight words from the text. They categorize the words to be selected as Tier Two words. Children should be familiar with the concepts represented by these words in their L1 or English, but do not know the actual words that represent the specific concepts. For example, they know what it means to tell someone they're sorry, but they may be unfamiliar with the word *apologize*. The teacher models the pronunciation of the word and provides a child-friendly definition together with several oral examples of usage. All children pronounce the word and a few children are invited to create sentences. It is important to mention that all of the instruction after reading takes place orally, so that children will have an opportunity to hear the words being used in multiple sentences that situate the words in different contexts. This format for vocabulary instruction is an excellent technique for teaching vocabulary more broadly for general reading comprehension. If you are using Text Talk with English learners (or this effective vocabulary instruction protocol), then we recommend that you show the words and sentences in print as you explain them, being sure to use illustrations, photos, or gestures to demonstrate the meanings of the selected vocabulary.

The Text Talk lesson plan in the text box on the next page is a script written by a kindergarten teacher for her read-aloud of *In November* (Rylant, 2000). Most teachers find that writing a detailed lesson plan such as this one enables them to craft the best questions, identify the most useful Tier Two vocabulary, and provide precise definitions and example sentences for the vocabulary. The distractions in a classroom often prohibit this level of effective spontaneous execution, so many teachers find that writing themselves a detailed script or cheat sheet is helpful. Primary-level students have short attention spans so every moment of the read-aloud time block is precious. Plus these lessons can then be taped on the inside of the book or in a file, revised for improvement, and reused the following year. Time well spent one year saves time in the future.

Informational Text Read-Alouds

Children enjoy read-alouds about real things in the world just as much as they enjoy their favorite storybooks. Informational books are especially engaging when

Text: *In November* by Cynthia Rylant (2000)

Common Core State Standards

- Speaking/Listening K2: Confirm understanding of a text read aloud or information presented orally or through other media by asking and answering questions about key details and requesting clarification if something is not understood.
- Language K4: Determine the meaning of unknown and multiple-meaning words and phrases based on kindergarten reading and content.
- Language K5: With guidance and support from adults, explore word relationships and nuances in word meanings.

Set

"Today is the first day of November. Today I am going to read the book *In November* by Cynthia Rylant. This book is about many things that happen in the month of November. Raise your hand if you can tell me about something that happens in November. What else happens in nature in November? Today as I read I want you to think about what is happening in the story and make a picture in your mind before I show you the picture. After I finish reading a page and I can tell that you have a picture in your mind or we have talked about what's happening, I will show you the picture that the illustrator drew."

Implementation Procedure

- Read page 1.
  - Ask, "What picture did you draw in your mind?"
  - Follow-up: "What words by the author helped you make that picture in your mind?"
- Read page 2.
  - Ask, "What does the author mean when she says that the trees spread their arms like dancers?"
- Read page 3.
  - Ask, "Why are some birds moving away?"
  - Follow-up: "Where will they go?"
- Read pages 4–7 and show picture.
- Read page 8.
  - Ask, "Do you know of any other ways that animals prepare for winter?"
- Read page 9.
  - Ask, "What does it mean when it says that the smells 'pull everyone from bed in a fog'?"
- Read page 10.

(continued)

- Read pages 10–11 and show picture.
- Read page 11.
- Read pages 12–13 and show picture.
  - Ask, "What does the writer mean, 'The world has tucked her children in, with a kiss on their heads, till spring'?"

Overview Discussion of the Text

Elaborated Vocabulary Instruction

"Creature"

- In our story it said that the earth is making a bed for flowers and small *creatures*.
- *Creature* is another word we use for a living being. Both animals and people can be creatures.
- Many little creatures live in that rundown building where there aren't any people.
- Some creatures live inside trees.
- Some people dress like scary creatures on Halloween.
- Tell us about some creatures that you know about.

"Shiver"

- In our story it said that the air is chilly and the animals *shiver*.
- When it is very cold, our bodies start to shake to help make us warm. When our bodies shake it is called *shivering*.
- Can someone show me what it looks like when you *shiver*?
- I was shivering when my clothes got wet during the storm.
- I was shivering when I went outside without my coat in the winter.
- I was shivering when I jumped in the ocean.
- Are there times when you *shiver*? Tell me about it using the word *shiver* in your sentence.

"Treasure"

- In our story the author says all the berries the birds find will be *treasures*.
- A *treasure* is something that is very important to us, something that we love.
- My niece treasures her new sneakers that light up when she walks. Those sneakers are treasures to her.
- This dolphin bracelet is a treasure to me because my mother gave it to me.
- To me, the smell of the ocean is a treasure. I love closing my eyes and smelling a special smell that you can only smell in one place . . . the seashore.
- Can someone tell me about a *treasure* you may have? Try using the word *treasure* in your sentence. You can use the word to describe your feeling about something or you can tell me something that is a treasure to you.

they are selected as part of a disciplinary theme that is the focus of sustained instruction. Reading informational books expands our students' knowledge of the world and their conceptual vocabulary. Building world knowledge and vocabulary in the early grades is one of the most powerful ways that we can strengthen our students' potential for listening and reading comprehension over time.

The amount and type of talk during a read-aloud of an informational text is distinctly different from a storybook (Smolkin & Donovan, 2001). During the informational text read-aloud, there are more meaning-seeking and meaning-making efforts by children and teachers, resulting in more conversational moves than occur during the typical storybook read-aloud. Often informational books have mixed text structures (i.e., description, sequence, cause and effect, comparison–contrast) that you will need to point out and discuss. Discussion of text features and text structures must go beyond simple identification to an elaboration on how an awareness of the organization supports comprehension and writing (see Chapter 7). During reading, you need to stop intermittently to take stock of student comprehension and to ask more *how* and *why* questions than *what* questions. Allow opportunities for children to interpret, elaborate, retell, hypothesize, make personal associations, and to generate questions. The considerations for informational texts should be applied not only during the teacher read-aloud but should also be applied during shared reading, small-group instructional-level text reading, and conferences following independent student reading. Additionally, providing students with opportunities for writing informational texts should be aligned with reading instruction in ways that deliberately consider text types and text structures.

Up until school entry, most children learn about the world from their experiences or television. Naive beliefs are widespread and difficult to transform because true scientific understanding is abstract and often counterintuitive. Teaching young children to learn about the world from words and from text evidence demands your persistence in employing intentional discussion and astute questioning. Navigating the tension among activating targeted prior knowledge, supporting the integration of prior knowledge with text-based information, and confronting conceptual inaccuracies require diligence and refinement as a teacher. The text box on the next page provides some instructional guidelines for planning and conducting an effective informational text read-aloud. They are in alignment with the CCSS K–2 standards for comprehending informational texts.

Shared Reading

Shared reading is providing support to students as they simultaneously read a common text with you. During shared reading, the teacher initially assumes more responsibility than the children, who may simply follow with their eyes or chime

INFORMATIONAL TEXT READ-ALOUD

Activate Prior Knowledge

- Before reading, discuss prior knowledge about the topic in a targeted way.
- During reading, use questioning and discussion to support ongoing integration of prior knowledge with text-based information.
- During reading, explicitly teach and model how to create a mental image of information in the text.
- During and after reading, explicitly confront inaccurate prior knowledge or conceptions through questioning, discussion, text evidence, and verification processes.

Link Portions of Text

- With prompting and support, teach students to form links among connecting words, sentences, and ideas in a text.
- Prompt and support students to be able to individually summarize and take stock using key ideas in a text.
- Teach text structure and text organization as a means of understanding how the book's macrostructure fits together. Prompt use of this structure and text features to enhance comprehension.

Foster Awareness of the Author

- Prompt a discussion of the author's perspective and background.
- Prompt and support fact checking and the identification of converging evidence in multiple sources on the same topic.
- Identify craft decisions made by the author and illustrator.

Note. Based on Smolkin and Donovan (2001).

in to read repeated phrases during the first reading. Texts used in shared reading are typically read more than once and children assume greater responsibility with each repeated reading. Shared reading is an important instructional context for all novice readers, but especially so for English learners.

Just as our notions of the teacher read-aloud have changed over time, so too has it been necessary to expand our vision of what constitutes appropriate shared reading (Stahl, 2012). The original model of shared reading is derived from Holdaway's (1982) classic description of the Shared Book Experience, which makes use of big books with emergent readers. The theoretical basis is the concept of scaffolding children to perform tasks at the highest level of their ZPD with teacher support. Therefore, as we move up through grade levels, shared reading should be designed to meet different developmental targets. Its function changes as children change as readers (see Table 3.2). If the teacher read-aloud is the "I do it," then shared reading and shared writing are the "We do it together." Shared reading should be distinctly different from a teacher read-aloud. Like the read-aloud, it is a place to develop a community of readers and writers. Therefore, it needs to be conducted in a whole-class, heterogeneous context. However, unlike the read-loud, children will assume increasing responsibility for reading the text over a few days' time. You should deliberately select a key theme-driven text that children will read as part of a community of learners.

In grades 1 and 2, shared reading serves an important function in developing reading fluency, reading comprehension, and vocabulary development. This is the time during the literacy block when we expect to see teachers and students collaboratively modeling the strategies and behaviors that were explicitly taught during the teacher read-aloud. We are on Step 2 of the GRR staircase of teacher–student ownership and participation.

Provide Visual Access to Text

Our definition of shared reading requires that students have visual access to the same text as the teacher, either in the form of a big book, a personal copy of the text, or a digital display. If you are the only person with a copy of the text and the children are listening to you read, that is a teacher read-aloud, even if children are later returning to their desks to perform the key strategy with a *different* book at their instructional reading level. In order for novice readers to successfully read complex text that might be above their instructional level (CCSS Anchor Standard 10), they need to have their eyes on the text while scaffolding is being provided.

TABLE 3.2. Meeting Developmental Needs with Shared Reading

Grade level	Instructional targets	Texts
PreK–early grade 1	• Print concepts • Phonemic awareness • High-frequency vocabulary • Oral language	• Big books • Poetry charts • Alphabet books
Late grade 1–early grade 3	• Fluency • Comprehension • Conceptual vocabulary	• Complex picture books (narrative and informational) • Poetry

Note. Based on Stahl (2012).

Select Theme-Based Stretch Texts

Including time in the day for *high-quality* shared reading has intensified in importance since the CCSS (NGA & CCSSO, 2010) have increased the readability demands on all children. Primary classrooms now must be vigilant in exposing students to a wide range of text types and text difficulty. Simply reading challenging texts to the children will not prepare them to fluently read, comprehend, and respond to stretch texts in independent settings, including real-life settings and high-stakes tests. Shared reading provides a depth of support that allows children to feel confident when reading and responding to unfamiliar stretch texts. In light of the strong level of reading support, the texts that you choose for shared reading should be at the top of the students' ZPD. They are likely to be the same type of texts that you choose for teacher read-alouds: high-quality picture books with sophisticated vocabulary and rich themes or new information. They are conceptually dense but a bit easier to read than the teacher read-aloud. Caldecott Medal winners, Coretta Scott King Book Award winners, Pura Belpré Award winners, American Indian Youth Literature Awards, or classic authors (e.g., Kevin Henkes, Patricia Polacco, Tomie dePaola, Gail Gibbons) are good starting points. The CCSS Appendix B (NGA & CCSSO, 2010) also lists several books that are appropriate for shared reading at each grade level, although they should be viewed as exemplars, not a canon. Like the teacher read-aloud, the texts should be chosen deliberately as part of a themed unit. Teaching in units provides embedded support that is important for all students, but essential for children of linguistic diversity. You know that you have hit the right level of difficulty if most of the children in the class can read the text comfortably after a few days of exposure to it.

Preschool through Early First Grade

The Shared Book Experience with big books or other enlarged texts is an appropriate model of shared reading for preschool through early first grade (Holdaway, 1982). Teachers and the emergent readers gather together on the carpet to jointly read simple or predictable texts. The primary goal of these sessions is to identify high-frequency vocabulary, develop any unfamiliar conceptual vocabulary, and increase awareness of print concepts such as directionality, capitalization, punctuation, and word boundaries. Many of these books have rhymes and sound play that are good vehicles for developing phonological awareness. Stories with predictable patterns or repeated language structures encourage students to read along. Some of the same questioning techniques that are useful for dialogic reading may be applied to big book lessons. Following the Shared Book Experience, time is allocated for the children to read the big book or a small version of the text with a partner or independently. Many teachers schedule this follow-up reading by students as a center or station during the guided reading time block.

Late First Grade through Second Grade

We believe that a very particular kind of shared reading is crucial for children within this grade and age range. These novice readers must have supported opportunities to read compelling texts with high volumes of words and complex linguistic structures. In our experience, shared reading within this grade band must integrate the development of reading fluency and comprehension. Shared reading of this kind is as essential for accelerating the consolidation of decoding abilities as it is for promoting deep thinking about rich texts. You can bootstrap students' abilities to read texts that are beyond their traditionally identified instructional reading levels through the use of supportive reading techniques such as echo reading, choral reading, and partner reading. Echo reading is when the teacher reads a paragraph or page of text followed by the children reading aloud the same passage; choral reading is when all children read simultaneously. Partner reading is when two children take turns, alternately reading the pages of a text. All of these techniques provide effective graduated support.

Most teachers assign students a reading level based on their ability to read graded passages from an informal reading inventory or little books in a benchmark

TABLE 3.3. Criteria for Interpreting Reading Levels

Level	Word recognition	Comprehension
Betts (1946)		Based on the ability to answer questions[a]
Independent	99–100%	90–100%
Instructional	95–98%	75–89%
Frustration	90% or lower	50% or lower
Fountas & Pinnell (2011) Levels L–Z		Based on a qualitative rating system[a]
Independent	98–100%	Excellent or satisfactory
Instructional	95–97%	Excellent or satisfactory
	98–100%	Limited
Frustration	Below 95%	Any comprehension
Fountas & Pinnell (2011) Levels A–K		Based on a qualitative rating system[a]
Independent	95–100%	Excellent or satisfactory
Instructional	90–94%	Excellent or satisfactory
	95–100%	Limited
Frustration	Below 90%	Any comprehension

[a]Criteria for this rating scale are not clearly defined. No psychometric data are available for the questions that follow each story. Use of questions is based on teacher judgment as a supplement to the retelling.

assessment kit. The Betts (1946) criteria define the instructional level for native English speakers as the highest level at which children can read an unrehearsed text with 95–98% accuracy and 75% comprehension (see Table 3.3). Clay (2006) and Fountas and Pinnell (2011) use a 90% accuracy rate cutoff for the instructional level of beginning readers (through Level K, or mid–second grade) because the instructional format they each recommend for novice readers is more supportive than the traditional whole-class basal reader lesson structure typical of Betts's era (see Table 3.4 for a grade-level translation of Fountas & Pinnell text levels.) *Instructional level is malleable and contingent on the level of instructional support.*

By placing challenging texts in students' hands and providing high levels of instructional scaffolding, there is evidence that children can consolidate isolated skills in accelerated ways to yield fluent, meaningful text reading (Kuhn, Schwanenflugel, & Meisinger, 2010; Stahl & Heubach, 2005). Fluency-oriented reading instruction (FORI) and wide reading FORI are two similar shared reading protocols that have robust research validation in second grade but are also useful during the second half of first grade. The procedures require 30 minutes of shared reading time each day (see Figure 3.3). FORI provides assistance, coaching, and practice reading challenging texts. It also increases the awareness of reading purposes. Equally important, struggling readers who have often been limited to decodable texts or little books are now reading books that have an emotional hook or informational texts that pique their curiosity about the world. Selecting books that are related to the instructional theme provides an additional means of scaffolding children and enabling them to read more challenging texts.

	Monday	Tuesday	Wednesday	Thursday	Friday
FORI	• Prereading activities • Teacher reads the text as class follows along • Discussion of the big ideas and text themes	• Teacher and students echo read the text • Ongoing comprehension discussion and word work coaching	Choral reading	Partner reading	Extension activities
Wide Reading FORI			Extension activities and written responses to text	• Teachers and students echo read a second text selection • Comprehension activities	• Teachers and students echo read a third text selection • Comprehension activities

FIGURE 3.3. FORI and wide reading FORI lesson plan. Based on Schwanenflugel et al. (2009).

Guided Reading

Our model of guided reading for young children is in keeping with the recommendations of Fountas and Pinnell (1996) and Boushey and Moser (2009). Teachers bring together small groups of readers who have similar instructional text reading levels and similar developmental processing behaviors. During guided reading you hold readers accountable for reading text at their instructional level. In kindergarten and first grade, we recommend using a refined gradient of books that have been leveled according to a consistent, well-defined leveling system (Peterson, 1991). The Fountas and Pinnell leveling system is one good example that considers qualitative features such as content familiarity, text structure, page layout, degree of predictability, literary features, degree of text–illustration match, text length, sentence complexity, and word identification (see Table 3.4). However, other commercial or home-grown systems may be used. Nevertheless, schools must conduct periodic professional development to ensure that teachers understand the rationale behind the leveling system and its implications for instruction. Also, it is likely that schools will want to buy books from many different vendors that may use different leveling systems. It is up to the teacher to know the text characteristics that are likely to support or challenge a particular group of readers. This knowledge is also essential in selecting texts for novice readers that will nudge them to the next developmental level of awareness.

We do not believe in using decodable books during the guided reading lesson. Children do need the opportunities to practice reading high concentrations of newly taught letter–sound patterns that are afforded by decodable text. However, we believe that the place for that practice is during the word study component of your literacy block.

TABLE 3.4. Guided Reading Text Reading Level Expectations

Grade	Months of the school year									
	1	2	3	4	5	6	7	8	9	10
K				A	A/B	B	B	C	C	C
1	C/D	D	E	E/F	F	G	G/H	H	I	I
2	I/J	J	J	J/K	K	K/L	L	L	M	M
3	M/N	N	N	N	O	O	O	P	P	P
4	P/Q	Q	Q	Q	R	R	R	S	S	S
5	S/T	T	T	T	U	U	U	V	V	V
6	V/W	W	W	W	X	X	X	X	Y	Y
7	Y	Y	Y	Y	Y/Z	Z	Z	Z	Z	Z
8	Z	Z	Z	Z	Z	Z	Z	Z	Z	Z

Note. From Fountas and Pinnell (2011). Copyright 2012 by Heinemann. Reprinted by permission.

It is beyond the scope of this section to fully describe how to conduct an effective guided reading lesson, as novice readers' developmental needs change across time. Studying books written on the topic (e.g., Boushey & Moser, 2009; Fountas & Pinnell, 1996), viewing videos of small-group instruction at different text levels, and ongoing professional development are the best ways to learn how to conduct effective guided reading lessons. Fountas and Pinnell (1996) provide detailed descriptions of how to deliver developmentally appropriate new book introductions and how to use running record data to inform teaching decisions in the guided reading lessons for kindergarten and first graders. Boushey and Moser (2009) do a particularly good job of providing organizational suggestions for planning teacher-led guided reading lessons and the independent student centers. In this section, we focus on the *comprehension* considerations at early and later levels of the text reading component of the guided reading lesson.

Reading Level: Kindergarten to Mid–First Grade (Fountas & Pinnell Levels A–G)

Novice readers need small-group opportunities to orchestrate the reading process and to monitor that what they are reading makes sense, looks right (letter–sound correspondence), and sounds right grammatically. Level A–G books do not have the fodder for rich comprehension instruction.

We want to get books in children's hands as early as possible. When children are in the earliest stages of word recognition, they can read caption books and be held accountable for one-to-one matching of two or three words on a page that label the pictures. This is the stage at which we begin to call the emergent reader a novice reader. Novice readers are print driven, rather than relying *solely* on the pictures and patterns to "read." The child's oral reading should make sense, follow the text's structure, and look right (letters match spoken sounds). A brief new book introduction (three sentences) by the teacher should provide an overview of the meaning, text structure, and syntax of the story. A *brief* picture walk-through of the book helps the children get an overview of how the book's parts contribute to the whole (macrostructure) and establishes both the syntactic structure (often predictable language structures) and the text structure to propel reading. It is the child's job to apply his or her word-recognition abilities (at this stage, making a voice–print match) to arrive at an accurately read message. Over time, the child will progressively need to apply knowledge of first letter, one-to-one matching, final letter, and vowel patterns in order to accurately read the increasingly difficult texts. However, throughout the ongoing development of refined word-recognition abilities, the child self-monitors his or her comprehension by mentally asking, "Did what I read make sense?"

In text Levels A–G, the teaching points that follow reading typically focus on self-monitoring and cross-checking the three cueing systems: meaning, structure, and visual (letter–sound relationships). This juggling act is difficult for the novice reader and worthy of teaching thoroughly during the guided reading lessons at these early text levels. Regular running records of oral reading with an error analysis can provide strong evidence at this stage of development about the degree to which a novice is reading for meaning. Do the child's errors make sense but consistently ignore the letter–sound relationships being taught during word study? Or is the child inefficiently stopping to sound out concrete words that are blatantly indicated by the context of the story or in the picture? At this stage of reading, you must be acutely aware of each child's developmental word-recognition stage (Bear, Invernizzi, Templeton, & Johnston, 2011) and hold him or her accountable for applying the word-recognition skills indicated at that developmental stage while nudging the child's awareness forward to the next stage. Fluency and phrasing also provide evidence of meaning making at this stage. The anecdotal notes that you take during text reading and running records inform teaching points that immediately follow the children's reading in the guided reading lesson.

Because these texts are so meager, it is essential for rich, high-level comprehension instruction to be occurring during the teacher read-aloud and shared reading. If you have strong comprehension instruction happening during the teacher read-aloud and shared reading, you don't need to feel pressured to create contrived comprehension responses to these simple texts. For that matter, a 15-minute guided reading lesson that includes attention to text reading, word work, and guided writing does not allow time for deep comprehension probes or instruction. Often, well-intentioned teachers may overdo prediction before reading and force conversations in response to easy texts that lack fully developed narrative structures with cohesive plot episodes or a comprehensive set of story grammar elements.

Level F and Level G books are likely to have episodes or information that provide fruitful opportunities for a simple retelling. Because these texts are short, we like to ask a single child to give a comprehensive retelling or to share the key information with the person sitting next to him or her. For example, when reading the book *Our Dog Sam* (Bacon, 1988), it is logical to prompt the children by saying, "Tell your partner some of the things that Sam liked to do." In addition to the explicit instruction on how to retell a story or information provided during read-alouds and shared reading, you can prompt and provide verbal scaffolding in the small-group context. One of the functions of the guided reading group context is to informally assess who can't retell these short instructional-level texts and to provide immediate, specific, and individualized feedback.

Often children have difficulty providing an individual comprehensive retelling when prompted during benchmark testing because during instruction they have only been asked to provide a bit of what they have read, not recount the entire story or detailed information. In light of these factors, *when assessing students who are reading in early text levels, accuracy should trump comprehension in deciding whether or not to move a child to the next level.*

Reading Level: Mid–First Grade to Mid–Second Grade (Fountas & Pinnell Levels H–K)

The texts at these levels change in ways that cause a shift in book introduction and student accountability. The texts become longer, less repetitive, and less predictable. Because the stories are longer, and children still need to read them at the teacher-led table, time management becomes trickier when we work with these groups. Although your new book introduction should still consist of a brief overview of the story or defining the purpose for reading, the picture walk needs to be reconsidered because the words on the page only relate in a general way to the illustrations. As the readers are still novices, they need to approach their first reading of the text with the gist of the story or key ideas in mind. Picture walks at this stage need to be very brief, with the children doing most of the talking to set purposes for reading. We have found that the directed reading–thinking activity (DR-TA) often supports comprehension and new knowledge acquisition more effectively than a picture walk, especially for informational texts at this level (Stahl, 2009; Stauffer, 1969). In planning a DR-TA lesson, the teacher identifies logical stopping points. Just before the children read the first section, the teacher asks them to make predictions about what will happen (in fiction) or what they will learn (in informational text). The children then mumble-read or read silently. When the group reaches each stopping point, the teacher first guides them as they revisit their predictions, helping them clarify confusions and taking stock of what was read. Then the teacher asks them to make new predictions for the next section. This cycle is repeated for each section of text. Additionally, since these books tend to be longer and address more complex content than easier books, novice readers benefit from having intermittent opportunities to monitor understanding and to take stock of what has been read (see the text box below). Chapter 5 provides more information on using the DR-TA more broadly.

PLANNING A DIRECTED READING–THINKING ACTIVITY FOR GUIDED READING

- Divide the text into sensible two- to three-page sections.
- Students generate predictions and justify their predictions for a single two- to three-page section of text.
- Students mumble-read or silently read the section of text.
- After reading each section of text, students verify or revise their prediction and discuss that section of text.
- The process is repeated for each section of text.

Children may softly mumble-read and transition to silent reading. There should not be any finger-pointing at this level except to focus on a tricky word. Teaching points after reading are likely to focus on word-recognition strategies for multisyllabic words and supporting students in keeping the meaning at the forefront while they apply the most efficient word-recognition strategy to achieve an accurate reading. These longer texts are likely to have narrative episodes or simple information about a disciplinary topic. Running-record error analyses are still valuable for evaluating whether children are reading to make sense of text. Children should be expected to retell what they read. During guided reading lessons at this level, you should provide verbal scaffolding and prompting to instruct the children what a good retelling or informational text summary includes. During benchmark assessing of texts at Levels H and I, your decisions about instructional text level should still rely more heavily on accuracy than a student's comprehension rating. This is especially important if your assessment system does not provide a detailed scoring guide for the retelling (as explained more fully in Chapter 8) or a set of 8–10 explicit–implicit questions that are specific to the text. However, if your assessment meets that criteria and you are confident that you have provided your students with explicit instruction on how to generate a good retelling or summary and that this instruction was followed by many guided instructional opportunities for the children to individually construct a retelling or text summary, applying specific comprehension scores to the criteria for determining a child's instructional text level is appropriate.

Reading Level: Beyond Mid–Second Grade (Fountas & Pinnell Level L)

As Fountas and Pinnell (2011) indicate by their shift in criteria for determining instructional level (from 90% accuracy to 95% accuracy), the focus now becomes comprehension. Brief new book introductions, comprehension instruction, reinforcement, and comprehension strategy application occur at the table, but typically the reading occurs before children arrive for their 20- to 30-minute small-group lesson with the teacher. The accuracy criterion for the instructional level increases from 90 to 95% because students are receiving less instructional support *during* reading than they received at the earlier levels. With less instructional support, there is a lower threshold for the process breaking down. It will take fewer errors to result in meaning-making hurdles.

Now the readability gradient for leveling texts widens because the pressure points that influence a student's ability to successfully read the book are less tied to the linear development of word recognition and more tied to other pressure points such as prior knowledge, conceptual vocabulary, genre, text structure, conceptual density of the text, and self-regulation. At this stage of reading development, the measurement tools used to develop Lexiles begin to be more sensitive to what makes a book easy or hard for a student than a qualitative scale, such as the Fountas and Pinnell (1996) leveling system.

During guided reading, students apply the comprehension strategies that were taught during the read-aloud and shared reading to personal reading materials at their instructional level. Now, the small teacher-led group becomes the setting for discussion and to insert follow-up questions that lead to high levels of thinking about the common texts that students are reading away from the table. Although writing in response to text often occurs away from the guided reading table, it is shared with teacher and peers for feedback during the guided reading lesson. This level of scaffolding is very different from a workshop model, which involves meeting each child individually for a few minutes once a week for a conference. Instead, the model we are describing provides an additional layer of instructional support before the child is asked to be accountable independently. The children in the guided reading group have common developmental needs or may be working on a common project, so children are learning from the teacher and from one another around a common text. Also, because the lessons are 20–30 minutes two or three times a week instead of 5 or 10 minutes once or twice a week, the lessons achieve a greater depth of processing than is possible during a conference.

Scheduling Guided Reading

In a classroom literacy block, 45–60 minutes need to be allocated to guided reading (see Figure 3.2). In kindergarten and first grade, that allows the teacher to meet with each group daily. In second and third grades, the teacher would meet with the neediest group daily, grade-level groups two or three times a week, and high-performing students twice a week. During the time that students are not with the teacher, they work in productive stations or centers that are the sites of differentiated practice, follow-up activities to the guided reading lesson, and independent reading. Appendices 3.1, 3.2, and 3.3 (at the end of the chapter) provide sample time distributions for literacy activities at Mott Haven Academy, a charter elementary school.

Independent Reading

Children should be given time for independent reading each day. Typically in primary classrooms, this independent reading time is one of the workstations or centers offered while the teacher is meeting with the guided reading groups. In kindergarten and first grade, independent reading ranges from 10 to 15 minutes. In second grade, it ranges from 20 to 30 minutes or the length of a single guided reading lesson. Independent choice reading is also assigned as homework each day for equivalent time frames.

Conclusion

The GRR is an important pedagogical understanding when teaching comprehension because, unlike constrained skills, comprehension is never mastered. The GRR is a structure that allows for a reader to receive high levels of support when engaging in a difficult task and gradually assuming ownership for the task. This model of support allows for children to continue to grow so that they can meet more difficult reading challenges.

Organizing the literacy block to include the four instructional contexts described in this chapter provides a range of teacher support that allows children to be exposed to texts that range in level of difficulty. When the support by teachers is complemented by engaging, supportive content, it creates a classroom where readers can achieve their highest potential in developing reading comprehension. In Chapter 4, we discuss the role that content plays in helping students thrive in a rich learning context.

APPENDIX 3.1. Kindergarten Schedule (January to June)

	Time frame	Text
Teacher read-aloud*	30 minutes (2 × 15 minutes each *or* 15+ follow-up activities)	Complex text Whole class and small group Reading may be followed by dramatization, small-group discussion, writing/drawing in response to text.
Shared reading*	30 minutes (10 minutes = morning message + 20 minutes = big book or other themed text)	Grade-level text Whole class
Writing in response to reading*	25 minutes	Process writing tied to disciplinary theme in response to teacher read-aloud or shared reading—narrative, explanatory, persuasive.
Guided reading (**skill/text-level driven, not theme**)	45 minutes (4 groups × 10 minutes *or* 3 groups × 15 minutes)	Teacher-led reading group Possible stations: independent reading, high-frequency word practice, handwriting, partner reading, listening station, computer station
Independent reading	1 guided reading station (10 minutes) + 10 minutes at home	Student choice reading
Decoding/spelling	30 minutes	
Interactive writing	10–15 minutes	Language experience and foundational skills

*These activities are derived from the thematic literary or disciplinary unit.
Thanks to Mott Haven Academy for kindly supplying the schedule in this table.

APPENDIX 3.2. Grade 1 Schedule (January to June)*

Semester 2	Time frame	Text/grouping
Teacher read-aloud**	20–30 minutes *Text Talk protocol 2 days/week*	Complex text Whole class
Shared reading**	30-minute block	Grade-level text—stretch texts Whole class—Fluency-Oriented Reading Instruction
Writing in response to reading**	30 minutes	Process writing tied to theme
Guided reading (text-level driven, not theme)	45–60 minutes (15–20 minutes/group)	Small group
Independent reading	1 guided reading station (15 minutes) + 15 minutes at home	
Decoding/spelling	30 minutes	
Interactive writing	10–15 minutes	Language experience to foundations

*Schedule for first grade September through December resembles kindergarten (January to June).
**These activities are derived from the thematic literary or disciplinary unit.
Thanks to Mott Haven Academy for kindly supplying the schedule in this table.

APPENDIX 3.3. Grade 2 to Early Grade 3 Schedule

	Time frame	Grouping/text
Teacher read-aloud*	20–30 minutes *Text Talk protocol 2 days/week*	Whole class Complex text
Shared reading*	30-minute block	Whole class—Fluency-Oriented Reading Instruction Grade-level text—stretch texts
Writing in response to reading (theme driven/CCSS)*	30 minutes *Process* writing—similar to writing workshop but driven by accountability to CCSS and content standards *Mindful of GRR* Three writing rubrics	Whole class—writing in response to same topic or prompt. This writing might be *collective*, *collaborative*, or *independent*. It is process writing—narrative, explanatory, and persuasive—of various lengths tied to theme.
Guided reading (text-level driven, not theme)	1 hour	Small group Differentiation by text level
Independent reading	One guided reading station (20–30 minutes) + 20–30 minutes at home	
Decoding/spelling	20 minutes	This may be included as an independent work station during the guided reading time block.

**These activities are derived from the thematic literary or disciplinary unit.
Thanks to Mott Haven Academy for kindly supplying the schedule in this table.

CHAPTER 4

Using Content
to Create Engagement

- How do disciplinary themes support reading and writing processes for young children, English learners, and diverse learners?
- What are the essential steps in planning integrated disciplinary instructional units?
- How is student learning assessed?

Setting the Stage

The boys and girls in K-Blue at Mott Haven Academy are studying a unit on insects. Glass cases containing the immature forms of butterflies and ladybugs sit on counters around the room. A wide variety of books about insects are displayed on shelves within easy reach. Some are beautiful hardback, photographic essays, but a closer look around the room also reveals a few little leveled books and piles of photocopied, teacher-created class sets of books about insects. This morning the children sing "The Fuzzy Caterpillar" as part of their morning message routine. The song is posted on chart paper, and their teacher, Erin Jeanneret, points to each word as they sing. The song describes the life cycle of the butterfly.

ERIN: I noticed yesterday when you were writing that you did a good job of looking around the room to find some of the insect words that we've been learning. So I thought it would be useful to make a handy list of some of the words that you'll need. First, let's look in our song to find some of the words that will be helpful to you when you do your writing about insects.

[The children identify the words *butterfly, caterpillar,* and *chrysalis*. Erin has a picture ready to match with each written word.]

ERIN: What are some other insect words that might be useful to have on our vocabulary chart?

STUDENT: *Beetle.*

ERIN: Does anyone know how to spell that? [The children call out the salient sounds as Erin correctly spells the word on the chart.]

STUDENT: *Bug.*

ERIN: Is *bug* a word that we can tap out? [Leads the children in tapping out sounds as she writes it on the chart.]

ERIN: And how about the fancy word for bug?

STUDENT: *Insect.*

ERIN: [Writes the word.] As we continue our insect unit, we will add the words to our word chart that will be helpful when you are doing your writing and research.

Making Sense of the World: Building Bridges from Experience to Texts

Before children come to school, they learn about the world through their life experiences and the social interactions that accompany those experiences. Today children also learn about life beyond their immediate experiences through television, movies, and technology. For most of our lives, the greatest means of learning about the world is through text. Whether we are reading a novel to be in touch with the human experience, following a recipe for baking a cake, using a subway map, reading the newspaper to find out how our favorite team performed, or researching a topic on the Internet, beginning in the intermediate grades we come to rely on text sources for increasing our knowledge of the world. Building these mental representational knowledge systems creates a self-extending system of learning. The more one reads, the more one expands one's knowledge of the world; the more prior knowledge one possesses, the greater one's ability to comprehend text, generate inferences, remember what we have read, and acquire new information about the world.

When children are learning in real time from real experiences, they have the opportunity to acquire knowledge in concrete ways. Learning from a book requires attention to and comprehension of the language in the text. Most children's initial exposure to text is through picture books, so the pictures provide a scaffold for understanding. However, eventually children need to make sense of decontextualized language, language that is not associated with the present experience of the reader. Engaging children in read-aloud experiences like Text Talk that require children to derive meaning from the language of the text with the support of teacher prompts is a good way to scaffold meaning making from print for native English-speaking children (Beck & McKeown, 2001). As children move from being emergent readers to novice readers, children need modeling, questioning, and intermittent opportunities to take stock of their own comprehension processes.

Vocabulary, Text, and Knowledge

In order for children to learn about the world from text, they need to be familiar with the language of the text. Proficiency in English is no guarantee that students will be able to meet the vocabulary demands of most books. The language of text varies from the conversational register, or how we informally speak with each other. The vocabulary of a typical children's book ranks higher in difficulty than an adult television program and above that of a typical conversation between two college-educated adults (Hayes & Ahrens, 1988). And although knowledge of the vocabulary is necessary for understanding text, a child doesn't need to know all of the words or have a deep understanding of every word in the text. Vocabulary knowledge is one of the pressure points that dynamically interacts with purpose for reading, context, level of instructional support, and ease of word identification to result in a level of understanding.

A variety of experiences with words are needed to support students' vocabulary growth. Reading text with sophisticated vocabulary, incorporating that vocabulary in discussions, and written responses provide the repeated exposures that result in increased vocabulary knowledge. Refined vocabulary knowledge also refines concept development. For example, being able to distinguish an arachnid from an insect has implications for conceptual understandings of the animal classification system.

Using Themes and Disciplinary Content to Support Meaning Making

Beginning in kindergarten, the CCSS for English language arts (NGA & CCSSO, 2010) emphasize the need for all children to read, write, speak, listen, and use language effectively in the literary, science, and social studies content domains. However, using themed units to teach literacy should not be viewed as policy driven.

Integrated instruction actually applies good learning theory, and once organized, it is practical in terms of classroom time allocation.

Creating themed disciplinary content units to be used during the literacy block accomplishes multiple goals simultaneously. First, it creates an effective scaffold for uniting learning from experiences and applying that knowledge to texts. It makes sense to have hands-on experiences planting seeds, caring for the seeds, charting the growth of seeds, and identifying the parts of the mature plant as we read and write about the process. It makes text–world connections and text–text connections explicit. By providing the experiential knowledge required for understanding the text, we create a context that fosters comprehension. Having a set of common experiences that relate to the texts that are used during whole-group read-alouds and shared reading allows for teachers to model and prompt high levels of thinking about the topic and the texts.

Building knowledge about a topic across a sustained unit allows for digging deeply into the topic rather than the superficial exploration that occurs when everyone is reading a book on a different topic. A teacher's enthusiasm for a topic is contagious. Sustained interaction creates engagement with a topic. The community knowledge shared among classmates serves as a springboard for children to develop their individual interests about the topic and to pursue independent research on a specialized area. Even the youngest children can be held accountable for becoming class experts on particular aspects of a unit of study. Independent reading and writing for authentic purposes expands the group's knowledge base and further enhances student engagement and motivation. This results in an increase in the quantity and quality of student reading. Children are able to read more difficult texts independently because knowledge of the topic, vocabulary, and text types have been bolstered by the community experiences of reading, writing, and talking about the topic. Because common experiences and readings serve as the foundation of the unit, children are held to higher levels of accountability for close reading, leading to higher levels of thinking in response to both shared reading and independent reading. You can more easily detect superficial responses to text and use verbal scaffolding to redirect students' higher levels of thinking.

Using Themes and Disciplinary Content to Support Vocabulary Development

When children engage in a sustained unit on a disciplinary topic, the vocabulary is recurring. In order for children to acquire ownership of vocabulary and to know words broadly and deeply, they need repeated exposures to the words. Theme study provides the repeated exposures organically. Children are able to recognize the words more quickly when they occur in novel text, can use the words effectively in their own writing, and understand the words at a deeper level as they encounter them across the unit in multiple contexts. Familiarity with target disciplinary vocabulary raises a child's comprehension threshold, enabling him or her to successfully read more complex text fluently and meaningfully. These experiences are supportive for all learners, but they are essential for the English learner. Teaching reading using themed units increases the likelihood that the English learner can be a full participant.

The Value of Authentic Experiences in Classroom Settings

Throughout the school year, Erin's kindergartners engage in a series of themed units. In January, they study the features and needs of plants during their bulb unit. Hands-on experiences accompany a wide range of reading, writing, speaking, and listening activities. They also engage in a 5-week rain forest unit and a 4-week insect unit. During the rain forest unit the children visit the nearby botanical garden, where a rain forest is housed in a conservatory. During the insect unit they engage in daily observations of the life cycle of butterflies and ladybugs. They visit the butterfly garden at the local zoo. The children read and write both informational and narrative texts throughout the units. The units also incorporate songs, poems, drama, and art projects. Erin believes that by pairing authentic disciplinary content experiences with literacy instruction she is making reading and writing come alive for her students. Erin's students live in a high-poverty urban community. At this school, 65% of the children are either in foster care or members of families that are being supervised by Family and Children's Services. Without integrated instruction, it is unlikely that 30 minutes a day of science instruction could teach them the science content needed to acquire age-appropriate world knowledge. Most of these children are entering school having rarely left their urban neighborhood. Therefore, without the hands-on experiences it is unlikely that the content and vocabulary found in many texts would be comprehensible to them. By planning her integrated curriculum carefully, Erin believes that she has expanded the amount of time that she spends teaching both disciplinary content and literacy skills to her students (see the appendices at the end of Chapter 3 for sample schedules).

Concept-oriented reading instruction (CORI; Guthrie et al., 1996) is an instructional framework for integrating science and literacy instruction. Research investigating CORI has determined that students who were engaged in this integrated model of instruction performed higher on reading comprehension, reading strategies, and engagement than students who participated in strategy instruction alone or a more traditional model of instruction (Guthrie et al., 2004). Although

CORI has primarily been tested in grades 3–5, we think that several components of CORI are relevant for planning a primary-level integrated curriculum. Comprehension strategy instruction is embedded within the framework. A gradual release of responsibility model is used to teach the children activation and application of prior knowledge, questioning, summarizing, and how to search for information. Their consistent key finding during years of research is that concept development, strategy application, motivation, and social interaction are the key contributors to student engagement.

How Do You Plan an Integrated Curriculum?

School Planning

The interdisciplinary perspective of the CCSS (NGA & CCSSO, 2010) has caused many schools to undertake the process of integrating disciplinary content and literacy instruction. Regardless of the existing literacy program that a school has adopted, steps can be taken to make instruction more integrated. If a school has already purchased a commercially produced core reading program, much of the work has already been completed and only calendar modifications for disciplinary units may be needed in the primary grades. Themed units do not interfere with the instruction of foundational skills and guided reading groups. The latter continue to adhere to the scope and sequence prescribed in the program. However, the themes are strengthened and tailored to include and develop the mandated science and social studies standards. In the primary grades it is easier to map the disciplinary units to the sequence of the core materials rather than trying to completely rearrange the basal reader. That is not to say that some stories can't be omitted or that some themes can't be placed in a different sequence to strengthen the unit.

Those schools that use a different model for literacy instruction, such as a reading–writing workshop model or The Daily Five (Boushey & Moser, 2009), will have more flexibility in mapping their new integrated curriculum on a calendar. However, you may need to walk through the process of teaching reading and writing processes with authentic content in sustained ways before becoming convinced that nothing is lost from teaching reading and writing in isolation. Instead of using a teacher's manual to dictate when to teach particular reading competencies or processes of narrative, explanatory, and persuasive writing, the demands of the disciplinary content will dictate the best time for teaching reading processes and including particular writing genres and forms (see Figure 4.1).

The purpose of schoolwide planning is to ensure that all mandated disciplinary content units of study are covered, there is vertical alignment of the topics

Month	Topic	Content Discipline	Comprehension Strategy Focus	Writing Focus
September	Our Community: School and Neighborhood	Literary and Social Studies	Activating prior knowledge Purposeful predictions	Narrative Explanatory
October	Harvest—Plants	Science	Visualizing Sequential text structure	Explanatory
November	Farm to Supermarket	Social Studies/ Economics	Determining importance Clarifying	Explanatory Argument
December– mid-January	Polar regions	Science	Descriptive text structure Summarizing	Explanatory
Late January	Life's Lessons—Fables	Literary	Narrative text structure (beginning, middle, end)	Narrative
February	Life's Lessons—Realistic Fiction Biographies	Literary	Question generation	Narrative Argument
March	The Human Body	Science	Question generation	Explanatory
April	Kings and Queens in Life and Literature	Literary and Social Studies	Narrative text structure (characters and setting)	Narrative
May	Our Favorite Characters	Literary	Narrative text structure (characters' point of view)	Narrative

FIGURE 4.1. Grade 1 yearly unit plan.

from grade level to grade level, spiraling (revisiting topics in contexts of increasing complexity) occurs across grade levels for anchor standards and conceptual development, and there are no voids or redundancies in content across the years. Schoolwide planning also guarantees that at some point in their elementary schooling the students have received exposure to each text type and subgenre as specified in the CCSS. It is not enough to say that the children will have opportunities to read narrative and informational texts. You might ask, "When will students be familiarized with fables, mythology, and legends?" or "What units call for students to comprehend and complete forms or schedules?" Cross-grade-level planning ensures that all text types are explicitly taught as part of the school's curriculum.

There are many resources that are now available to support schools undertaking this process. The Internet has many examples of integrated units designed to meet the CCSS (*www.coreknowledge.org/curriculum-planning-tools*; *www.engageny.org/english-language-arts*). Electronic management systems that use a common template allow individual teachers to add plans and lesson materials that can be shared by the school faculty. These templates are becoming an increasingly popular means of making instructional curriculum planning more transparent, collaborative, and dynamic (e.g., *www.sungard.com/publicsector/productofferings/ curriculumconnector.aspx*).

Grade-Level or Classroom Planning

Once the unit topics have been determined for each grade level, it is useful for a grade-level team or classroom teacher to create a general table that charts the course for the year (see Figure 4.1). A first-grade team created this table preceding their first year of aligning their literacy curriculum to the CCSS. Their state website included learning modules based on the Core Knowledge Curriculum (*www. engageny.org/english-language-arts*). The administration and teachers at Mott Haven Academy decided to apply these modules discriminately, teaching to the standards rather than being dictated by a set of materials. Cheers to them!

During the summer planning meetings, a combination of preexisting content units and state modules were combined to create a cohesive yearlong plan. Once the topics were chosen, the grade-level teams decided what key texts would be used for shared reading, what comprehension strategies would be most helpful in making sense of the texts within each unit, and what types of writing would be the most logical means of expressing comprehension, creativity, and new learning during each unit.

When implementing themed units, teachers tied read-alouds and shared reading to the theme. However, guided reading materials did not always adhere to the theme due to the lack of availability of themed materials at each text level. Everyone accepted that this was a process that would continue to evolve. For example, the first-grade teachers had been very happy with their preexisting "School–Community" unit, "Harvest" unit, and "Farm-to-Supermarket" unit. They had reading materials, writing and research projects, and field trips in place. "The Polar Regions" and "Favorite Characters" (e.g., *Henry and Mudge, Olivia, Frog and Toad*) units were also already well developed. These units needed fine-tuning and alignment with the CCSS because they had never before included complex texts for shared reading using FORI. However, in previous years they had spent several months teaching some units of reading and writing in isolation, such as "Picking the Right Book," "Building Stamina," or "Bringing Stories to Life." Therefore, they had a few months without any specific disciplinary themes. To fill those time slots, they selected some of the recommended state modules (e.g., "Kings and Queens," "The Human Body," and "Fables") so they would not need to develop every unit from scratch. They selected these new units with an eye to maintaining a literary, social studies, and science balance. They also considered the availability of materials and the units being taught by other grade levels.

They were willing to acknowledge and accept that building the collection of materials to support the units would have to occur across the next few years.

Making Powerful Text Selections

In 2000, Nell Duke wrote an article that exposed the scarcity of informational texts found in first-grade classrooms. She determined that first graders only spent an average of 3.6 minutes per day engaging with informational texts. Duke hypothesized that this deprivation in the early grades might be a contributing factor to the fourth-grade slump. Chall and Jacobs (1983) described this phenomenon as the shift that occurs around fourth grade, when children begin to encounter difficulties as they are expected to read longer, conceptually dense texts and shift from "learning to read" to "reading to learn." Teachers had long recognized that children enjoyed reading about their world as much as they enjoyed storybooks. After Duke's article, publishing companies began increasing the availability of beautiful photographic essays for the youngest readers. Many publishers created boxed sets of paired fiction and nonfiction titles on a common topic. The publishers of basal reading series became more intentional in including informational texts as key selections in the anthology, adding highlights from primary sources or magazines, and balancing the genres of add-on texts for guided reading instruction. The synchronicity of these events caused a sea change in the balance of reading material in primary-grade classrooms. So today, as we enter the era of the CCSS, even kindergarten classroom libraries have a collection of informational texts.

However, what the CCSS seem likely to change is the level of competence that children need to demonstrate with a wider range of more difficult texts than has ever been expected. As a result, teachers need to be deliberate in making the most powerful text selections possible to prepare their children to engage joyfully and accountably with rich texts. Although it is time-consuming, expensive, and mentally demanding work for teachers to plan and deliver this balanced, nourishing diet, it restores the bliss and creativity that reminds us why we became teachers. And for our students, these texts and the related social interactions are the keys to the magical world of reading.

Genre Considerations

The CCSS recommend that children be exposed to a collection of texts on a single topic that allows for sustained study. The CCSS explicitly call for children to experience both narrative and informational texts beginning in kindergarten. However, within those two general categories there is a wide variety of text types that need to be included as part of our students' reading diets. Teaching integrated units (even before kindergarten) ensures that children receive exposure and instructional support by reading a wide variety of texts in purposeful, authentic settings. As an outcome, children are likely to be intrinsically motivated to self-select a genre that might not have been a preference before the unit of study. Repeated, sustained opportunities to work with each type of text increase children's comfort level and the likelihood of comprehension success. So just as sustained study of a topic is recommended for deep learning, sustained exposure to particular genres that effectively address particular topics allows students to have opportunities to receive explicit instruction that characterizes the genre and supports student reading and writing processes with that genre. Shared reading and collaborative interactions can occur before the student is required to independently read and respond to a text.

Readability Considerations

In addition to the variety of text types, we must assume that children need to increase their degree of comfort with texts that span a wide range of difficulty. By the end of third grade, children who take the new standardized tests used to measure CCSS proficiency will need to read unfamiliar texts that according to traditional readability formulas range from second- to fifth-grade reading levels. A detailed explanation of the reading-level determinations and expectations for each grade level is provided in CCSS Appendix A with text examples provided in CCSS Appendix B (NGA & CCSSO, 2010).

Children deserve to be offered a diet of texts at varying levels of difficulty. As we have discussed, by situating texts within a unit, we are providing a degree of conceptual and vocabulary scaffolding so that children may be able to read books slightly above their identified reading levels. Additionally, sometimes children read books for a very specific purpose. As a result, there is a high tolerance in those contexts for unknown words. One of us (Kay) had each child in her second-grade classroom research a self-selected sea mammal early in the school year. Children had a template that was used to gather information such as length, weight, ocean home, food, predators, and two interesting facts. Even though the children were using books and Internet sources that were clearly beyond their independent reading levels, the purpose of the reading task was so constrained that they were able to conduct their research successfully with minimal assistance and high accountability.

By applying a classroom organizational model that offers read-alouds, shared reading, guided reading, and independent reading each day, you can provide children with text interactions that span a wide range of difficulty. Table 4.1 is only a suggestion. However, it has been constructed with consideration of the CCSS expectations for second grade in consolidation with the Fountas and Pinnell (2011) expectations for guided reading (see Table 3.4). These decisions will always require

TABLE 4.1. Text Difficulty Range Suggestions for Scaffolded Instruction

	Read-aloud	Shared reading	Guided reading[a]
Kindergarten	H–J	Wide variety	A–D
Grade 1	L–M Lexiles 400–500	G–K	D–J
Grade 2	N–P Lexiles 500–700 (Minimum, may range as high as 820L)	L–N Lexiles 400–600	J–M Lexiles 300–500

Note. All levels are presented using the Fountas and Pinnell (1996) leveling system. [a]Guided reading levels are based on Fountas and Pinnell (2011) progress monitoring grade-level recommendations.

appraisal of the texts, assessment of the children, and analysis of the learning context by a knowledgeable teacher. We want to challenge children and provide support as needed so that learning can be maximized, with our target being the high end of the ZPD during teacher-led activities.

Helping Students Process Multiple Texts

The CCSS require third-grade students to comprehend and analyze two texts written on a common topic. Therefore, teachers in the primary grades need to expose and support students in comprehending, discussing, and writing in response to multiple texts on a common topic. This will not be an easy task.

Stahl, Hynd, Britton, McNish, and Bosquet (1996) conducted a study of high school students' comprehension and written responses to a set of historical documents written on a common topic. In short, the researchers found that these students had difficulties processing multiple documents. One challenge was that the students had minimal prior knowledge about the Gulf of Tonkin Incidents, the topic addressed in the documents. The students gained knowledge from the first piece they read but despite the differences in the documents, they did not acquire new knowledge from reading additional documents. They had difficulty picking main ideas from longer documents. The students were asked to either write a description of the historical event or to express an opinion on the event. They tended to pick a few big ideas from the shorter documents and focus on them in their written responses rather than attending to the nuances expressed in different pieces. Students who were asked to write a description stayed fairly close to reporting the events as described in the first text they read. Those who were asked to express an opinion made global comments about their personal thoughts and beliefs with few references to their sources of information.

We think this study is interesting and important to share with you for a few reasons. The students who encountered difficulties comprehending, learning from, and writing in response to reading multiple documents were 10th graders in Advanced Placement classes. However, today's third graders are being held accountable for performing these tasks on high-stakes tests. Whether students are in third grade or high school gifted classes, we cannot assume that they will acquire these skills naturally or that the ability to perform well on comprehension measures of a single text guarantees effective processing of multiple documents. Most of the work investigating the comprehension of multiple texts has been done with older students. However, there are some common findings that we need to consider since younger students are being asked to process multiple texts. Building integrated units supports this process.

The First Text Is Important

The first text that students read within a set of texts is important because it is likely to be the source of the readers' global understanding of a topic. This is especially true if the students don't have much prior knowledge about the topic. The first text will be a mental anchor as they read additional texts. With your help, as students read additional texts they should deconstruct, prune, and then reconstruct a new mental representation, or what Kintsch (1998) calls a situation model. Therefore, when you are planning your units you want to select the introductory texts and the shared reading texts to address these needs for essential understandings of the topic or theme. Later in the unit, you will want to introduce texts with different perspectives and refined information about the topic, so that you can use think-alouds to model how we reconstruct our new situation model or how we address contradictory information in sources. The texts that children self-select for independent reading should enable them to assume more responsibility for this process. However, teachers must have an intimate knowledge of each book that is included in their classroom collections and available for student-selected reading. Otherwise, conferences, written responses, and research projects are likely to perpetuate superficial understanding of the topic similar to those reflected by the 10th-grade history students.

Teaching Children to Evaluate Sources

Part of a genre study includes helping children to develop a set of criteria for evaluating the quality of texts within the genre (Stahl, 2014b). As a result, readers will have a basis for comparing the texts within a unit with the universal criteria. For example, when evaluating literary texts, a discussion of author craft and critical literacy elements (point of view, issues of power, stereotypes) becomes a part of the classroom discourse. Different criteria are used to help children evaluate the merit of historical and scientific texts. Historians evaluate a document's source, the level of corroboration for information in the document, and contextual factors such as when and where it was written. Scientists evaluate the source, data, visual evidence, precision of methodology, clarity of writing, and level of corroboration. These guidelines provide useful starting points to enable children to approach multiple texts. A single mini-lesson isn't adequate. Learning is best accomplished across a series of lessons within your units using the gradual release of responsibility.

Knowledge of the above criteria will also help children refine their self-selection process for independent reading and study. It will enable them to evaluate the usefulness of a particular book to accomplish specific reading purposes compared with other choices. It will provide a basis for thinking interpretively and flexibly about the contents of their self-selected texts. Finally, it will provide the framework for composing their own written products.

Expanding to Include Internet and Hypermedia

Application of strategies for dealing with multiple sources is imperative for effectively approaching hypertext. The architectural platform of the Internet involves engagement with hypertext. Hypertext is made of chunks of nonlinear text, pictures, sound, and video that are chained together by electronic links that may be accessed by clicking a mouse or touching a computer screen. There are many new challenges to comprehension presented when we introduce the Internet and hypertext reading. For the youngest readers, we may want to structure Internet experiences to match our comprehension goals. Since neither comprehension nor hypertext exploration is linear, instruction is best accomplished embedded within a unit to achieve particular reading and writing purposes. Then apply the gradual release of responsibility to directly teach, model, think-aloud, and guide students through the process.

For example, most kindergarten classrooms that are reading Eric Carle's books and becoming familiar with him as an author would be likely to make use of the Eric Carle website (*www.eric-carle.com/home.html*). However, rather than simply sharing the visual information with the children, you can take advantage of the opportunity to teach both navigation skills and ethical use of Internet sources. Opening the Eric Carle home page provides the fodder for a powerful lesson on interpretation of the home webpage options, how to make selections, and the meaning and seriousness of copyright protection. Since most award-winning authors have extensive webpages, this provides a good way to introduce and gradually release responsibility to children for primary navigational skills. Often as teachers we already take advantage of Internet content; however, with a few extra steps we can make our instruction more effective by making our navigational processes and evaluative processes "public" in our classrooms and by using a gradual release of responsibility to guide our students' hypertext usage.

Incorporating Instructional Videos in New Ways

New technologies have made it possible for us to transport students to places that they might never be able to visit. Digital videos can be used to build prior knowledge, conduct comprehension strategy instruction, develop conceptual vocabulary, and expand student research capabilities.

Evidence indicates that the brain processes information through two separate channels: verbal and nonverbal (Clark & Paivio, 1991). If information is simultaneously entering both channels, the brain connects it, thereby strengthening our ability to learn and remember that information. Particularly for young children who are accustomed to learning experientially, providing support in both verbal and visual channels serves as a powerful scaffold. Picture books often serve this function, but new technologies can allow us to take greater advantage of this biological system. The verbal and nonverbal information that is presented simultaneously in digital media can be used in powerful ways to enhance the comprehension development of young children (see Hall & Stahl, 2012).

Recent research with videos and young children has some important implications for comprehension instruction (Kendeou et al., 2006; Lynch et al., 2008; Sharp et al., 1995). The ability to comprehend a narrative seems to transfer across media (print, video, audio). Additionally, narrative comprehension skills applied by young children to video and audio presentations predict later comprehension skills when reading printed material. This is not to say that this knowledge cannot be applied to informational texts, only that it was tested with narratives. What does this mean for the classroom teacher of young children?

Use Videos to Provide Vicarious Experiences

The most basic reason for interjecting videos into a disciplinary unit is to create a vicarious experience for children. Showing brief documentary videos and tuning in to live web cams that provide a close look at animals in the wild, outer space, unfamiliar habitats, or famous speeches can enrich any unit and provide prerequisite prior knowledge that will enhance our students' reading comprehension (Neuman, Newman, & Dwyer, 2011).

Apply Comprehension Lessons to Short Videos

Incorporate storybooks, poetry, and documentaries in video formats into your unit planning. Conduct comprehension instruction and questioning just as you would with a read-aloud. Since children have the visual support, their comprehension and inference generation may be pushed to a higher threshold. The video is actually a more highly scaffolded learning opportunity than a teacher read-aloud of a picture book (Stahl, 2014a). Chapter 9 contains more details about the ways that video can be used to extend comprehension instruction for children who need something extra to support their learning.

Use Videos as a Conceptual Scaffold

Use the video dynamically before other, less-scaffolded reading and writing activities. For example, the book *The Adventures of Taxi Dog* (Barracca & Barracca, 1990) is a Level E (early first grade) storybook that describes the adventures of Maxi, a dog that was rescued by Jim, a New York City taxi driver. Now Maxi lives with Jim and rides around the city with him on his driving shift. The book is a rhyming account of their adventures. This text would be a valuable addition to a late kindergarten or early first-grade unit on cities, transportation, or friendship. The *Reading Rainbow* video (*http://vimeo.com/6277109*) is 8 minutes long and provides a visual demonstration of the role of taxis within a city's transportation infrastructure, an explicit visual demonstration and explanation of the characteristics of taxis using domain-specific vocabulary (*rate, meter, fare, passenger, cabbie, receipt*). After the factual introduction, a New Yorker with a very distinct accent reads the book. Some of the book's original illustrations have been animated. A teacher would be hard-pressed to convey more information and get the story read in a more engaging manner within an 8-minute time frame. Particularly for children who do not live in a city, the video makes the experience of New York City traffic and being in a cab come alive. Following a brief discussion of the video, the children can read the text independently or with a partner. Providing such high levels of support increases the likelihood that students with an identified instructional level of C or D will be able to read this Level E text independently or with a partner.

Depending on the unit of study and purpose for including the text, the children could create a written response to a teacher prompt: (1) "Describe why Maxi and Jim make a good team. Use evidence from the story" or (2) "What skills does a person need to be a good taxi driver in a city?" The children could also create a written response or have a small-group discussion that addresses the more general prompt: "We have studied several methods of transportation that might be used in a city. Compare the advantages and disadvantages of cabs, buses, and subways for the passengers."

In this example, the short video is using verbal and nonverbal information to convey factual information and tell a story. However, despite the vast amount of information being conveyed, the use of video engages the students and serves to reduce the cognitive load so that more classroom time and student energy can be applied to the follow-up comprehension tasks of writing and discussion. Children seem to be able to remember more and make more complex inferences when cognitive demands are reduced through video presentation (Goldman, Varma, Sharp, & Cognition and Technology Group at Vanderbilt, 1999; Sharp et al., 1995). This finding has proved to be especially true for younger children and children who have more difficulty in school.

Use Videos to Support Vocabulary Development

Video clips are also a good way to support vocabulary development, especially for English learners (Silverman, 2013). Although videos should not be used in isolation, they provide an effective means of introducing new words and concepts. However, it is important to use the videos as only one component of a more comprehensive vocabulary effort that includes direct instruction, conversation, and written activities.

Formative Assessment and Themed Instruction

Themed instruction provides opportunities for a range of assessment formats. The assessment of comprehension calls for a collection of artifacts that reflect in-head processes. Both spoken and written artifacts may be used as evidence of comprehension. As we have discussed, reading comprehension is influenced by text factors (genre, topic, and readability), reader factors (decoding abilities, prior knowledge, strategic control, self-regulation, and engagement), and contextual factors (level of instructional support and purpose for reading or writing). Therefore, assessment of comprehension is never a unitary measure. It is a measure of a particular comprehension experience. In order to fully evaluate a student's comprehension, we must look at student performance across a range of comprehension tasks. These formative assessments can provide an ongoing gauge of children's ability to meet the large-grained reading goals or standards (including CCSS), as well as smaller-grained, specific literacy objectives. In standardized reading assessments that are commercially produced, we have no control over texts and tasks. However, in our classroom we can provide a range of opportunities for children to demonstrate their ability to make sense of a variety of texts and reflect that understanding through speaking and writing.

While a formative assessment may target a particular kind of text, it is likely to provide you with information about a collection of standards or objectives in a holistic way. It is unlikely that there will be a one-to-one task–standard match. According to the CCSS, the richest tasks actually combine multiple standards and "each standard need not be a separate focus for instruction and assessment" (NGA & CCSO, 2010, p. 3). By collecting written and spoken evidence across a range of texts that include the same standards, we will be able to see a portrait of our student's comprehension strengths and weaknesses. By incorporating assessment tasks into themed units, we are increasing our students' likelihood of success because the conceptual knowledge that we have developed as part of the unit supports comprehension processing.

The formative assessments that we use in our classroom may span the continuum from informal observations to what we call *common formative*. Informal assessments include anecdotal records, conference notes, and questioning. However, *common formative* assessments are administered, scored, and interpreted in clearly defined, standardized ways, often by all teachers in the grade-level cohort of a school or district. Informal assessments that fall midway along this continuum can often be converted to common formative assessments by creating guides or scripts to accompany the assessment process to ensure that the assessments are administered, scored, and results interpreted in uniform ways from student to student, from year to year, and across different classrooms.

Pretesting

We have found that administering a unit pretest for first and second graders serves multiple functions. It helps us gauge what our students already know about a topic and serves as a road map for planning instruction. It provides a clear demonstration of student growth and the assurance of accountability to external stakeholders. It is a morale booster for teachers and children to see evidence of the growth from the beginning to the end of the unit.

The pretest shouldn't be complicated. At a minimum, we recommend some informal measure of the target vocabulary administered to the whole group (see Stahl & Bravo, 2010). A knowledge rating scale or the vocabulary recognition task works well for novice readers and also for English learners (see Figures 4.2 and 4.3).

Bravo, Cervetti, Hiebert, and Pearson (2008) created a Vocabulary Assessment Magazine to measure students' science knowledge, strategy use, and reading comprehension of science texts before and after each unit was taught. Students wrote open-ended responses to text passages on the topic of study. The researchers were able to trace a clear increase in the use of technical vocabulary and depth of conceptual understanding using this format. The posttest or culminating assessment should measure the same general learning goals but to a higher standard and more comprehensively. Grade-level teams can easily transform these three vocabulary assessments into common formative assessments that provide useful information to teachers at each grade level who are teaching a common unit.

For sophisticated second graders, some form of pretest might also be done individually on the computer as a center, the week before the unit officially begins. Another simple assessment is to ask English learners to identify unknown words by having them circle and count all the words they do not know in a text.

	I have never heard of this.	I have heard of this, but I can't tell you much about it.	I can tell you what this is and draw a picture of it.
	CCSS Language 1.4. Determine or clarify the meaning of unknown and multimeaning words and phrases based on grade 1 reading and content, choosing flexibly from an array of strategies. CCSS Language 1.6. Use words and phrases acquired through conversations, reading and being read to, and responding to texts, including using frequently occurring conjunctions to signal simple relationships.		
ocean			
plankton			
coral			
current			
tide pool			
kelp			
estuary			
shoreline			

FIGURE 4.2. Pretest knowledge rating scale for grade 1 unit on marine habitats. The pretest would be read aloud by the teacher. Posttest would also require children to demonstrate their knowledge of each term through drawing, labeling, and describing each term.

Intermittent Assessments

Throughout the unit, students can respond in a variety of formats to individual or sets of texts. These products might be as simple as a written response that is composed during a single class period or they might be more sophisticated hypermedia projects that are constructed throughout the unit. You and the students would use a rubric to evaluate the product. For longer written responses to text, it is a good idea to use the same rubric that will be used to evaluate your students on your state's high-stakes standardized test in the upper grades. Alternatively, the 6 + 1 Writing Trait Rubric does a good job of clearly describing a generic progression of written expression. For shorter writing products or speaking performances, a teacher-made rubric with clearly established criteria works well.

Taffe and Bauer (2013) describe a third-grade classroom that was studying the works of Grace Lin. After viewing the author's website and building on the students' interest, the teacher suggested that students contact Lin using the author's

CCSS Language 2.4. Determine or clarify the meaning of unknown and multimeaning words and phrases based on grade 2 reading and content, choosing flexibly from an array of strategies.

CCSS Language 2.5. Demonstrate understanding of word relationships and nuances in word meanings.

CCSS Language 2.6. Use words and phrases acquired through conversations, reading and being read to, and responding to texts, including using adjectives and adverbs to describe.

"We have been learning about the human body. Below you see a list of words. Put a circle around the words that you can read *and* are sure have something to do with the human body. Do not guess because wrong answers will lower you score."

heart	*brain*	*way*
nerves	*muscles*	*esophagus*
telescope	*motor*	*blood*
intestines	*circulation*	*whiskers*
skeleton	*stomach*	*digestion*
joint	*lungs*	*respiration*
trachea	*bones*	*roots*
tail	*creation*	*skull*
	tendons	

"Put the words that you circled in the right group."

```
                    ┌──────────────┐
                    │  The Human   │
                    │    Body      │
                    └──────────────┘
   ┌──────────┬──────────┬─────┴────┬──────────┬──────────┐
┌─────────┐┌─────────┐┌─────────┐┌─────────┐┌─────────┐
│Respiratory││ Skeletal ││Digestive ││Circulatory││ Nervous │
│ System  ││ System  ││ System  ││ System  ││ System  │
└─────────┘└─────────┘└─────────┘└─────────┘└─────────┘
```

FIGURE 4.3. Vocabulary recognition task—human body.

blog or a personal letter. After a lesson comparing and contrasting letters, e-mail, and blog posts, the students created blog posts and letters to the author. This type of assignment serves as an ideal intermittent, authentic assessment for CCSS writing standards for grade 3 (see the text box on the next page).

Projects

Integrated units lend themselves to project-based learning that incorporates reading, writing, speaking, listening, and technology. These projects can and should take a variety of forms across the year for each unit. Projects provide children with opportunities to choose an area of interest that they deem worthy of an investment of their time and energy. Independent reading and writing is in service to their

CCSS WRITING STANDARDS FOR GRADE 3

CCSS Writing 3.1: Write opinion pieces on topics or texts, supporting a point of view with reasons.

CCSS Writing 3.4: With guidance and support from adults, produce writing in which the development and organization are appropriate to the task and purpose.

CCSS Writing 3.5: With guidance and support from adults, develop and strengthen writing as needed by planning, revising, and editing.

CCSS Writing 3.6: With guidance and support from adults, use technology to produce and publish writing (using keyboarding skills) as well as to interact and collaborate with others.

project. Most projects involve reading a wide range of texts, some difficult, for an authentic purpose. Typically, work on the project starts a few weeks into the unit or close to the end of the unit. Time blocks typically devoted to reading or writing become more malleable at the end of the unit as the students' reading and writing inform each other. Teachers can create engaging projects for literary units as well as other disciplinary content areas.

The expectations for the children's contribution should grow across the year. Early in the year, the projects are more structured and supported by the teacher and involve high levels of peer collaboration. Across the year, the students own more independent responsibility and the projects become more comprehensive. Children should be reading and writing for authentic purposes, including but not limited to sharing their specialized expertise about a unit subtopic, taking social action to support a cause, and performing a function as a member of a family or a community citizen. More information on the actual writing process involved in a research project is addressed in Chapter 7. Rubrics with explicit reading, writing, and speaking criteria serve as production guidelines and criteria for evaluation.

For example, you'll recall that Kay's second graders were required to complete a fairly limited research project on a single sea mammal in the beginning of the school year. The children used a template to guide their research. As resources, they read from a single website and a collection of books on the topic. By the end of the school year, each child was responsible for generating a research question on a topic related to the unit "Our Changing Earth." They each had to select an open-ended question that had not been studied by the class. The children were not allowed to research a specific dinosaur. Although a large percentage of the children in this school came from high-poverty homes, the children were always

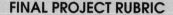

FINAL PROJECT RUBRIC

_____ **Reading**

- Able to fluently read all material that is displayed.
- Project accurately represents at least three reference sources.

_____ **Writing**

- Writing and visuals represent time and effort.
- Formal, correct use of writing mechanics.
- Effective synthesis of information.

_____ **Speaking**

- Oral presentation demonstrates knowledge of topic.
- Expert demeanor.

_____ **Listening**

- Listens respectfully to other presentations.
- Asks questions about other displays/presentations.

held to high learning expectations. Some of the inquiry projects that Kay's second graders wanted to explore included:

- How are trilobites alike and different from today's arthropods?
- What plants lived during the Cretaceous period?
- What was Earth like during the Cambrian period?
- Is Earth still changing? How do scientists know?

Research findings were displayed on a trifold board with explanations, illustrations, and artifacts. These projects were presented in a museum format to their classmates, other second-grade classes (that also studied the state-mandated science unit), and as a second-grade preview to the first graders. A project rubric was used to guide and assess their project.

Conclusion

Teaching themed disciplinary units builds the experiential knowledge required for comprehension and inference generation. The sustained coverage of a topic promotes engagement and motivation. Opportunities for repeated exposure to related sets of academic vocabulary leads to concept development and word recognition that can be used when reading and writing. Throughout a themed disciplinary unit, children have multiple opportunities to familiarize themselves with the genres and text types that are associated with the area of study.

Planning disciplinary study works best if it is conducted at both school and grade levels. School-level planning ensures vertical alignment and comprehensive coverage of the most important disciplinary content. Grade-level planning considers the texts, resources, and experiences that will best help students master the unit learning goals. Reading, writing, and speaking tasks facilitate and demonstrate student learning.

Formative assessments are used as evidence of the children's disciplinary knowledge and their ability to express that knowledge through speaking and writing. Pre- and posttests, projects, and measures of targeted vocabulary knowledge can all be used to provide evidence of students' literacy standards, performance proficiency, and disciplinary knowledge.

CHAPTER 5

Comprehension Strategy Instruction and Self-Regulation

- What is comprehension strategy instruction, and why do researchers think that it can improve children's reading comprehension?
- What is the role of self-regulation?
- How can teachers use the GRR to teach comprehension strategies?
- What types of comprehension strategy instruction have been developed, implemented, and tested?
- What are the strategy traps that teachers need to avoid?
- What have we learned about the comprehension strategy use of English learners?
- How can teachers evaluate students' use of comprehension strategies?

SETTING THE STAGE

Five second graders are sitting around a table (three girls and two boys). One child, Tamika, is serving as the leader of the group. She begins by showing the other children the cover of the book *Rap a Tap Tap: Here's Bojangles—Think of That!* (Dillon & Dillon, 2002), and asks them what they think the story is about. Based on the book cover, two children provide predictions. Tamika says, "Let's see if your predictions are true."

Tamika begins to read the book aloud as she shows the children the first three pages. She then asks Lydia to summarize what has happened so far. Lydia uses AAVE (explained in Chapter 2) to respond, "There a man all dressed up who make people happy cuz he always be dancing." Ralph chimes in, "My prediction wasn't true. I thought he was dancing on a stage. He's dancing in the street." Catherine voices a concern: "Oooh, I hope he doesn't get hit by a car!" The children in the group, including Tamika who is acting as the teacher, have learned how to enact comprehension strategy instruction in a student-led small group to discuss a text.

Overview of Research

Comprehension Strategy Instruction

If you are interested in improving your students' reading comprehension, one of the best things that you can do as a classroom teacher is to ensure that your students know how to use metacognitive and cognitive strategies flexibly as they interact with texts. Metacognitive and cognitive strategies are mental approaches or tools that readers consciously use to monitor, repair, and facilitate their comprehension of narrative and informational text (Almasi, 2003; Baker & Brown, 1984). Many times the two terms—*metacognitive* and *cognitive*—are collapsed into the single term *cognitive strategies*. However, when the terms are separated, *metacognitive* usually refers to readers' talk about text or reflection on how they are monitoring their reading comprehension or reasoning about text. An example of a metacognitive strategy is when a child states, "Oh, no, I don't understand this part." Cognitive strategies are the mental approaches that students use to proceed through text to resolve a comprehension problem or to enhance their comprehension. Two examples of cognitive strategies are invoking prior knowledge to make sense of a text (e.g., "Oh, I remember we read about what it means to be _____."), and making an accurate inference by stating what an unspecified part of the text means (e.g., "It doesn't say, but I think that he went to the school yesterday"). When we use the terms *comprehension strategies* or *comprehension strategy instruction* in this chapter, we are referring to both metacognitive and cognitive strategies. Comprehension strategy instruction has its origins in investigations of what expert readers do to repair and enhance their comprehension as compared with less successful readers.

Studies have demonstrated that teaching comprehension strategies to primary-grade students has positive effects both on standardized measures and formative measures (Shanahan et al., 2010; Stahl, 2004, 2013). Table 5.1 lists and describes the comprehension strategies that studies have shown to be effective in improving reading comprehension for primary-grade students. Interestingly, there is no evidence to show that students who were taught how to use comprehension strategies

TABLE 5.1. Comprehension Strategies Supported by Research

Strategy	Description
Targeted activation of prior knowledge and purposeful predictions	Students activate their existing, relevant knowledge and integrate it with text-based information to hypothesize what will happen in the text, followed by verification and taking stock.
Text structure: Narrative and expository	Students are able to use the organizational structure of narrative and informational texts to enhance meaning making and recall.
Visualizing	Students create a mental image or representation of text.
Questions: Answering high-level questions and generating questions	Students are able to both answer and ask important questions about the text.
Taking stock/summarizing/retelling	Either orally or in writing, students can identify and report the key elements of a text.
Generating inferences	Students retrieve information related to the text that is not explicitly stated and they are able to generate new ideas based on text concepts (deductive reasoning).
Monitoring and applying fix-up strategies	Students are aware of the need to make sense of text in an ongoing way, to identify the point at which they do not understand either the vocabulary or ideas in a text, and what they might do to overcome comprehension hurdles.

Note. Based on Shanahan et al. (2010) and Stahl (2013, pp. 226–227).

while reading actually used the specific strategies that were taught when reading on their own (National Reading Panel, 2000; Rosenshine & Meister, 1994). Rather, researchers speculate that when students are taught how to use strategies flexibly while reading, their interactions with and thinking about text are heightened, leading to deep, or close, reading that, in turn, improves their reading comprehension (Taylor, Pearson, García, Stahl, & Bauer, 2006). Another benefit of comprehension strategy instruction, whether the strategies are taught singly or in combination, is that students' motivation to read is enhanced, frequently resulting in their reading more text than they did prior to the instruction (National Reading Panel, 2000).

A good question to ask is, what about younger students in preschool through first grade? One of the multiple strategic approaches, Reciprocal Teaching (discussed later in this chapter), has been used effectively with first graders. However, in general, the multiple strategic approaches have been taught explicitly to students in second grade and above. Yet, we know that students in preschool, kindergarten, and first grade can be taught to use comprehension strategies as they listen to a teacher read-aloud, watch a video, participate in a guided reading lesson, or read on their own. In fact, there is some evidence to show that children as young as kindergarten benefit when their teachers prompt them to activate their prior knowledge, ask questions that require them to use prediction or consider story grammar elements, and participate in retellings (Morrow, 1984, 1985). Teacher questioning that prompts children to apply comprehension strategies can be considered the precursor to explicit strategy instruction.

Consequently, when you ask kindergartners or first graders to retell what they have heard read aloud or what they themselves have read, and you show them how to use a story map to guide their retellings, you are introducing them to summarization. Other comprehension strategies appropriate for young children include comprehension monitoring, activating prior knowledge, visualizing, hypothesis testing (making and testing inferences), requesting clarification, and using fix-up strategies when confused (reread, read ahead, talk with others). Teachers usually introduce these strategies by modeling their own thinking as they read aloud stories or informational text, stopping at key points to model and invoke students' use of specific strategies.

Self-Regulation

For comprehension strategy instruction to be effective, classroom teachers need to teach their students how to self-regulate their reading. Self-regulation occurs when students set their own goals for reading, monitor their own reading comprehension, and apply strategies flexibly to repair and enhance their comprehension. How these three tasks look in real life will vary according to the developmental level of the reader. For example, when young children (preschool through second grade) are asked about their goal or purpose for reading a book or text, they may say, "To learn about sharks," or "I love reading about princesses. I really like the stories."

Comprehension monitoring occurs when young children interrupt their reading or that of the teacher to say, "Wait, I don't understand that part." Young children demonstrate the flexible use of strategies when they spontaneously say, "Uh, oh, I better reread that part because I don't understand what is happening here." As students become older, they should be able to select strategies according to what they know about themselves as readers, the text they are reading, the task or activity for which they are reading, and the context in which the reading act takes place (National Reading Panel, 2000; Stahl, 2013).

An important aim of self-regulation is for students to internalize the strategies, so that they can use them on their own to repair and facilitate their comprehension as needed. To help students internalize their use of strategies, Almasi (2003) recommends that you make sure that your students (1) know the purpose and usefulness of comprehension strategies, (2) have a variety of comprehension strategies at their disposal, (3) have heightened metacognitive knowledge so that they know when they are not comprehending, (4) be able to "analyze the reading task or activity, and (5) be motivated to use the appropriate" strategies (p. 13). Most important, your students need to know how to select and apply comprehension strategies *as needed* to repair or facilitate their text comprehension. Self-regulated readers do not use strategies in a lock-step fashion, but choose from a repertoire of strategies according to what they need to improve their comprehension. Making the right choice means that they have to know how to transfer what they have learned in the classroom about comprehension strategy instruction to their own independent reading of texts. Therefore, it is important to explicitly tell your students that they can use the strategies they are learning in literacy when reading other types of texts and about other topics (e.g., science, social studies) both in and out of school. As you work with your students to develop their use of comprehension strategies while reading, it is important to keep the self-regulation goals in mind.

Implementing Comprehension Strategy Instruction

Using the GRR

Following the GRR, introduced in Chapter 3, is an excellent way to ensure that your students learn how to use comprehension strategies so that they become self-regulated readers. As shown in Figure 5.1, the GRR approach applied to

Task	Share of Responsibility for the Task				
Explicit Instruction of Strategy: Declarative, Procedural, and Conditional Knowledge					
Modeling of Strategy					
Collaborative Use of Strategy					
Guided Practice of Strategy					
Independent Application of Strategy					

☐ Teachers   ☐ Students

FIGURE 5.1. GRR for Comprehension Strategy Instruction. Based on Duke and Pearson (2002), Pearson and Gallagher (1983), and Shanahan et al. (2010, p. 15).

USE OF EXPLICIT INSTRUCTION TO INTRODUCE A STRATEGY

Teacher introducing her first graders to visualization:

Declarative Knowledge: "It is a good idea to make a picture or a movie in our mind as we are reading. We call this strategy 'visualization.'"

Procedural Knowledge: "For instance, if the author is describing a really scary monster, it will help you to understand the story better if you make a picture in your mind of what the monster looks like. To make the picture, you need to use the words that the author has written and what you know about scary monsters."

Conditional Knowledge: "Visualization is an important strategy because many books that you will read, especially when you are a little older, do not have pictures. Making a movie in our mind as we read or hear a story helps us monitor whether we understand what the author wrote. It also helps us remember what we are reading. We can use visualization when the author has described something, but doesn't include a very good illustration. For example, a story is really like a movie and the illustration is often only one snapshot of what is happening but it leaves out lots of other important information about what is happening. You don't need to use visualization when there is a really good illustration in the book that shows what the author is describing or if a scientific picture tells more than the words in an information book."

comprehension strategy instruction includes explicit instruction, teacher modeling, collaborative use, guided practice, and independent practice. Although the goal of strategy instruction is for students to flexibly select strategies that are useful for their comprehension of specific texts, we recommend that you use the GRR to introduce each strategy individually through explicit instruction. When you introduce a strategy through explicit instruction, you should state *what* it is (declarative knowledge), explain *how* to use the strategy (procedural knowledge), and state *when* and *why* it should and should not be used (conditional knowledge). The text box above shows how a teacher used explicit instruction to introduce her first graders to the strategy of visualization.

After providing the students with declarative, procedural, and conditional knowledge about a new strategy, you should model how to actually use the strategy with authentic text. The next two stages of the GRR are collaborative use and guided practice. The text box on the next page shows how a classroom teacher used the first parts of the GRR (explicit instruction through guided practice) in a teacher read-aloud of the *Used-Up Bear* (Carmichael, 1998). The last GRR stage is independent application, in which primary students use the strategy in student-led small groups, in pairs, or by themselves. We talk more about the use of student-led small groups for independent practice in the section below.

PARTIAL USE OF THE GRR TO TEACH QUESTION GENERATION WITH *USED-UP BEAR* (CARMICHAEL, 1998)

Explicit Instruction: "Today we are reading a story about a stuffed bear that has become old and worn."

[*Declarative knowledge:*] "During the story we will be asking questions to help us understand the story, to help us think about the story more deeply, and to help us make connections to the story."

[*Procedural knowledge:*] "As I read the story, think about parts of the story that are not clear or that you are not sure about and turn them into questions. Sometimes, when I am reading a book, I just think about my questions and try to answer them as I am reading. Today, we will answer them as a class."

[*Conditional knowledge:*] "Asking yourself questions while you read helps you know whether or not you understand the text. You can do this with stories and informational texts."

Modeling: "As I read the book, I will ask you the kinds of questions that will help us to understand the book. . . . Okay, I have read a few pages. I am going to stop here because I don't think the book tells us Bear's problem. So I am going to ask the question: 'What is Bear's problem?' Do a think–pair–share to come up with your answers; then we will share some of them." (In the discussion of answers, point out that Bear's problem is not stated in the story, although there are clues.)

Collaborative Use: "What question do you have about what has happened so far? Share your question with your partner. Discuss whether the question's answer is in the story. Then, see if you can answer your partner's question. . . . Okay, let's share the questions that didn't have complete answers in the story. "

Guided Practice: "Okay, after I finish reading this part of the story, I want you each to write down on a sticky note a question that will help you understand this part of the story better. Okay, I've finished reading this part. Please write down your question on the sticky note." (Collect the sticky notes and post the questions on the white board for discussion.)

Note. Adapted from unpublished grant materials (García, Pearson, Taylor, Stahl, & Bauer, 2007) and Stahl (2009, p. 355).

Developing Expertise with Comprehension Strategy Instruction

A number of multiple comprehension strategy programs have been developed, taught, and tested by researchers and/or teachers. Table 5.2 presents a list of the more popular programs along with the names of the strategies explicitly taught in each program. All of them have been found to be effective in improving students' reading comprehension performance (National Reading Panel, 2000; Stahl, 2009). If you are teaching PreK–K, then we recommend that you implement the

TABLE 5.2. Comprehension Strategies Explicitly Taught in Different Types of Multiple-Strategy Programs

	Directed Reading/ Thinking Activity (DR-TA or DR/L-TA)	Reciprocal Teaching (RT)	Synthesized Comprehension Instruction (SCI)	Transactional Strategy Instruction (TSI)
Clarification		X	X	X
Comprehension monitoring				X
Confirming (verifying)	X	(X)	(X)	X
Disconfirming (verifying)	X	(X)	(X)	X
Fix-up kit (may overlap with individual strategies): guessing, rereading, skipping, using picture clues				X
Predicting	X	X	X	X
Prior knowledge (invoking)			X (included with prediction)	X
Problem solving				X
Question generation and answering		X	X	
Rereading or looking back				X
Setting reading purpose	X			
Summarization (taking stock)	(X)	X	X	X
Think-aloud				X
Using text or picture clues				X
Visualizing			X	X
Vocabulary			X	

listening component of the Directed Reading/Listening–Thinking Activity (DR/L-TA) described below. For first and second graders who are new to comprehension strategy instruction, we recommend that you begin with the Directed Reading–Thinking Activity (DR-TA), followed by reciprocal teaching (RT). As you become more experienced at implementing comprehension strategy instruction, then you should implement transactional strategy instruction (TSI) and/or synthesized comprehension instruction (SCI).

Directed Reading–Thinking Activity

Stauffer (1969) initially developed DR-TA for reading, but later expanded it to include listening (DR/L-TA) for younger students who cannot read the texts for themselves but who can understand the text when the teacher reads it aloud (Richek, 1987).

Teachers who implement the DR/L-TA or DR-TA emphasize the reading–thinking relationship by teaching students how to identify a purpose for the reading; how to select, comprehend, and learn information in the text; how to analyze the text according to the reading purpose; how to "suspend judgments"; and how to make decisions based on the information "gleaned from reading" (Tierney & Readence, 2000, p. 21). One of us (Kay) tested the use of DR-TA with second graders reading at a first-grade level (Stahl, 2008) and found that it was very effective at helping the students to read texts closely, one of the aims of the language arts CCSS. The children achieved high levels of reading comprehension and acquisition of new science knowledge when reading the informational texts that were used in the small-group setting. We have adapted the instructions presented below so that DR/L-TA can be used with children who are listening to the text being read, orally reading the text in partners, chorally reading it with the classroom teacher, or mumble-reading it (i.e., reading the text orally, but softly). For explicit directions on using DR-TA during guided reading, see Chapter 4.

Per Stauffer (1969) and Stahl (2008), we recommend that you first select and segment an authentic text into meaningful units of about two to three pages. Then, you should lead a discussion in which each student in the classroom or small group establishes his or her own purpose for reading the text. Next, help students generate predictions for what will happen in the next segment of text. Then, the students read (or listen to) that segment. Last, you lead a small-group discussion of the text, during which students confirm/disconfirm their predictions (called proving or verifying the prediction). You continue the process, helping students to revise their predictions (i.e., thinking about the text) as more of the text is read and discussed until you complete the reading and discussion of the text. The DR/L-TA or DR-TA can be used with both narrative and informational text.

Reciprocal Teaching

Originally developed for low-performing readers who were adequate decoders but poor comprehenders, RT is a multiple-strategy program that has resulted in the improved reading comprehension of students in first through eighth grades (Palincsar 1988, 1991; Palincsar & Brown, 1984). It can be used with students as they listen to a text being read aloud or as they read a text. To begin RT, the teacher first discusses with the students why some texts may be difficult to comprehend, and how having a strategic approach such as RT can help them to monitor and improve their reading comprehension. Then, he or she explicitly teaches the students how to use each of four strategies (questioning, summarizing, clarifying, and predicting) while reading a passage from an authentic text. It also is recommended that you post the four strategies where students can see them throughout the time that they are participating in RT. Next, in small groups, the teacher models a structured dialogue format that gets the students to use the four strategies to discuss their comprehension of the text. Later, the teacher's role fades as each of the students in the group takes over the teacher role in leading the dialogue and guiding the other students in their use of the four strategies. Depending on the age of the students and their success at implementing the dialogue, the teacher may provide scaffolded support throughout the small-group work. In the excerpt below (Palincsar & Brown, 1986, p. 771), a small group of first graders are implementing RT with their teacher's scaffolded support:

STUDENT 1: My question is, what does the aquanaut need when he goes under water?

STUDENT 2: A watch.

STUDENT 3: Flippers.

STUDENT 4: A belt.

STUDENT 1: Those are all good answers.

TEACHER: Nice job! I have a question, too. Why does the aquanaut wear a belt? What is so special about it?

STUDENT 3: It's a heavy belt and keeps him from floating up to the top again.

TEACHER: Good for you.

STUDENT 1: For my summary now . . . This paragraph was about what the aquanauts need to take when they go under the water.

STUDENT 5: And also about why they need those things.

STUDENT 3: I think we need to clarify gear.

STUDENT 6: That's the special things they need.

TEACHER: Another word for gear in this story might be *equipment*, the equipment that makes it easier for the aquanauts to do their job.

STUDENT 1: I don't think that I have a prediction to make.

TEACHER: Well, in the story they tell us that there are "many strange and wonderful creatures" that the aquanauts see as they do their work. My prediction is that they will describe some of these creatures. What are some of the strange creatures that you already know about that live in the ocean?

STUDENT 6: Octopuses.

STUDENT 3: Whales?

STUDENT 5: Sharks!

TEACHER: Let's listen to find out. Who will be our teacher?

First-grade teachers who have used RT as a listening activity or who have modified RT instruction have reported success in implementing RT with first graders (Coley, DePinto, Craig, & Gardner, 1993; Palinscar, 1991). For example, a group of first-grade teachers collaboratively used RT as a listening activity with expository texts at the third-grade level (Palincsar, 1991). Their first graders demonstrated significantly higher quantitative gains in their abilities to answer comprehension questions, solve novel problems based on information from the texts, and in their strategy use compared with other first graders who had not received RT instruction.

Craig adjusted how she introduced RT to her first graders (Coley et al., 1993). She spent 3 months teaching her students how to use each of the four strategies before she introduced them to the RT dialogue routine. Then, she paired her students and had them work in groups of four pairs or eight students in each group. She assigned a different strategy to each pair within a group, and gave them 15 minutes to prepare for the discussion. Each set of partners wrote their summary, prediction, clarification, or question on a note card. Next, she assigned a leader for each group and had the students use the note cards to participate in the small-group discussions. Based on her observations of her students' RT participation, she considered her modifications to be effective (Coley et al., 1993).

The RT guidebook (Palincsar, David, & Brown, 1989) also has explicit instructions for implementing RT. Although this method takes a while to train your students to enact RT, you need to remember that their comprehension will steadily improve during the training period, and the training period can be spread over a semester or the school year. According to the guidebook and a synopsis of the RT procedures in Hacker and Tenent (2002), you should teach the strategies explicitly and individually before using all strategies in the RT routine. Once students are comfortable with the RT protocol, instead of sharing questions, points of clarification, summaries, and predictions with the entire class, students do their

LONG-TERM RECIPROCAL TEACHING ROUTINE

Step 1: Introduce each strategy explicitly (one strategy/day) with review on Day 5. Young children are likely to need more than a day to become familiar with how to apply each strategy.

Step 2: After children have mastered the individual strategies, select and copy a short text (narrative or informational) related to a disciplinary-themed unit and/or for which your students already have background knowledge. Segment the text into meaningful reading and discussion sections.

Step 3: Form small RT groups with each student assigned to a heterogeneous group of six, with a partner at a similar reading level, so there are three sets of reading partners at different reading levels in each group.

Step 4: After students have their reading partners and are sitting in their small groups, you should introduce the text to the entire class by describing how it relates to what else the students are studying or reading about. Then, talk about the title and illustrations, and ask students to predict what they think the text is about. After generating predictions, tell students to pay attention to their predictions as they read the story with their partner. Explain and model for them how they will follow the reading by asking a question about the text and circling any words or parts of the text that they do not understand.

Step 5: Distribute student copies of the segmented text, and have students begin their partner work within their RT groups.

Step 6: After students have completed their partner work with the first text segment, have students meet in their RT groups to share their questions and discuss the parts that were confusing or unclear.

Step 7: Each group selects a question to share with the larger class and identifies any parts that still require clarification.

Step 8: During the whole-group community share, each small group will ask their question and answer the questions formulated by the other small groups. Additionally, confusions will be clarified by the class members or by you.

Step 9: Summarization of the passage occurs next. With primary-level readers, we recommend that you call on each group to help you write a collective summary on chart paper for the text they have read.

Step 10: Finally, ask the primary-level readers to meet in their groups to predict what will happen next in the text. Call on each group to provide their predictions, which you list on the board. The above cycle is repeated until the first text has been read and discussed.

Note. Based on Hacker and Tenent (2002) and Palincsar, David, and Brown (1989).

sharing within their RT groups, with a student assigned the teacher role. This long-term method of teaching RT might be useful in second grade to support the close reading of complex text that is now commonly used to support achievement of the CCSS. Consider using this with informational texts, *Time for Kids*, or other news article formats that children might be reading. As you implement RT, it is important to remember that the goal is for your students to be self-regulated readers so that they internalize the strategies and use them on their own flexibly as they read both narrative and informational text.

Transactional Strategy Instruction

As you gain experience in helping students match strategies to texts, to their reading purposes, and to what they know about the larger reading context and themselves as readers, you may be ready to try TSI (Pressley et al., 1992). TSI is more challenging to implement because it involves more strategies than RT and much less of a routine to guide students' use of strategies. The primary aim of TSI is for students to jointly construct interpretations of authentic texts by using comprehension strategies as they read the texts (Brown & Coy-Ogan, 1993). Although the teacher explicitly teaches certain strategies (see Table 5.2), students are also taught how to set goals and make a plan for reading, how to provide aesthetic and personal responses to texts, and how to share their textual interpretations with others. Probably the easiest way to initiate TSI is with a program called Students Achieving Independent Learning (SAIL; Bergman, 1992; Pressley et al., 1992).

According to Bergman (1992), a classroom teacher who implemented SAIL, the purpose of SAIL is to teach students comprehension strategies "to monitor [their] understanding and solve problems as they read" (p. 599). Problem solving includes students' resolution of comprehension problems as well as word recognition or decoding problems. SAIL explicitly teaches students how to predict, summarize, think aloud, and visualize. In addition, when students select and use a strategy, they have to justify or verify its use by explaining their rationale for using it. For example, when they make predictions, they have to explain what in the text or in their own personal experiences caused them to make the prediction. Then they have to read to confirm or disconfirm the prediction. In addition, students are taught to read for gist, so that they can tell what a story is about by figuring out the problem and solution in a narrative text. In SAIL, teachers use think-alouds while reading authentic texts aloud to model how to monitor, problem-solve, and use comprehension strategies while reading. Then, as students select and use strategies while reading, teachers coach them by asking for verifications, providing prompts, elaborating on their responses, and asking them questions to clarify their use of strategies and resolution of comprehension problems. Teachers are also encouraged to accept all student answers or responses, focusing more on how students arrive at their answers or responses than on providing them with predetermined answers. Teachers need to listen carefully to student responses in order to provide follow-up questions that force children to think more deeply and to justify their initial responses. According to Bergman, two of the major differences she made in her reading instruction when using SAIL were that she helped students to activate their background knowledge and figure out unfamiliar text vocabulary *while* reading rather than before reading the text.

Although a precise routine for classroom teachers' implementation of TSI is not provided, the effective TSI instruction of a second-grade teacher who was in her third year of implementing TSI provides us with several guidelines (Brown & Coy-Ogan, 1993). Based on the teacher's third-year experience, we recommend that you provide your students with intensive and explicit strategy instruction, following the GRR model, during the beginning of the school year. During this time, it also is important to start student-led reading groups, assigning student leaders to lead the groups by calling on specific members of the group, resolving any disputes, and asking group members to identify comprehension and word-recognition/decoding problems, and to raise and verify interpretations. We encourage you to let your students discuss in student-led small groups their text interpretations, without insisting on your own interpretation. Similarly, you need to accept all of your students' interpretive responses, as long as they can support them with references to the text. At the end of the year, compared with students in the first and second year of the teacher's implementation of TSI, the third-year students were observed to integrate information across their discussions of text segments, make more personal connections across the segments, and state and support their interpretations more effectively by using world knowledge, personal experiences, and text information.

Synthesized Comprehension Instruction

SCI combines three comprehension approaches that teachers previously taught separately to students in grades 2–5: cognitive strategy instruction (CS), responsive engagement (RE) instruction, and intentional vocabulary instruction (García, 2006; García, Pearson, Taylor, Bauer, & Stahl, 2011; García, Pearson, Taylor, Stahl, & Bauer, 2007; Stahl, 2009; Taylor et al., 2006).

CS draws from both RT and TSI. Teachers use the GRR model to explicitly teach students how to use five strategies flexibly (purposeful prediction, taking stock/summarization, question generation and answering, clarification, and visualization) according to the text, the task, and themselves as readers. The end goals are for students to use the strategies flexibly and as needed in student-led small groups as the students read and discuss texts (often with a student serving as the teacher, similar to RT), and later as they read independently.

Instructional Conversations (Saunders & Goldenberg, 1999) and Taylor and colleagues' (Taylor, Pearson, Clark, & Walpole, 1999) findings on characteristics of effective reading instruction in high-poverty schools influenced the development of RE. The aim of RE is for teachers to engage their students in high-level talk and thinking about text. In RE, primary teachers use shared reading or teacher read-alouds of rich texts with themes (for narrative texts) or open-ended issues (for informational texts). After reading the text, teachers ask their students to complete literature response logs in which the students make personal connections to the text and identify open-ended questions related to the theme or issue ("big juicy questions"). Then, in small, student-led groups, they are encouraged to use their logs to ask and answer open-ended questions related to the theme or issue, to make personal connections, and to provide elaborated responses in support of their points of view or those of other students. Young children could draw their responses to texts, meet in pairs or small groups to collaboratively write their responses, and/or complete graphic organizers that indicate their responses.

Intentional Vocabulary Instruction emphasizes the work of Beck, McKeown, and Kucan (2002) and focuses on teaching Tier Two vocabulary items found in the texts. Tier Two words are words known by sophisticated language users that occur often in texts, and for which students have conceptual understanding without having knowledge of the particular word. For example, children would be more likely to identify a traffic light or a school bus as yellow than amber. Students are intentionally given multiple opportunities to use and learn the words after they hear the texts read aloud, not before, with the teacher quickly pointing out the meanings of key words as he or she reads the text aloud.

The three approaches were combined into SCI because considerable evidence shows that each of them contributes uniquely to students' reading comprehension (García et al., 2007, 2011; Stahl, 2009). It was hypothesized that a combined approach would be a much more powerful way to improve students' reading comprehension than any of the individual approaches. Teachers are supposed to implement SCI at least three times per week for 30–45 minutes in addition to their other literacy instruction. Second-grade teachers who compared how they did with SCI after a year of instruction—compared with one of the three previous approaches or with conventional reading instruction—reported that they were able to focus on Intentional Vocabulary Instruction, provide explicit instruction in the five strategies, and get their students to participate in engaging, high-level discussions of texts with themes and open-ended issues, although the movement to student-led small groups was not realized on a large scale. Most important, the teachers reported that their second graders' comprehension of text substantially improved compared with students who previously had not received SCI (Stahl, 2009).

If you are interested in implementing SCI, we recommend that you review the principles for SCI instruction listed in the text box on the next page (García, 2006; García et al., 2007; Stahl, 2009, p. 355). Then, we suggest that you begin by using explicit instruction to teach your students in a whole-class setting how to use each of the five strategies. At the same time, we recommend that you select texts for teacher

PRINCIPLES OF SYNTHESIZED COMPREHENSION INSTRUCTION

- Effective comprehension instruction for rich text includes instruction in vocabulary, strategy, and responsive engagement.
- To effectively provide comprehension instruction, teachers need to select and preread text and decide on the vocabulary, strategy, and responsive engagement emphases appropriate to each text.
- The amount of attention devoted to each of the three approaches (vocabulary, strategy, responsive engagement) will vary according to student needs and instructional goals.
- Each of the approaches requires some explicit instruction.
- For vocabulary instruction, students need to learn how to identify unfamiliar words and unlock the meanings of these words.
- For strategy instruction, students need to learn and apply a range of strategies to resolve comprehension problems and enhance their comprehension.
- For responsive engagement instruction, students need to learn how to respond to and identify themes, answer and ask big juicy questions, make relevant personal connections, and state and elaborate their reasoning.
- Teachers need to vary the support and amount of responsibility given to students based on their ongoing assessment of students' progress toward independence.
- A key component of the comprehension framework is small-group discussions about texts. Teachers need to provide students with explicit instruction on how to participate in and hold strategic and rich conversations about texts.

Note. Based on unpublished grant materials (García, Pearson, Taylor, Stahl, & Bauer, 2007) and Stahl (2009, p. 355).

---

read-alouds with "well-developed plots, sophisticated vocabulary, and compelling themes" (Stahl, 2011, p. 233) so that you can implement Intentional Vocabulary Instruction and show students how to ask and answer "big juicy questions" related to the theme or an open-ended issue. For example, for *The Paper Bag Princess* (Munsch & Martchenko, 1980), a set of big juicy questions that could be asked of second graders would be "What do you think the author means when he talks about a 'real' prince or a 'real' princess? Is there such a thing? Why or why not?"

As you read aloud the texts, we recommend that you use think-alouds to model how to use specific strategies, identify themes, and make personal connections. Once students are familiar with the three components of SCI, we encourage you to use the GRR model to get them to integrate all three components. For example, you can provide them with opportunities for collaborative use and guided practice when you have them think–pair–share in the whole-class setting, later followed by teacher-directed small-group instruction. As you move to student-led groups, you will want to use shared reading or partner reading of the texts in addition to the occasional teacher read-aloud. You may want to assign student leaders or captains and provide an initial protocol to organize and prompt student use of strategies and high-level discussion of texts. More recommendations will be provided in Chapter 6 for implementing and increasing the effectiveness of small-group discussions. Throughout the small-group work, you need to observe students' use of SCI in their groups, remembering to coach students as they implement SCI. A drop-in visit to the small group in the primary grades is not enough support until you have conducted many small-group discussions. The GRR needs to include many discussions that involve you as facilitator, then moving to the side with the occasional interjection, followed by the stage that allows you to circulate among multiple groups. In your discussion with students, you will want to remind them to use the SCI approach when they read other texts inside and outside the classroom.

Avoiding Strategy Traps

It is important to remember that the purpose of comprehension strategy instruction, and any of the instructional programs reviewed earlier, is for students to internalize the strategies so that they can use them *as needed* to enhance their comprehension of a range of texts (narrative and informational) inside and outside the classroom. The end goal is enhanced comprehension of text, not mastery of each strategy in isolation. Teaching students so that they demonstrate mastery of the strategies without emphasizing self-regulation defeats the purpose of comprehension strategy instruction. Similarly, the various strategy instructional programs and protocols provide a way for teachers to introduce and get students to use strategies while reading. The programs or protocols need to be viewed as temporary scaffolds. Being able to follow a program or protocol in a formulaic manner is *not* the goal. Finally, a side benefit of comprehension strategy instruction is students' deep thinking about text and increased interest and motivation to read texts. We need to reconsider how we are implementing comprehension strategy instruction when it does not promote students' deep thinking, textual engagement, and motivation to read texts.

Considerations for English Learners

Different types of short- and long-term comprehension strategy instruction (RT, CS, SCI) have resulted in improvements in the Spanish and English reading comprehension performance of Spanish-speaking English learners (García, 2003; García, Bray, Mora, Carr, & Rinehart, 2008), and there is no reason to believe that this type of instruction would not be beneficial for other language groups. However, if you are teaching English learners to use comprehension strategies in English, we remind you to shelter or scaffold your English by using the instructional principles explained in Chapter 2, so that English learners understand your instruction.

Also, it is important to let English learners use their L1 to discuss their use of strategies or responses to text or to write their responses in their L1 in their literature response logs even if you do not understand them. Many English learners will be able to explain their thinking much better when they are encouraged to use their L1. If you do not understand their L1, you can place them in mixed-proficiency groups from the same L1 with a strong bilingual student, or provide them with a bilingual tutor or volunteer who can explain to you in English what they are saying in the small groups or writing in their response logs. The use of small groups of English learners of mixed proficiency from the same L1 also provides them with the means to explain to one another aspects of your instruction that they may not all have understood.

It is also important for you to realize that English learners may demonstrate the use of bilingual strategies unique to their bilingual status to clarify or explain their understanding of text. We discussed these strategies in Chapter 2. They include recognizing cognates (the identification of words that are similar in appearance and meaning from two languages that have a common ancestry, such as Spanish and English), code mixing (use of a word from one language while speaking or writing in another language), code switching (alternate sentences in the two languages), paraphrased translating (use of their L1 to explain in their own words what they have read), and summary translating (use of their L1 to explain the gist or main idea of the text). These are not deficit strategies, but strategies that should be encouraged, especially when bilingual readers are working together to comprehend a text, because they facilitate the students' general communication proficiency as well as their comprehension of text (García, 1998).

We encourage you to find out whether English learners have learned about comprehension strategy instruction in their L1 and/or already use strategies to monitor and facilitate their text comprehension in their L1. As explained in Chapter 2, many bilingual students are able to use comprehension strategies taught in one language while reading in the other language, indicating cross-linguistic transfer. Those students who have a uniform view of reading across their two languages are more likely to exhibit the use of comprehension strategies in both languages than those students who think they have to keep their two languages separate. Therefore, when you are teaching English learners, it is important to remind them that they can use what they have learned about reading comprehension in one language (such as comprehension strategies) to approach reading comprehension in the other language.

In terms of the vocabulary instruction included in SCI, there are a few caveats for teaching English learners when SCI is applied to English reading. The three-tier system of vocabulary selection developed by Beck and colleagues (2002) will need to be adapted for English learners. The first thing to figure out is whether English learners know the English and/or L1 versions of Tier One and Tier Two words. If they know the L1 versions but not the English versions, and the two versions are equivalent in meaning and function, then it is helpful when you ask bilingual adults, tutors, or peers to show the students the English versions of the L1 items, and require the students to keep their own bilingual dictionaries of the terms (such as *lazy* and *perezoso* or *perezosa*). If the English and L1 versions are cognates, then showing students the cognate relationships and having them indicate the cognate relationships in their bilingual dictionaries will be helpful for future use (such as *baseball* and *béisbol*). Here is where disciplinary thematic units across the different instructional settings (bilingual, ESL, and/or English) can be very helpful. When English learners don't know the meanings and functions of the words in the L1, then you will have to work collaboratively with their bilingual and/or ESL teachers to teach the meanings and functions of the vocabulary and use the ESL principles described in Chapter 2.

Assessment of Comprehension Strategies

It is important to know how and when your students use strategies so that you can monitor their progress and improve your instruction accordingly. A simple way to do this is to keep a clipboard with a strategy checklist on it with each child's name and the date of your observation. Then, you can use the chart to record how well individual students demonstrate their knowledge and appropriate use of an individual strategy or sets of strategies while participating and reading a text in small groups. Form 5.1 (at the end of the chapter) provides a sample checklist for RT instruction. A more systematic way to record student progress is to meet with students individually in a periodic reading conference, in which each student participates in a short think-aloud or strategy interview.

Think-Alouds

A think-aloud assessment is a way for readers to make their thinking during reading public (see Pressley & Afflerbach, 1995). Before you ask a child to participate in an open-ended think-aloud or a prompted think-aloud, you need to model the procedure with a short segment of text (different from the text you are using for the think-aloud). If you are assessing the child's specific use of certain strategies with an open-ended think-aloud, you want to specifically remind the child that the class has been practicing how to use a particular strategy or strategies. Tell the child that you want him or her to stop reading the passage (orally or silently) every time that he or she uses that strategy and to explain why. As the child is reading and explaining his or her strategy use, you'll want to use a checklist similar to the one in Form 5.1 (at the end of the chapter) to document the child's use of the taught strategy and explanation. If the child does not interrupt his or her reading of the passage, then when the child has finished, you can ask him or her to look at the passage (reread it) and tell you whether he or she used the specific strategy, point to where the strategy was used, and explain why.

When you want to compare your students' performance, it often is easier to use a prompted think-aloud. In a prompted think-aloud, you choose a passage ahead of time and analyze it according to where you think there are opportunities for your students to use specific comprehension strategies, putting consecutive numbers on the text. (See Figure 5.2 for an excerpt of a passage with consecutive numbers for a prompted think-aloud; there are opportunities in this short passage for the children to predict, visualize, clarify, ask and answer a question, and summarize or take stock.)

Then, after modeling how to do a prompted think-aloud with a different text, tell individual children to begin reading the text aloud or silently, stopping their reading when they come to a number in the text. At the number, ask the children to tell you what they are thinking or doing to understand the text. Form 5.2 (at the end of the chapter) shows a chart that you can use to track each child's strategy progress in a prompted think-aloud. This chart also includes a place for the students to set personal goals for their individual strategy use and to self-evaluate their attainment of the goals. A benefit of encouraging students to set their own goals and self-evaluate their strategy use is that the process heightens their metacognitive awareness about their strategy use.

Strategy Interviews

In the individual reading conferences with students, you can also assess their metacognitive awareness about strategies by asking them to participate in a strategy interview. McKenna and Stahl (2009) identify and include several interviews that can be used to learn more about your students' awareness of both general and particular purposes for reading, as well as their strategy knowledge. Form 5.3 (at the end of the chapter) shows some of the types of questions that you can ask in a strategy interview. You should be sure to add other questions pertinent to your

---

Holiday Adventure (1)

It was an icy day. Steve and his family got in the car to go to the airport. (2) His dad turned on the radio to hear the news. Just as he got to the highway, he stopped the car. (3) He didn't know if he should go to the airport or return home. There were accidents all around them. Other drivers had slid off the road. (4)

FIGURE 5.2. Example of a prompted think-aloud.

classroom instruction and students' progress. By dating the interview, and asking your students to answer the same or similar questions periodically throughout the school year, you can monitor their development of metacognitive awareness and self-reported use of strategies.

Conclusion

Comprehension strategy instruction teaches students how to use metacognitive and cognitive strategies flexibly to resolve comprehension problems and to enhance their comprehension of narrative and informational texts. Primary-grade students who have received comprehension strategy instruction have significantly outperformed their peers on a range of reading comprehension measures. Researchers think that the improved reading comprehension of students who have received strategy instruction is a result of their heightened thinking about text and increased motivation to read additional text.

To make sure that students know how to self-regulate or transfer their use of strategies from the instructional setting to other settings, you need to teach them how to select and use appropriate strategies according to what they know about themselves as readers, the texts they are reading, the tasks for which they are reading, and the contexts or settings in which the reading takes place. The GRR—with its focus on explicit instruction, teacher modeling, collaborative use, guided practice, and independent practice—provides you with a way to introduce and support students in their strategy development so that their use of strategies is self-regulated.

There are several types of strategy protocols or programs that you may implement. The DR/L-TA may be used as early as PreK–K. The DR-TA, RT, TSI, and SCI have research validation for students in grades 1–2 and higher. Two strategy traps that teachers need to avoid are teaching strategies to mastery or rigidly following a strategy program or protocol.

English learners benefit from strategy instruction in their L1 and/or English. If you teach them in English, you need to shelter or scaffold their strategy instruction by using ESL sheltering and bilingual techniques and make sure that their vocabulary instruction is appropriate. Some English learners may use strategies unique to their bilingual status, which facilitate their text comprehension. Many of them can transfer what they have learned about strategy instruction in one language to the other language.

There are several assessments that teachers can use to monitor their students' use of strategies and to inform their instruction. These include a strategy checklist, a think-aloud interview, and a strategy interview. In the next chapter, we discuss how the implementation of high-level discussions of texts can improve students' reading comprehension.

FORM 5.1

Reciprocal Teaching Strategy Checklist

Date _____   Title of Text _____

Student Names	Prediction (confirmation or disconfirmation)	Summarization	Question Generation and Answer	Clarification	Comments

Student Strategy Chart

Date _____ **Title of Text** _____

Student Name	Prediction	Verification of Prediction	Taking Stock or Summarization	Question Generation and Answer	Clarification	Visualization
Declarative Knowledge						
Procedural Knowledge						
Conditional Knowledge						
Appropriate Use						
Teacher's Comments and Goal for Next Time						
Student's Evaluation and Goal for Next Time						

FORM 5.3
Questions for Strategy Interview

Student Name _____ **Date** _____

1. What do you do when you don't understand what you are reading? (Tell me all the things you can do when you don't understand what you are reading.)

2. What do you do when you are reading a story, and something in it does not make sense?

3. What do you do when you don't understand all the words in a story?

4. What types of things does your teacher have you do when you read?

5. What can you do easily when you read? Why?

6. What is difficult for you to do when you read? Why?

7. What makes a good reader?

8. How well do you read? What makes you think that?

9. What does a poor reader need to do to improve his or her reading?

10. What things do you need to do to improve your reading?

CHAPTER 6

Let's Talk About It

HIGH-LEVEL DISCUSSIONS

GUIDING QUESTIONS

- What are high-level discussions of texts?
- Why do researchers encourage high-level discussions of texts in grades K–2?
- How can teachers organize and support high-level discussions of texts?
- How can English learners benefit from high-level discussions of texts?
- How can teachers evaluate the effectiveness of high-level discussions of texts?

SETTING THE STAGE

In the spring semester of first grade, Ms. Spacey has just finished reading aloud the picture book *The Lazy Lion* (Hadithi, 1990). (Ms. Spacey already has introduced her first graders to the RE component of SCI introduced in Chapter 5.) To prepare for a high-level discussion of the text, she asks her students to write their answers to a yes/no question ("Would you want the lion to be your friend?") along with a one- to two-sentence explanation ("Why or why not?"). In the story, the lion demands that all the other animals that live on the African plain build him a big house so he does not get wet when the big rain comes. When each group of animals builds him a home, he arrogantly dismisses their efforts, demanding that another group build him an appropriate home. In the end, the big rain arrives before the lion has a home, so he lives in the open on the plain and gets wet, while all the other animals seek shelter in the homes they built for him.

Then, during the week, Ms. Spacey meets with small groups of four to six heterogeneously grouped students to help them discuss their answers to the question. Each group brings its answers to the discussion group, and know that they are supposed to use them to respond to the other children's answers and explanations by saying, "I agree with _____ because _____ or I disagree with _____ because _____." Throughout the discussion, Ms. Spacey asks the students to elaborate on their answers by explaining why they said what they did or what in the story prompted their responses. If students' responses are not linked to the story, she reminds them that they are discussing what is in the story. Next, in preparation for another small-group discussion about the book, she asks them to think about what the author wanted them to learn from reading the book, and to share their thoughts with a partner. She then has the students draw and/or write their answers to the following question: "What lesson did the author want us to learn from the story?" The students then meet in their small groups to discuss their answers to the question.

Overview of Research

High-Level Discussions of Texts

How you participate or interact with your students and how they interact with one another during literacy instruction and disciplinary themed units affects your students' reading comprehension development and performance. When we talk about "high-level discussions of texts," we are referring to teacher–student and student–student interaction patterns in which students are actively engaged in thinking about and sharing their thoughts about texts. Talking and writing are the two key ways that we express our comprehension of text and share ideas about text. Garas-York, Shanahan, and Almasi (2013) define discussions "as classroom events in which students and teachers are cognitively, socially, and affectively engaged in collaboratively constructing meaning or considering alternative interpretations of texts to arrive at new understandings" (p. 246). The CCSS for speaking and listening for K–2 emphasize comprehension and collaboration so that students are engaged, critically thinking about texts, and sharing their interpretations with their classroom teacher and peers. The CCSS also specify getting students to participate in high-level discussions of texts in small groups because it is the collaborative teacher–student and student–student discussions of texts that help students to become more engaged with text and to internalize their critical thinking about text.

High-level discussions of texts are in direct contrast to the teacher initiates–student responds–teacher evaluates (I-R-E) framework that often characterizes teachers' instruction (Cazden, 1988) and may result in only one- or two-word answers, as illustrated below:

TEACHER (I): John, what color was the doctor's jacket?

JOHN (R): Yellow?

TEACHER (E): Yes, you are correct.

In high-level discussions of texts, teachers ask and model higher-order questions that motivate students to think deeply and explain their answers. The questions require students to make personal connections to the themes and characters in the books being read. In small groups, students learn how to ask their own questions and share their own thoughts with each other and the teacher, as shown in Form 6.1 (at the end of the chapter). In the following excerpt (Garas-York et al., 2013, p. 269), first graders, who have been learning how to implement conversational discussion groups (CDGs; O'Flahavan, 1994/1995), share their thinking about the book *How Smudge Came* (Gregory & Lightburn, 1997):

ASHLEY: I wonder where the dog came from? Like when she was just sitting there.

ASHLEY: I wonder if she [the main character, Cindy] found it and she just wanted to take it home?

ROSE: Maybe, it was just, like, there. Maybe the puppy ran away from its home. . . .

CYNTHIA: Maybe its mother died. . . .

High-level discussions of texts can characterize many different facets of your literacy and content-area instruction, such as how you lead a discussion about a book read-aloud, how you implement comprehension strategy instruction or disciplinary themed units, or how your students discuss texts in the whole class or in small groups. For example, when you spend time modeling and coaching your students' comprehension, rather than telling or informing students about comprehension or having your students participate in recitation exercises, in which you already know the requested answers, then you are helping to facilitate high-level discussions of texts (Taylor et al., 2003). Students in high-level discussion classrooms are active participants, asking and answering questions and elaborating on their thinking; they are not passive participants who listen to the teacher or rely on other students to do most of the thinking and talking.

Martínez-Roldán (2005) talks about the importance of developing an inquiry stance in your classroom, in which you encourage your students to ask for others' help in going beyond their own current understandings. Two characteristics of an inquiry stance are "I wonder" statements and authentic questions (for which there are no set answers). For example, Martínez-Roldán explains that in a discussion of the book *Oliver Button Is a Sissy* (dePaola, 1979), a teacher or student who states, "I'm still wondering whether Oliver Button is a boy or a girl" (p. 23) has made an I wonder statement, opening up the discussion for others' comments. When the teacher or student asks, "Do you guys think that Oliver should do whatever others tell him to do?" (p. 23), then he or she has asked an authentic question, eliciting others' opinions. A key feature of high-level discussions about texts is when students explain the reasons for their interpretations. Teachers provide feedback, not in terms of correctness of interpretation, but in terms of how students arrive at their interpretations and how they participate in the discussions.

The Impact of High-Level Discussions of Text

Three recommended practices identified in the What Works Clearinghouse publication entitled *Improving Reading Comprehension in Kindergarten through Third Grade* (Shanahan et al., 2010) relate to our discussion of high-level discussions of texts: "Recommendation 3: Guide students through focused, high-quality discussion on the meaning of text; Recommendation 4: Select texts purposefully to support comprehension development"; and "Recommendation 5: Establish an engaging and motivating context in which to teach reading comprehension" (p. 1). Although only one of the recommendations had moderate research evidence (Recommendation 5), the authors of the report felt that Recommendations 3 and 4 were extremely important, and that the reading field should not wait until enough researchers had conducted a sufficient number of "gold standard" studies to encourage teachers to implement these recommendations.

Other researchers have provided qualitative and quantitative evidence supporting the relationship between high-level discussions of texts and the improved reading comprehension of students in grades 1–2. For example, qualitative studies of high-level discussions of texts showed that students from a range of backgrounds (African American, Anglo, Cambodian, English learners, Hmong, Laotian, Latina/o) successfully participated in and benefited from teacher- and student-led small-group instruction that emphasized high-level discussions of texts (Klassen, 1993; Martínez-Roldán & López-Robertson, 1999/2000).

In a meta-analysis of research studies on high-level discussions of texts, Murphy, Wilkinson, Soter, Henessey, and Alexander (2009) reported that effective use of high-level discussions of text resulted in increased amounts of student talk, reduced amounts of teacher talk, and improved student comprehension of texts, especially students' literal and inferential comprehension of efferent (informational) texts. The approaches that included students in grades K–2 were CDGs (O'Flahavan, 1994/1995), instructional conversations (Goldenberg, 1992/1993), and literature circles (Martínez-Roldán, 2005), among others.

Taylor and her colleagues (2000, 2003) investigated the types of literacy instruction that "beat the odds" in high-poverty schools (grades 1–5)—that is, approaches that overcame low expectations based on SES. They reported higher student comprehension growth rates for students in classrooms where teachers facilitated higher-order thinking through the questions they asked and the tasks they assigned to their students. Higher-order thinking occurred when students made and voiced their own personal connections to text; identified and discussed thematic features of text; considered characters' motives and actions; and demonstrated comprehension strategies, such as "retelling or summarizing the text . . . and making predictions before and during reading" (Taylor et al., 2003, p. 22). Taylor and colleagues (2003) also identified two types of participation, regardless of the whole-class or small-group setting, that did not result in high-level discussions of texts: round-robin oral reading and teacher-assigned oral turn taking.

Implementing High-Level Discussions

High-level discussions of texts can occur in the whole-class setting with the entire class taking part, in teacher-led small groups, and in student-led small groups. Although student participation usually is enhanced in small-group instruction, the grouping arrangement is not as important as how the teacher and students interact in the different grouping alignments. For example, a teacher in the Taylor and colleagues (2003, p. 20) study used teacher-led small groups and asked high-level questions but limited her students' active engagement and thinking when she answered her own questions and did not provide her students with opportunities to state their own ideas and explain their thinking, as illustrated below:

TEACHER: Why do you think they wrapped the [dinosaur] bones?

STUDENT: [*silent*]

TEACHER: So, they wouldn't break.

We agree with Johnston's (2004) observation that "if a student can figure something out for him- or herself, explicitly providing the information preempts the student's opportunity to build a sense of agency and independence" (p. 8).

To get started with high-level discussions of texts, we recommend that you either start with the whole-class setting, using the idea of the GRR introduced in Chapter 3 to help you move to teacher-led small groups for guided practice and to student-led small groups for independent application, or that you implement an instructional program designed to promote high-level discussions of texts by students. We explain each of the configurations below (whole-class settings, teacher-led small groups, and student-led small groups) as well as three instructional programs: CDGs, literature circles, and the RE component of SCI, previously introduced in Chapter 5.

Whole-Class Settings

Whole-class settings do not present the same opportunities for collaborative work and student participation as teacher-led small groups or student-led small groups. So if you just use whole-class settings and avoid small groups, you are not addressing the CCSS for speaking and listening and not really facilitating the use of high-level discussions of texts in your classroom. However, the whole-class setting is useful when you are demonstrating the types of questions and answers you want your students to share, scaffolding students' thinking about texts, and modeling how students should participate in small groups (Garas-York et al., 2013). For example, you can use any of the following questions to get a high-level conversation started about a narrative text introduced in a teacher read-aloud (see Peterson & Taylor, 2012):

> "What is the big idea that the author wanted you to learn? Why do you say that?"
> "What is the main thing you learned from the story or the text?"
> "What personal connections can you make to the text?"
> "Which of the characters would you want to be and why?"

Many times, you will need to scaffold your students' answers by asking them to think more deeply. Peterson and Taylor (2012) encourage you to get them accustomed to elaborating on their responses. They recommend that you prompt them by saying, "Please tell me more about that" or asking them, "What makes you think that?" (p. 303). Other times, you will want to help students to extend their ideas so that they can make personal and textual connections. In the excerpt below (O'Flahavan, 1994/1995, p. 355), the teacher asks the student to provide evidence for the inference made:

> STUDENT 11: Well, the mother is probably very mad at Laurie, but it would be better if Laurie just told the truth in the first place.
>
> TEACHER: How do you know the mother might be mad at Laurie? It doesn't say in the story. So how did you arrive at that conclusion? What made you think that?
>
> STUDENT 11: Well, for one thing, I would. I would be a little upset.
>
> TEACHER: So, you're putting yourself in the mother's shoes. This story is written through the mother's eyes.

You can use the whole-class setting to model the types of questions that you want students to ask each other in small groups. In the example below (Peterson & Taylor, 2012, p. 298), the teacher already had asked the students to write down their own questions after hearing a trickster tale being read. She then asked a student to share one of her questions. After the student gave the question, the teacher asked what she could do to provoke more discussion:

> STUDENT: Would you be happy to be a hungry spider?
>
> TEACHER: What could you do to add to that question to get more discussion?
>
> STUDENT: I could ask, "Why or why not?"

Using the whole-class setting to model how you want the teacher- or student-led small groups to work can be effective. For example, before implementing teacher- or student-led small groups, we advise you to work with your students in the whole-class setting to develop rules for participation. Next, it is helpful for your students to practice implementing the participation rules in small groups as they discuss texts. When you have a small group that is doing fairly well, we recommend that you have them participate in a fishbowl. In a fishbowl, the group that is being observed is placed in the center of the class, and the rest of the class sits outside of the small group. You give each member of the large group sitting outside of the fishbowl a checklist with the participation rules on it. Their job is to use the checklist to evaluate whether members of the fishbowl group followed all the participation rules or needed to improve. Then, after the fishbowl group has completed their discussion of a text, and members of the larger group have completed their checklists, you ask members of the larger group to use their checklists to point out one thing that the group did well and one thing that could be improved. When you ask the students to point out an item for improvement, it is important to let them know that they should direct the negative feedback to the group as a whole and not to an individual student or students. Form 6.1 (at the end of the chapter) presents a checklist of participation rules that could be used for the high-level discussions of texts and for the fishbowl.

Teacher-Led Small Groups

In organizing teacher-led small groups, we recommend that you follow the guidelines for high-level discussions provided above. Students can discuss texts that you have read to them or texts that they already have read on their own. You can select the texts to be discussed or let students select them, but for high-level discussions to occur, you need quality narratives with interesting plots and characters and informational texts with compelling issues that will engage your students. Because teacher-led small groups usually are preceded by teacher modeling and scaffolding or a fishbowl in the whole-class setting, and involve prereading and selection of the texts being discussed, they usually meet once per week. It is not unusual for teachers to purposefully assign students to the small groups to ensure that the small-group dynamics are positive. However, all students, even those who are not strong decoders or independent readers, can participate in teacher-led, high-level discussions of texts in small groups.

Throughout the small-group discussion, you will need to support students' participation by encouraging them to share ideas, scaffold their thinking, and coach their interactions. O'Flahavan (1994/1995) provides guidelines for implementing the CDG, a teacher-led small-group program that emphasizes high-level discussion of texts with children in grades 1–2. He recommends that CDGs be used with small groups of five to six children, who meet periodically to discuss texts. The teacher or the students themselves choose which students will participate in the specific groups. Prior to the discussion, the students read the selected text and individually create responses to it 1 day before the discussion. They use their responses to discuss the text in their small groups.

According to O'Flahavan (1994/1995), each CDG session lasts for about 30 minutes. The session includes a teacher opening (5 minutes), a small-group discussion (20 minutes), and a teacher debriefing (5 minutes). In the opening, you review the rules of participation and model different ways for the students to interpret the text being read. As students discuss the text, each group keeps a two-column chart in which they list the rules for participation they used and the reader- and text-based interpretations they made. These interpretations could include "character feelings," "author's clues," "challenging author's organization," "conflicts, solutions," "relate to personal life," "diverse viewpoints of the story," "author's purpose," and so on (p. 355). Form 6.2 (at the end of the chapter) presents an example of a two-column chart. During the debriefing, you provide feedback on the students' interpretations, have students evaluate how well they implemented the small-group discussion, and encourage them to set participation and interpretation goals for their next discussion. The cycle then is repeated with a different text.

Throughout the CDGs, as the classroom teacher, you take on various roles. For example, you are the elicitor when you help students to "elaborate or extend" their thinking: "What made you suspicious? What did you read there that made you suspicious?" (O'Flahavan, 1994/1995, p. 355). You are a framer when you enhance your students' thinking: "So, you're putting yourself in the mother's shoes. This story was written through the mother's eyes" (p. 355). You are the monitor when you remind students of the participation rules: "Let her finish. Don't interrupt" (p. 355).

For the students in prekindergarten and kindergarten, it is particularly important to have teacher-led small-group discussions following teacher read-alouds of high-quality literature. We know that conversations with adults help young children to develop their oral language skills. Whole-class teacher read-alouds do not provide enough opportunities for large numbers of children to respond in elaborate ways to the texts. Typically, the children who need the most opportunity to develop their language skills talk the least in the whole-class setting. Therefore, you should be deliberate in scheduling small-group conversations following rich read-aloud experiences. Chapter 9 addresses this in more detail.

Student-Led Small Groups

For student-led small groups to work effectively, it is important for you to spend considerable time preparing your students for how they are to participate and what they are to discuss. Martínez-Roldán (2005) highlights the importance of emphasizing an inquiry approach and a rich language arts curriculum that get students to connect with books prior to implementing student-led small groups. She recommends that you establish literacy activities—such as story time, writing workshops, guided reading groups, and literature discussions in small groups—because these activities set the context for student-led small-group discussions. Students also need to be comfortable working together in guided reading groups.

If you are interested in implementing student-led small groups, Martínez-Roldán (2005) and her colleague (Martínez-Roldán & López-Robertson, 1999/2000) recommend that you try literature circles with students in grades 1–2. In literature circles, you group students heterogeneously according to the text that they have chosen to read and discuss. The text can be read aloud by the teacher or the students, or read independently by the students, depending on their reading proficiency levels. However, the texts need to be quality literature that link to disciplinary themes or the students' cultures, or in which the students can see themselves. The aim of literature circles is for students to take an aesthetic stance (Rosenblatt, 1995), in which they make connections from the text they read to their own lives and to other texts, in addition to learning what types of texts they like and appreciate. Texts selected for literature circles often focus on social issues or universal open-ended themes for which there are no definite answers. The literature circle discussions usually last between 15 and 30 minutes in primary classrooms.

To get the groups started, you may want to assign specific roles to the students. For example, one student could be the captain or the discussion director, another student could be the summarizer, another could be the word wizard, and a fourth student could be the literary luminary who addresses author craft (Daniels, 2002). If using roles, it is important to remember that the children should rotate the role assignments. The purpose of the role is to serve as a temporary scaffold for the type of thinking and talking that should contribute to the discussion. Therefore, roles should not persist longer than two or three role rotations.

You, as the classroom teacher, still have a role to play in student-led literature circles. Your job is to encourage the children to listen to each other, speak spontaneously without raising their hands, take a turn when they are prepared, and respond constructively to their peers' comments and thoughts. In addition, Martínez-Roldán (2005) recommends that you mediate the discussions by listening to the children, requesting clarifications, asking questions, or making comments that get children to expand or elaborate on their thoughts.

In the RE component of SCI, discussed in Chapter 5, second-grade students participated in student-led small groups similar to literature circles. However, in RE and SCI, both informational texts, with open-ended issues, and narrative texts with universal themes are supposed to be used. In RE and SCI, students read the texts or hear them being read, write a response to a "big juicy question" related to a major theme or issue in the text, and then discuss their responses in small groups. An example of a big juicy question related to the rain forests might be something like "Should rain forests be preserved when people need the lumber or medicines made from plants that live in the rain forests? Explain." A big juicy question for a narrative text might be "What is friendship? Explain." You need to encourage students to elaborate on their responses by identifying the sources of their ideas (personal experiences, the current text being read, or other texts) and by responding to each other's ideas by stating, "I agree with . . . because. . . . Or I disagree with . . . because. . . ." As students become familiar with the big juicy questions, you can ask them to write their own big juicy questions, and to select the questions that they want to discuss in their small groups.

For small-group discussions in the primary grades to be productive, it is likely that you will need to take an active role in scaffolding each conversation group several times (Stahl, 2009). Circulating among simultaneous discussion groups should only occur after you are confident that the students can distribute talk time fairly equally among group members, respond to one another's comments rather than engage in parallel talk, and discuss text themes and big juicy questions.

Considerations for English Learners

Literature circles have been used effectively with English learners. Martínez-Roldán and López-Robertson (1999/2000) explain that even first- and second-grade English learners who are still learning to decode can participate in student-led literature circles. In Spanish–English bilingual classrooms, books in the L1 and English typically are read and discussed.

In organizing teacher- or student-led small-group discussions for English learners, we recommend that you let the students choose the language in which they want to respond: their L1 or English. A teacher who was teaching a class of all-English speakers and English learners remarked that the bilingual, Latina/o students with low proficiency in English participated more in the small-group discussions when they were placed with speakers of their L1, and allowed to use their L1 (in this case, Spanish) to discuss the English text (García, Bray, et al., 2006). Martínez-Roldán (2005) reported that bilingual students (Spanish–English) who effectively implemented literature circles in a second-grade class decided on when they each had a turn, and let each student decide how they would talk by using English, Spanish, or code switching. In keeping with the above findings, we recommend that, when possible, you place students of varying English proficiencies but from the same L1 background together in small groups, and that you encourage the students to individually select how they want to respond to English text—in English, their L1, or through code switching. If you only speak English, then the students can negotiate how to explain to you in English what they are discussing about English text. The latter discussion actually heightens their higher-order thinking across both languages.

Even in whole-class discussions, we recommend that you let English learners respond to text you have read in one language by using the language they know best or want to use. A second-grade bilingual teacher found that when she let her Spanish-speaking students use Spanish to discuss the English texts she was reading aloud, the students participated more than when she restricted them to just using English.

English learners' participation in high-level discussions is usually enhanced when you give them the opportunity to write or create a response to a text (by drawing or creating a craft) before participating. By having the response in front of them, they have mentally rehearsed what they are going to say, increasing their confidence. We recommend that you let individual children choose the language in which they want to respond to text. If it is absolutely necessary for students to construct their response(s) in English, then pairing students from the same home language but of different English proficiency levels encourages them to discuss the response in their L1, in English, and/or through code switching. As a group, they can decide how to convey the meaning of their response to the teacher in English.

English learners often differ from Anglo students in terms of their cultural backgrounds, experiences, and histories, so we encourage you to use multicultural literature for high-level discussions of texts. Martínez-Roldán and López-Robertson (1999/2000) observed that the bilingual Latina/o first graders in their study responded to texts that focused on political, cultural, and social issues relevant to them and their families. They also reported that the students sometimes extended their discussions of texts to include related storytelling—something that the Anglo students in the class did not do. They later realized that the storytelling was part of their Latina/o students' cultural tradition, and "gave students space to create meaning together on threatening topics and simultaneously, a feeling of power as storytellers" (p. 278).

The Evaluation of High-Level Discussions

Because it is often difficult to monitor how you are interacting with your students, we recommend that you periodically video-record your implementation of high-level discussions of texts in the whole-class setting for about 10–15 minutes. Then, on your own or in a professional learning community with other teachers who are learning how to implement high-level discussions of texts, we recommend that you review the video recording to document who you called on, how you interacted with students, and how your students responded.

Teacher Self-Assessment of Instruction

It is often difficult to know if you are calling on all the students in your classroom and giving all of them opportunities to participate in high-level discussions of text. For example, it is not unusual for teachers new to high-level discussions of texts to only call on their high-performing students. To offset this situation, you want to make sure that you are calling on everyone in the classroom, modeling and scaffolding students' responses as necessary. If you (or someone else) can periodically video-record your implementation of high-level discussions of texts, then it is helpful to use a rubric to evaluate how well you are doing. Form 6.3 (at the end of the chapter) provides an example of a rubric that you could use to evaluate how you are implementing high-level discussions of texts with your students in the whole-class setting. We recommend that you date the rubric, keep it in a notebook, and use it across the school year to document your progress. You also can adapt this rubric to fit your role in teacher- and student-led student groups.

Student Self-Assessment of Small-Group Work

It is also helpful for your students to evaluate how they are participating and discussing texts in their small groups (teacher led or student led). Form 6.4 (at the end of the chapter) provides a rubric that we adapted from our work with SCI. We recommend that students use this rubric after they have participated in a high-level discussion of text in a small group to evaluate how well they and each member of their group worked with one another and interacted with text. We recommend that you have students complete this rubric across the school year, being sure to date each rubric so that students can see their progress. You can also use this rubric to provide collective feedback to the students on how they are doing individually and as a group. Students can use the rubric immediately following their discussion or after viewing a video recording of their group's discussion. In an era of smartphones, video recording is both convenient and unobtrusive. In our study of SCI, we found that the most effective teachers frequently video-recorded their students' discussions and replayed them instructionally to teach their students the conventions of high-level discussions.

Conclusion

Researchers have reported that high-level discussions of texts, where students actively share how they are responding to and thinking about text, typically result in reading comprehension improvements. To implement high-level discussions of texts, you should use the GRR to model, support, and scaffold students' participation first in whole-class settings, then in teacher-led small groups, and later in student-led small groups. Throughout, you need to remember to model, scaffold, and coach students' participation in high-level discussions of texts. You can also use several instructional programs with students in grades 1–2 to implement high-level discussions of texts, such as CDGs, literature circles, and the RE component of SCI.

English learners' participation in high-level discussions of texts typically is increased when you let them choose the language (L1, English, or code switching) in which they prefer to respond, write, or create a response to the text they are going to discuss, and use the response in their discussion. When you use multicultural literature related to their life experiences, then you facilitate their connections to the texts being discussed. Allowing them to use cultural literacy activities, such as storytelling for Spanish-speaking Latina/o students, increases their level of participation.

To evaluate how well you organize and implement high-level discussions of texts, we recommend that you or someone else video-record and evaluate your students' participation in high-level discussions. In the next chapter, we discuss the reciprocal relationship between reading and writing, and how to get your students to develop written responses to and about texts that can be used for high-level discussions of texts.

FORM 6.1
Participation Checklist

Participation Rules	Always	Sometimes	Never	Comments
Take turns.				
Don't interrupt each other.				
Don't dominate the conversation.				
Don't embarrass anyone.				
Be respectful.				
Pay attention.				
Listen carefully.				
Focus on discussing the text.				
Build on what others say.				
Explain why you agree or disagree with someone.				

What the group did well:

What the group needs to improve:

Participation Rules Used and Text-Based Interpretations Made

Participation Rules Used	Interpretations Made

Based on O'Flahavan (1994/1995).

Rubric for Evaluating Teacher's Implementation of High-Level Discussions

Date	No or None	Some	Lots	Comments
I-R-E interactions				
One- or two-word student answers				
Text with a compelling theme or issue				
Teacher asks/models "I wonder" statements				
Teacher asks/models authentic questions				
Teacher asks/models big juicy questions				
Teacher prompts or extends student thinking				
Teacher accepts multiple interpretations				
Teacher asks for sources of interpretations and provides appropriate feedback				
Students ask questions				
Students make connections to book themes or characters				
Students make "I wonder" statements				
Students ask authentic questions				
Students ask big juicy questions				
Students present their interpretations and sources				

Rubric for Student Self-Assessment
of High-Level Discussion of Texts

Name _____ **Date** _____

Interact with the Text

   a. Work together to understand the text
   b. Discuss the theme or big ideas
   c. Use and discuss big juicy questions
   d. Make personal connections with the theme, big ideas, or characters
   e. Make "I wonder" statements
   f. Ask "real" questions
   g. Present interpretations and sources

Interact with One Another

   a. Take turns talking
   b. Listen carefully
   c. Be respectful
   d. Build on what others say
   e. Explain why you agree or disagree

Draw a smiley face for excellent work: ☺

Draw a so-so face if some improvement is needed: ☺

Draw a sad face when lots of improvement is needed: ☹

Group Member	Interact with Text	Interact with One Another	Reasons
Yourself			

CHAPTER 7

Written Responses to Texts and Writing Projects

GUIDING QUESTIONS

- What is the relationship between reading and writing?
- How can writing improve students' reading comprehension?
- What are appropriate writing activities for children in PreK–2?
- What are the considerations for English learners?
- How can teachers evaluate students' written responses to texts and writing projects?

SETTING THE STAGE

Ms. Lyons is meeting with five students in one of her guided reading groups, while the rest of her class is doing work at four literacy centers. In the guided reading group, she is reviewing what her second graders wrote about a story they previously read. Each student completed a five-finger graphic organizer that listed key story map features of the story. On the thumb, the students wrote the characters; on the index finger, the setting; on the middle finger, the problem; on the ring finger, the beginning, middle, and end; and on the little finger, the solution to the problem. In the middle part of the hand, they wrote the major events that led to the solution. As Ms. Lyons was conferencing briefly with each student, she noticed that several of them had listed events in the middle of the hand that were not even in the story. Ms. Lyons addressed the students in the guided reading group:

"Wait, some of you wrote ideas that weren't even in the story! How did that happen? Remember, you are only to list the important ideas from the story you just read. This is not a creative writing assignment where you write your own story."

Just like Ms. Lyons, when you ask your students to respond to what they have read by completing a story map or informational text rubric or by writing personal responses, you are facilitating and assessing their reading comprehension.

Overview of Research

When students draw or write responses to texts, they facilitate their comprehension of texts as well as reveal how they are making sense of them. Many researchers call reading and writing reciprocal processes because they "share many of the same developmental components" and mutually reinforce each other (Fitzgerald & Shanahan, 2000, as cited in Schisler, Laurice, Konrad, & Alber-Morgan, 2009, p. 137). For example, when you read, you generally are aware of the writer who has created the text you are reading. Similarly, when you write, you orient your writing to an audience who will read your text. Encouraging young students to draw their responses to texts is also a form of communication that represents comprehension (Hubbard, Winerbourne, & Ostrow, 1996).

Gammill (2006) explains that "the act of writing, whether in short sentences or lengthy paragraphs, helps students make connections between what they read, what they understand, and what they think" (p. 754). Others argue that the act of writing actually improves your thinking and learning because you have to make your thinking explicit, and your writing choices (e.g., words, text structure, genre, and rhetorical style) affect how you represent knowledge (Hebert, Gillespie, & Graham, 2013).

Most of the quantitative research conducted on the relationship between writing and reading comprehension has shown that writing about texts improves the reading comprehension of students in grades 3–12 (Graham & Hebert, 2010). Although fewer researchers have examined the relationship between students' writing and reading comprehension in grades 1–2, the findings are similar, in that writing about texts appears to enhance students' reading comprehension, even when students are in grades 1–2 (Duke, Purcell-Gates, Hall, & Tower, 2006; Graham & Hebert, 2010; McMahon & Raphael, 1997). Teacher-written case studies show improvements in young students' appreciation and interpretation of reading when they write in response to reading (Grattan, 1997; Scherer, 1997).

The CCSS actually specify that students in kindergarten should be able to write the name of "the book they are writing about and state an opinion or preference about the topic or book (e.g., My favorite book is . . .), with increased elaboration and a conclusion as they progress through second grade" (NGA & CCSSO, 2010, p. 19). Students in kindergarten through second grade are also expected to participate in shared research and writing projects. For example, in first grade, they are "to write a sequence of instructions" based on their exploration of several "how-to-do books on a given topic" (NGA & CCSSO, 2010, p. 19). In second grade, they are supposed to "gather information from provided sources to answer a question" (NGA & CCSSO, 2010, p. 19). We explain how you can work with your students to address the CCSS standards in our discussion below.

Writing to Express and Extend Comprehension

To get students to write in response to texts, we recommend that you use the GRR model presented in Chapter 3. Table 7.1 applies the GRR to writing. In the whole-class setting, we encourage you to model and demonstrate how you want your students to draw and write in response to text. For example, a second-grade teacher, Pam Scherer (1997), used think-alouds as she was reading aloud to model a variety of ways to respond. In one response, she drew a picture to show what she was thinking. In another, she wrote and answered questions. When personal memories were prompted by what she read, she showed her students how to write about them. When she taught her students about reading strategies, she modeled how to respond to text by writing predictions and retelling or summarizing a favorite part of the story.

Kristen Grattan (1997), a first-grade teacher who used response logs with her first and second graders, thought it was important for her students to have

TABLE 7.1. The GRR in Writing

Level of responsibility	Context	Who does what
Teacher control	Shared writing	Teacher holds the pen, instructs or models writing process, children share composition process (e.g., Language Experience Approach).
Shared teacher and student control (teacher led)	Interactive writing or collaborative writing	Teacher and students share the pen, collaborative composition process.
Student control with support from teacher (more supportive) or peers (less supportive)	Guided writing (small group or conference)	Student controls the pen with support and feedback from teacher or peers.
Student control	Independent writing	Student controls the writing process.

an opportunity to share their responses. She chose to use a community share, in which everyone in the classroom shared. You can also have students share their responses in pairs, small groups, and individually with you in a student–teacher conference. Grattan also recommends that you organize a system for the children to record and save their responses, so they can refer to them later for extended writing projects, and so you can use them to assess their comprehension.

Response Journals and Logs

Teachers often use response journals and logs to encourage their students to record their ongoing thoughts or questions about the texts they hear being read or are reading (Garas-York et al., 2013; McMahon & Raphael, 1997). These responses tend to be short and focused. For example, beginning readers and writers can put drawings and short written comments ("Like," "Don't like") or questions or question marks (?) on sticky notes that they post on the pages of the text as they read, later referring to the sticky notes to write in their journals. In one case, a first-grade teacher provided her beginning writers with sticky notes she previously had made that contained question marks, sad faces, and smiley faces (Garas-York et al., 2013), which her students placed in their copies of the story that the teacher was reading aloud. The children later used the sticky notes to write a response in their journals and discuss their response with their partner.

In preschool through first grade, some teachers prefer to use response logs rather than journals. In a log, students draw, combine drawing and writing, or write in response to what they have heard read or read. Students usually keep the log in a notebook, in which the title of the book or story, the author's name, the date that they heard the book read or read it, and the date on which they entered the response are listed (by you, the classroom teacher, or by the student). The logs provide a record of the students' ongoing reading, writing, and thinking about texts. Teachers typically use response logs to enhance and check on their students' comprehension and writing development.

Double-Entry Journal

Sometimes teachers have their students keep their responses in a double-entry journal (Tompkins, 2009). In this type of journal, the page is divided into two columns. In the left-hand column, the students write down the part of the text that provoked their response. In the right-hand column, they write their response to the text. Figure 7.1 is a simulated example of a double-entry journal. This type of journal not only enhances students' understanding of text but also allows the teacher to see how students are making sense of it.

Date: November 10, 2013 **Title:** Mushroom in the Rain **Author:** Mirra Ginsburg	
He saw a tiny mushroom (page 2). They moved over, and there was enough room for the sparrow (page 9).	The ant, butterfly, mouse, sparrow, went under a mushroom. How can all the animals fit under the mushroom?

FIGURE 7.1. Simulated example of a second grader's double-entry journal.

Dialogue Journal

Another form of open-response writing is the dialogue journal. The student chooses what part of the story to respond to and draws or writes a comment or a question to which the teacher responds. If students are reluctant to initiate the dialogue, then you can initiate it yourself by asking the student to write about or draw the part of the story he/she liked best or least and to explain why. Teachers usually respond to the students' writing by briefly responding to the students' comments and answering any student questions. They often end the response with a question that extends the dialogue. However, because the point of the dialogue journal is to develop a sustained written conversation between you and the student, it is important not to correct the students' writing and avoid asking too many questions (Werderich, 2006). Instead, we recommend that you model appropriate spelling and syntax in your response, which you typically write below the child's entry and read aloud to the child. Figure 7.2 is an example of a simulated dialogue journal with the child's entry and teacher's response.

Regardless of the response format, you need to select texts that will provoke your students' responses. Grattan (1997) recommends that you use narrative texts with well-defined characters and sophisticated plots to stimulate students' responses. Narrative texts that have been used effectively with primary-age students are listed in the text box on the next page. Most of these texts are beyond the independent reading levels of primary-age students, but are the type of rich, stretch texts required by the CCSS. Additional texts may be found in Appendix B of the

December 10, 2013 I am sad win I read about Tacky becs he is diferent. He is different from the other penguins. Why are you sad?

FIGURE 7.2. Simulated dialogue journal about *Tacky the Penguin* (Lester, 1988).

CCSS or lists of award-winning children's books, such as the Caldecott Medal or the Coretta Scott King Book Award winners. Therefore, we recommend that you present these texts to your students in teacher read-alouds. If you want your students to provide written responses to texts they read independently or in guided reading groups, then Grattan recommends that you pose a question for them to respond to about the characters, setting, or plot because the texts usually are too simple to provoke an authentic response.

We also encourage you to read aloud informational text that is well organized and that focuses on an important or controversial issue, such as preservation of the environment, how to conserve energy, or on a topic for which your students are very interested (e.g., sharks or dinosaurs). The text box on the next page presents a list of informational texts that have been used effectively with primary-age students (Kletzien & Dreher, 2004).

If you are working with children who aren't reading or writing on their own, you can have them draw in response to a book or story you have read aloud, and encourage them to use their own words to explain the drawing. You can ask them to draw what was going on in their minds as they listened to the book or story

---

NARRATIVE TEXTS TO READ ALOUD TO PRIMARY STUDENTS WHEN WRITING IN RESPONSE TO TEXTS

Amazing Grace (Hoffman & Binch, 1991)

Amelia Bedelia (Parrish, 2002)

Cloudy with a Chance of Meatballs (Barret & Barrett, 1978)

The Day the Crayons Quit (Daywait, 2013)

Dragons Love Tacos (Rubin, 2012)

The Girl Who Loved Wild Horses (Gobel, 1978)

Hey, Al (Yorinks, 1986)

If You Give a Mouse a Cookie (Numeroff, 1985)

Jumanji (Van Allsburg, 1981)

Louis the Fish (Yorinks, 1980)

The Magic Finger (Dahl, 1966)

Mouse Soup (Lobel, 1983)

The Mysteries of Harris Burdick (Van Allsburg, 1984)

The Pout-Pout Fish (Diesen, 2008)

Rosie Revere (Beaty, 2013)

Used-Up Bear (Carmichael, 2000)

being read or have them draw the part they liked best or least. Grattan (1997) explains that she typically introduces first graders to the response log by giving each of them a little booklet of five pages stapled together. She then observes that at the beginning of the year, most of her students draw their responses with a few letters representing words. However, by the middle of the year, most of them are writing one or two sentences about the story and identifying the characters.

If you have word walls in your classroom (and we hope you do), you can encourage your students to use the words posted on the word walls to explain their drawings. We recommend that primary classrooms have a word wall with high-frequency, "no excuses" words listed in alphabetical order so that children do not have to repeatedly misspell irregular common words. We also recommend that classrooms have an attractive word wall that contains 12–20 target words that are associated with the disciplinary theme that is currently the focus of study. When students need a word that is not posted, we recommend that you encourage them

---

INFORMATIONAL TEXTS FOR PRIMARY STUDENTS WHEN WRITING IN RESPONSE TO TEXTS OR FOR PROJECTS

* *

Abraham Lincoln (Cohn & Schmidt, 2002)

Amazing Frogs and Toads (Clarke, 1990)

Arctic Foxes and Red Foxes (Meadows & Vail, 2002)

Bears (Merrik, 2000)

Biggest, Strongest, Fastest (Jenkins, 1995)

Dinosaur (Walker & Gray, 2001)

Growing Vegetable Soup (Ehlert, 1987)

How Big Were the Dinosaurs? Gigantic! (O'Brien, 1999)

I Love Guinea Pigs (King-Smith, 1994)

Leaves (Saunders-Smith, 1998)

The Life and Times of the Peanut (Micucci, 1997)

Lightning (Kramer, 1992)

Monarch Butterfly (Gibbons, 1989)

Prehistoric Record Breakers (Theodorou, 1998)

Slap, Squeak, & Scatter: How Animals Communicate (Jenkins, 2001)

Splish, Splash (Graham, 1994)

Terrible Tyrannosaurs (Zoehfeld, 2001)

———

Note. Based on Kletzien and Dreher (2004).

to write the word as they think the word should be (i.e., use invented spelling). Children's use of invented spelling often indicates how they are developing their knowledge of sound–symbol correspondence. When children use invented spelling, you may not always recognize what they are trying to say, so it is helpful to ask them to tell you what they have written. In fact, we encourage you to periodically ask your students to tell you what they have written and drawn in their response logs because by doing so, you are heightening their metacognitive awareness about the reciprocal relationship between writing and reading.

Sometimes, students are reluctant to draw or write responses to texts. To offset this problem, teachers often ask their students to respond to a specific question or to draw and write about a specific topic. For example, after students have read or heard the teacher read the introduction in Lobel's *Mouse Soup* (1977), a first-grade teacher might ask her students to provide (through writing, drawing, or a combination of the two) a response to the following questions: "Who do you think is smarter, the mouse or the weasel? Why?" If your students are not ready to write their own responses, you could have them work in pairs to complete a sentence frame, such as "I think the _____ is smarter than the _____ because _____."

Once students are comfortable writing their responses to texts, then you want to provide them with instruction that will get them to implement different types of responses that will heighten their thinking about text (Raphael, Pardo, Highfield, & McMahon, 1997). The easiest response for most students is a personal response, in which they discuss how their feelings were evoked by the text, how much they enjoyed the text, and how the text relates to personal memories or stories (Raphael & Boyd, 1997). However, getting your students to make creative responses is also important. In creative responses, students alter what happens in a text or extend the text. They imagine they are the author of the text or communicate with the author by asking questions or writing a letter (Raphael & Boyd, 1997). The last type of response in Raphael and Boyd's classification is the critical response. Critical responses occur when students analyze the author's message or theme, describe the literary elements in the text, and discuss how the author has created a textual effect. For example, if a student typically responds to texts by making personal connections, you might provide a mini-lesson on how to compare the text with other texts, or on how to analyze and compare plots across texts (Garas-York et al., 2013).

Many times, teachers have students write in their response logs before participating in high-level discussions of text. Students then bring their logs with them to the discussion. In this way, every member of the group is prepared to participate in the discussion. If a student's response duplicates a response that already has been shared, you can teach your students to extend their thinking by saying, "I agree with or disagree with _____ because _____." In presenting their rationale for their opinion, we recommend that you prompt their higher-order thinking by teaching them to support their opinion (i.e., the part after "because") by specifically referring to the text being discussed, by relating the text to another text, or by referring to a personal experience.

Participating in response journals, response logs, and dialogue journals prepare K–2 students for attaining the CCSS in which they are to write "about and state an opinion or preference about [a] topic or book (e.g., My favorite book is . . .), with increased elaboration and a conclusion as they progress through second grade" (NGA & CCSSO, 2010, p. 19). If you want to make sure that your students can attain this standard, then after giving them sustained practice in responding to texts, we recommend that you actually have them complete a response in which they do what the standard requires, according to their grade level.

Extended Responses and Writer's Workshop

Extended Responses

The writing that K–2 students do in response journals and response logs tends to be short. First and second graders also need opportunities for more extended writing in response to reading. CCSS Appendix C has samples of writing that children have completed at each grade level. Additionally, *In Common: Effective Writing for All Students* is an online resource that consists of a collection of hundreds of samples of student writing that are aligned with the CCSS (*achievethecore.org/page/507/in-common-writing-for-all-students*). These exemplars and the annotations are helpful for establishing grade-level expectations.

McMahon and Raphael (1997) propose that students be given the opportunity to think about a theme or big issue that emerges when they have read several related texts. For example, Scherer (1997) had her second graders read fantasy books and write and discuss how they were alike or different. Another idea in keeping with the CCSS Reading Anchor 9 and Writing Strand 7 would be for first and second graders to compare several versions of a fairytale. For example, there are multiple versions of the Cinderella fairytale from around the world, as well as modern-day books that counter the princess and prince images portrayed in many of the fairytales, such as the *The Paper Bag Princess* (Munsch & Martchenko, 1980) and *Part-Time Princess* (Underwood, 2013). The text box on the next page presents a list of possible books that you could use. The aim of this activity is for your students to work in pairs or small groups to write an extended text that gets them to think across the fairytales that were read. For example, a possible end result would be for the students to write a letter to a children's book publisher to request more books like *The Paper Bag Princess* or *Part-Time Princess*, with nonstereotypical roles for both girls and boys, or for the students to write about the various concepts of beauty and wealth that are portrayed.

When you first assign an extended response, it is helpful for you to model the process for your students before asking them to write extended responses in pairs

FAIRYTALE GENRE SELECTIONS

Bubba, the Cowboy Prince (Ketteman, 1997)

Cinder Edna (Jackson, 1998)

Cinderella, or the Little Glass Slipper (Brown, 1954)

Dangerously Ever After (Slater, 2012)

Estrellita de Oro/Little Gold Star: A Cinderella Cuento (English and Spanish edition) (Hayes, 2002)

Mufaro's Beautiful Daughters: An African Tale (Steptoe, 1987)

No Lie, I Acted Like a Beast! The Story of Beauty and the Beast (as Told by the Beast. The Other Side of the Story) (Loewen, 2013)

Not All Princesses Dress in Pink (Stemple, 2010)

The Paper Bag Princess (Munsch & Martchenko, 1980)

Part-Time Princess (Underwood, 2013)

Peach Boy and Other Japanese Children's Favorite Stories (Sadake, 2008)

Prince Cinders (Cole, 1997)

The Rough-Face Girl (Martin, 1992)

The Talking Eggs (San Souci, 1989)

Yeh-Shen: A Cinderella Story from China (Louie, 1982)

or individually (see Table 7.1). You begin by selecting multiple books on the same theme and/or the same genre. Then, you often identify a question that you think your children would enjoy addressing. Next, you pose the question (setting the purpose for the extended response) and read the books. As you are reading the books, your students are drawing or writing their individual responses in their response logs. You then have your children review their response logs and work with you on a collaborative response, which you shape by asking them questions and scaffolding. When you have finished writing the collaborative response, you post it, and everyone in the class reads it aloud with you. You then model and explain how the process will work with students working in pairs or small groups, and how they can choose their own question or topic after reviewing their individual responses and work together to write an extended response.

Students can also write extended responses to informational texts on themes tied to social studies and science standards, such as community members, civil rights, animal rights, animal or plant extinction issues, or the environment. We recommend that first and second graders use quick writes to initiate their responses to informational texts. According to Elbow (1998), in quick writes students respond

> Some black bears are big. They can weh almost 500 pounds. I don't understand how it can clim trees.

> Maybe, the black bear that <u>climbs</u> trees <u>weighs</u> less than 500 pounds. What do you think?

FIGURE 7.3. Simulated quick write about bears with teacher response.

to an idea that was read by writing without stopping. Students should not worry about their spelling or grammar in the quick writes, although they should be encouraged to use related word walls posted in the room to locate the correct spellings of words they do not know yet. As the teacher, you should periodically collect the quick writes so you can read and respond to them by using the correct forms of the misspelled words. Then, you can have your students use their quick writes in pairs or small groups or as the whole class to construct an extended response. Figure 7.3 is a simulated example of a second grader's quick write about bears and her teacher's response.

One of the CCSS stated at the beginning of the chapter requires first graders to write an extended response—to "write a sequence of instructions" based on their exploration of several "how-to-do books on a given topic" (NGA & CCSSO, 2010, p. 19). A form of extended response occurs when students study a particular genre of books and write their own little books by identifying and following a pattern (or genre) in the books they have heard read aloud or read in guided reading or independently. You may prepare students for the CCSS by having them create their own books by following the pattern in predictable picture books, such as *The Very Hungry Caterpillar* (Carle, 1989) or *Brown Bear, Brown Bear, What Do You See?* (Martin & Carle, 1992), as well as in informational and how-to-do books.

Writer's Workshop

So that your students are comfortable writing on their own, it is important for you to introduce them to the writing process approach by establishing a writer's workshop in your classroom. There are several sources where you can read about the writing process and the writer's workshop (Calkins, 1991; Graves, 1994). Officially, the writing process approach includes five phases: prewrite, draft, revise, edit, and publish. However, these phases are not supposed to be implemented in a rigid, linear fashion, and not all the phases have to be used with beginning readers or writers. For example, some first-grade teachers only have their students participate in prewriting, drafting, and publishing (Tompkins, 2010). Additionally, we advocate that writer's workshop activities be used in an integrated way to support communicating about the theme for authentic purposes rather than as isolated writing exercises without connection to content.

To begin, you need to establish a formal time each day for the writing workshop. Tompkins (2010) recommends that you allow about 25 minutes for first graders to write independently, 15 minutes for a teacher mini-lesson, and 10 minutes for students to participate in an author's chair or to share their publications with classmates. Then, you need to model and demonstrate through your own writing how you want your children to proceed through the various phases (see Table 7.1). Teachers usually conference with individual children throughout the time dedicated to students' independent writing, making sure to meet with one-fifth of the students each day, so that every child has met with the teacher by the end of the week (Tompkins, 2010). Children often have more to write about if the writer's workshop is situated as part of the comprehensive themed literacy unit. Texts that children are reading serve as anchor texts both stylistically and conceptually for their own writing. Children write more when they have an authentic purpose for writing.

Children often participate in the *prewrite* phase by responding to books that are read to them or that they read. However, in addition to their response logs, Calkins (1991) strongly recommends that they keep a bound idea notebook, in which they put drawings and short jottings about what they might write about. They should feel free to add ideas to the idea notebook throughout the school day, but the writing workshop is also a time when they can complete drawings or add ideas.

Next, students need to review their response logs and idea notebooks to select topics and genres for their writing. In this phase, they develop or *draft* their idea into an actual story, poem, letter, or report. Much of the writing workshop time is spent on their independently developing drafts.

Then, students share their rough drafts with others. They may do this with a small writing group of four to five students, in which they read aloud what they have written and receive constructive feedback from other students (and sometimes the teacher) on what was effective (compliments) and what needs to be improved for the writing to make sense or be effective. Then, based on the feedback, they will make improvements or *revise* their writing. Sometimes, the process will stop here, and you will post their writings for others to read or send them home for their parents to read.

In the next phase, students often will work with another student, a small group of students, or the teacher to proofread or *edit* the work. It is in this phase that spelling and grammar are corrected. If a student decides not to publish the work, then it is put in the student's writing folder or portfolio.

Once the writing has been edited, the student will recopy the edited piece or it will be typed on the computer. Sometimes the student will provide a cover and illustrate the writing. The student then will *publish* the writing for others to read. The published writings typically are shared with the entire class, during which time the writing efforts are celebrated (Tompkins, 2010).

Many times, prior to the revising and editing, you will provide a mini-lesson on how to write a quality story or informational piece, as well as on specific writing features, such as paragraphing, punctuation, capitalization, or word choice. The focus of the mini-lesson is usually based on what you are discussing in your writing conferences with your students and seeing in individual students' writing.

The Reader as Expert: Using Literacy to Promote Learning and Create Projects

The Language Experience Approach

An early writing–reading activity that can be used with children of all ages, even preschoolers, is the Language Experience Approach (Ashton-Warner, 1965; Stauffer, 1970). This approach emphasizes the reciprocal nature of writing and reading and the creation of informational text. After your students have gone on a field trip or participated in a project, such as collecting fall leaves or planting a garden, you gather them together around a flip chart or a white board, and ask them to think about what they would like to tell their parents or another class about what they did on the field trip or in the project. You then have the students dictate to you as you print on the flip chart or the white board.

A major advantage of the Language Experience Approach is that it creates a level playing field for students. Participating in the field trip or project means that they have acquired the necessary background knowledge to participate in the dictation. When they dictate to you, they are using familiar vocabulary and syntactic structures.

Before beginning the dictation, you should scaffold student responses by telling them that you first need a title. Then, through the questions you ask, you help students to sequence or organize their thoughts. When you have completed the narrative, you have everyone read and reread it with you, as you point to the individual words. As a follow-up activity, many teachers assign students to work in pairs or small groups to illustrate different parts of the narrative. The teacher, an aide, or parent volunteer types the narrative and inserts the illustrations or drawings at appropriate places, creating a small book. Students usually like to reread the little books that they create, so many teachers laminate the small books and put them in the classroom library so that students have the opportunity to "read" them.

Conducting the Language Experience Approach with older students is also an excellent way to teach them text structure. For example, if you are working with second graders and want them to explain what happened when you conducted a science experiment with them, you can have them use their notes to dictate a research summary to you that involves the sequence text structure (first, second, third, finally) or the comparison–contrast text structure. As you scaffold their dictation, you are teaching them the clue words for the respective text structure. Through the dictation experience or shared writing (see Table 7.1), and their reading of the text that was jointly created, students heighten their awareness about how text structure can help to organize their thoughts as both writers and readers.

Disciplinary Projects

In many primary classrooms, students use reading and writing to investigate and learn about topics in science and social studies, such as how plants grow; different types of mammals; the lives of inventors; and how families across the world live, eat, and celebrate special occasions. For example, in a second-grade classroom that one of us (Georgia) observed, the teacher used a variety of graphic organizers, along with tradebooks, movies, and short Internet articles, to help her students identify and learn the differences among mammals, amphibians, and reptiles. She then assigned a culminating project for which she modeled how each student was to create a poster of a specific animal (elephants, gorillas, tree frogs, etc.) after reading tradebooks about the assigned animal, as well as short articles that the teacher had found on the Internet and then printed. She showed the students how to take notes about their animal according to the following categories: physical description, habitat, diet, birth and care of their young, and animal group. She modeled how the students should use their notes to write a paragraph about their animal for each of the categories. Then she modeled and told them to write a title for their poster, draw a picture of their animal, draw a map to show where it lived, add labels for the five categories to their poster, and post their paragraphs under each category. The posters then were hung in the room for parent–teacher conferences.

When you ask students to create a poster or write a report about a topic, Kletzien and Draper (2004) recommend that you help your students find a variety of texts that they can understand so that they do not copy what others have written and can put their findings in their own words. They also point out that requiring your students to document their findings by completing graphic organizers, sentence frames, Venn or H diagrams, and flow charts encourages them to use their own words, which will make writing the project or report in their own words much easier. Both disciplinary projects, such as the one described above, and themed disciplinary units (described below) prepare students for addressing the last CCSS for writing: "Gather information from provided sources to answer a question" (NGA & CCSSO, 2010, p. 19). Additionally, writing for a particular purpose using a clear template helps children build a tolerance for reading and comprehending difficult texts that contain many unknown words. Children learn to say to themselves, "This text may be hard, but I can still read enough of it to answer some questions and generate a written product from it." This is a valuable lesson for the striving reader or English learner who is likely to encounter difficult text passages in the classroom and later on standardized tests.

Discipline-Specific Writing

Thematic units that cut across several fields present an excellent opportunity for students to use writing to enhance their learning. For example, Olness (2007) explains how a first-grade teacher, Anne Veer, incorporated language arts, science, and mathematics in a unit on the life cycle of insects. As part of their investigation, they read books (through teacher read-alouds and guided reading), such as *Lifetimes* (Mellonie & Ingpen, 1983), *A Ladybug's Life* (Himmelman, 1998), and *Beetles* (Coughlan, 1999). They observed how a kit of mealworms in their classroom moved through the life-cycle stages of larvae, pupae, and adults. They conducted mathematical assignments by counting the number of legs, antennae, heads, and arms. Prior to their observations, Ms. Veer gave her class science journals or logs in which to record their observations and to list what they individually learned.

If you decide to pursue a similar project, we recommend that you model and show your students how to keep track of their observations in the science journals or logs. For example, they need to know how to record the dates of their observations, complete drawings of what they observed, label the drawings, write brief comments about the observations, and conclude their journal or log with a statement of what they learned about the overall topic. Throughout the project, you can meet as a class to post students' collective observations on a chart, which you can read and review with them, helping them to enhance their learning.

Multimedia Projects

Given the increased presence of the Internet and multimedia (cell phones, desktop and laptop computers, tablets, digital audio recorders or old-fashioned tape recorders, cameras, YouTube sites, video games, and so forth) in students' lives today, even for students in K–2 (Taffe & Bauer, 2013), we encourage you to incorporate multimedia into your classroom and to assign your first and second graders a multimedia project. When you and your students use multimedia to read and write and research topics, you not only facilitate your students' learning about an academic topic, but also provide them with opportunities to learn about and practice the use of multimedia—or what frequently is termed *digital literacies, multiple literacies,* or *new literacies.* Several educators note that the skills needed to comprehend and produce digital texts are different from traditional text (Leu et al., 2008; Taffe & Bauer, 2013). Now, students need to learn how to navigate websites, critically evaluate the sources of information, and synthesize information across the various sites. They also need to know how to point and click, scroll down a page, and bookmark websites, among other skills.

There are a number of ways that you can introduce and model the use of multimedia for students in preschool through second grade (McKenna, Conradi, Young & Gee Jang, 2013; Taffe & Bauer, 2013). Several teachers have used the

Internet to help their students learn about the authors of favorite books when they do an author study, such as Alma Flor Ada, Eric Carle, Patricia McKissack, Bill Martin, or Pat Mora. Many children's authors have interactive websites with photographs, videos, and a listing of books written and published, as well as audios of them reading their books or poems aloud and so on. The website Reading Rockets also provides information and videos about key children's book authors (*www.readingrockets.org/books/interviews*). Investigating a favorite author is an activity that can be done with children in preschool through second grade. When you look up a children's author on a website, you can demonstrate how to point and click, scroll down a page, and navigate and bookmark websites. As a follow-up activity you can assign first and second graders to work in pairs to do their own investigations of children's authors.

Taffe and Bauer (2013) describe how a first-grade teacher used multimedia to implement the Language Experience Approach. First, the teacher used a digital camera to document classroom events. Then, he projected photos of the event on a white board and got his students to discuss what happened in the photos. Next, he assigned pairs of students to each photo and asked them to write a sentence about it. Then, he had each pair dictate their sentence to him, as he typed the sentence under the respective photo. He then saved the photos and captions to an electronic folder, which the students read and reread throughout the week as a class and in a computer center.

Once your first and second graders become accustomed to the use of multimedia to read, write, and learn, we recommend that you assign them a multimedia project. This type of project will allow them to learn how to comprehend and produce digital texts (McKenna et al., 2013). However, to offset the possible inequity of access to technology, which has been observed between high- and low-income communities, we encourage you to find out which of your students have access to the Internet and multimedia outside of school and which ones don't. Because parents may not always understand why you are asking their children to search the Internet or use YouTube videos and so on, we recommend that you send a letter home describing the project and its purposes, identifying the team members, and asking for parental help and support. The demands for using technology to generate texts and other multimedia products are embedded in the reading, writing, language, and speaking and listening K–2 standards. The projects could be as simple as corresponding with e-mail pals (keypals) in other states or countries about community life in the students' community. For first graders, they might involve describing how a particular holiday is celebrated. For second graders, projects might be as sophisticated as conducting oral history interviews with community members on the impact of a natural disaster (tornadoes, floods, hurricanes, earthquakes) and posting information on the community's response to the disaster or on how to be prepared for such a disaster. The Web application *www.voicethread.*

com allows students to create a digital story through the selection of documents, pictures, and other media (McKenna et al., 2013).

Considerations for English Learners

You should not delay the participation of English learners in written response or writing activities until they have attained a certain level of oral or written English proficiency. Even when English learners are receiving instruction in English, we recommend that you let them participate in written response activities in their L1. It is helpful for English learners to write in their L1 because they will write at a much higher level in the language they know best than in a language they are just learning, such as English. Also, several researchers have found that English learners can transfer what they learn about writing in one language to the other language (Herrera, Perez, & Escamilla, 2010). As soon as they receive some instruction in English, they should also be expected to participate in writing activities in English. However, when you ask English learners to participate in written response activities in English, you should use ESL sheltering techniques and modeling and hands-on demonstrations (as explained in Chapter 2) so that they understand your instructions and know what it is you want them to do.

For English learners in preschool through grade 1, and beginning English learners in general, we recommend that you begin their English response and writing instruction with the Language Experience Approach, response journals and logs (in which students place sticky notes on pages of texts to indicate what they liked, disliked, or had questions about), and dialogue journals before you assign extended responses, writer's workshop, or disciplinary, themed disciplinary, or multimedia projects.

Several researchers have documented the effective use of the Language Experience Approach with English learners (Bezdicek & García, 2012). For example, after a field trip to a post office, a preschool teacher helped her class of English learners recount what they learned about the post office by showing them photos of the field trip and listing what they observed happen at the post office when a package was mailed. After the students dictated the narrative, the teacher read it with the students several times, had a parent volunteer to type it, and assigned pairs of students to illustrate it. The narrative later was laminated and placed in the class library for adult read-alouds and for the preschoolers to look at the book on their own. The Language Experience Approach is beneficial for English learners because it builds common background knowledge, provides students with content vocabulary, and the teacher can show the students how to spell key words and put their oral comments in written English as he or she listens to their comments.

Beginning English learners can also participate in dialogue journals when you encourage them to draw in response to a reading and to label the drawing with a caption or title. Initially, we recommend that you let the students write the caption or title in whichever language they prefer. Over the course of a school year, Georgia observed beginning English learners move from writing the caption in their L1, to code mixing, to writing the caption or title in English, to writing a short sentence or paragraph describing the drawing in English.

Implementing an interactive dialogue journal, in which you respond to the child's drawing or writing, is also very effective with English learners. Georgia saw how beginning English learners moved from minimal writing in their L1 to more complex writing in English when their teacher briefly met with each student to find out what he or she had written, and then wrote and asked him or her a question in response. When the teacher wrote her question, she modeled how to use English related to the child's drawing, initiating an ongoing written dialogue with the children.

In implementing response logs, we recommend that you encourage English learners to draw, combine writing and drawing, and write in response to a text you have read to them or they have read themselves. They should also be allowed to write in their L1, English, or a combination of the two. To provide an authentic purpose for the response log, we recommend that your children bring their response logs to their discussion groups to discuss the text. Georgia found that the participation of Korean English learners in teacher-led discussion groups about the texts they were reading was enhanced when students brought their written responses to their small-group meetings, and then were asked to orally share their responses in English. Writing or drawing the response prior to discussing it allowed the English learners to mentally rehearse what they were going to say aloud. If students' oral English proficiency limits their confidence in sharing their response in English, let them meet in heterogeneous L1 pairs or small groups to figure out how to share their responses in English before asking them to share in a small group or with the whole class.

English learners will participate more effectively in extended responses when you have chosen a topic for which they have the appropriate background knowledge (e.g., comparing and contrasting multicultural interpretations of the same type of story, historical events, celebrations, or customs) and provided them with Venn diagrams, semantic maps, flow charts, and graphic organizers to organize their thinking and writing. We also recommend that you use the Venn diagrams, semantic maps, flow charts, and graphic organizers to teach them key English vocabulary, later posting the vocabulary items on the word walls in your classroom.

Again, we recommend that you let students use their L1, English, or a combination of the two to think about their responses and to write their initial responses. Encouraging them to discuss their responses in pairs prior to writing their own individual responses in English is also helpful. To keep track of their writing development in the L1 and English, we recommend that you date and collect the different writing activities in which they have participated (in L1 and English), along with their final responses in English, and keep the activities in a folder or portfolio.

In terms of disciplinary, themed disciplinary, and multimedia projects, these are all learning and instructional opportunities that should be provided for English learners. The description of the poster project on mammals, amphibians, and reptiles, in which second graders created a poster that described their assigned animal, its habitat, how the young were born, what it ate, and the animal group to which it belonged, was conducted in a bilingual classroom of Spanish-speaking English learners.

The one activity in which you need to make sure that you provide English learners with considerable scaffolding and support is when you ask them to write in English during the writer's workshop. It sometimes is difficult for English learners to use English to write about experiences that have occurred in their L1 (Herrera et al., 2010). Encouraging your students to complete quick writes in English about classroom activities or English readings and to keep these quick writes in an idea notebook is one way to make sure that they have ideas to write about during a writing workshop in English. To facilitate their writing in English, be sure to post and update word walls, in which you review and post new English vocabulary from your instruction and students' readings. Always ask your students to refer to the word walls in their writing. Having them keep and refer to their own bilingual dictionaries, in which they list words in their L1 and the English equivalents, is also helpful. Letting them work with another student or a small group of students to figure out how to explain a topic in English is also effective.

Several ESL teachers have had English learners effectively participate in a writer's workshop when they keep the topics open. If beginning English learners have difficulty identifying a topic to write about, you can ask them to write about a favorite television show that they watched in English. In one case, an ESL teacher had DVDs of television shows with a lot of physical humor, such as *I Love Lucy* and *The Three Stooges*, and allowed students to view a DVD and write a response to one of the shows (what they liked, did not like, and why) during the writing workshop.

However, you need to remember that your English learners will not have a "natural" ear for English, and may not be able to proof and edit each other's writing correctly. Therefore, asking them to peer-edit or proof each other's English writing will not be effective without additional support from you. It is important for you to find out the structural and phonetic differences in your students' L1 and English, so that you can provide direct instruction and practice on these differences. For example, Spanish-speaking students will need to be taught how to show possession in English because possession is shown differently in Spanish (see Figure 7.4). Some of you may voice concerns about the numerous home languages (or

---

English possession statement:

The <u>man's</u> red car was large and beautiful.

Spanish possession statement:

El carro rojo <u>del hombre</u> era grande y bella.

FIGURE 7.4. Possession statements in English and Spanish.

L1s) in your classroom. If this is your situation, we recommend that you start by learning about the L1 of the largest number of English learners in your classroom and identify L1 resources for this group.

Another step is to identify the writing and spelling errors that students from the same L1 group make to see if there are patterns in their errors. Once you have identified an L1 pattern of errors, then you can contact the bilingual or ESL teacher and school or community L1 resources to see if they can help you to understand the differences between the L1 and English. You want them to explain why the students are making the error and indicate how you can explain the error to your students. Alternative sources of information include the Internet and literacy texts on teaching English learners (see Herrera et al., 2010).

Finally, knowing how to interpret and evaluate the English writing of your English learners is very important. It is very likely that young English learners will use what they know about print or writing in their L1 as they acquire and experiment with English. This may often be difficult for you to understand, especially if you are not proficient in your students' L1. Herrera and her colleagues (2010) point out that when Spanish-speaking English learners write in English, they sometimes use the Spanish (L1) phonetic system and invented spelling in English characteristic of native English speakers. For example, a Spanish-speaking child who wants to write the statement "My favorite food is spaghetti" in English may write, "May fud favorita is espageti." In this case, the child has used the Spanish phonetic system to write "May" for *My*; spelled *food* by writing "fud," using invented spelling in English (similar to native English speakers); written the Spanish version of *favorite* and placed the word *favorita* after the noun, according to Spanish syntax rules; used *is* in English correctly, but used the Spanish spelling for *spaghetti: espageti.*

If you cannot figure out what English learners are trying to communicate in their writing, we recommend that you ask them to read or tell you what they wrote. Printing what they say underneath their writing may help you to figure out which parts of their writing are in the L1 and in English. Sharing students' writing with their bilingual and/or ESL teachers or other L1 speakers may help you to understand how much of their writing is influenced by their L1 and English. Finally, in evaluating their written responses and writing, we recommend that you emphasize the ideas and idea development in their written responses and writing.

When you ask English learners to proof their writing, then it is appropriate to evaluate their use of correct spelling of vocabulary posted on your word walls and the English syntactic features you specifically have taught them, but these writing features are less important than their ideas.

Assessment

To understand students' written responses to texts, writing development, and use of writing to learn, it helps to have a formative writing assessment system in place in your classroom. According to advocates of the CCSS, a formative writing assessment system informs your instruction, helps you to differentiate your instruction, and includes opportunities for your students to set goals and evaluate how well they have met their goals (Heritage, 2010; Osmundson, 2011). Student self-evaluation can be as simple as placing a smiley face, a neutral face, or a face with a frown on a writing piece or a rubric. A writing assessment system typically includes anecdotal notes, the employment of rubrics to guide students' work and your interpretation and evaluation of their work, and the use of writing conferences.

Anecdotal Notes

When you take systematic and periodic anecdotal notes (i.e., brief descriptive notes) on individual students' participation in written response to text activities, the different phases of the writer's workshop, participation in the Language Experience Approach, or work on a project, you are recording their ongoing progress. In taking anecdotal notes, McGee (2007) recommends that you describe the setting and the individual child's actual behavior or participation, but that you do not make inferences about his or her performance. You make inferences later when you have had time to read and reflect on several sets of anecdotal notes for the individual child.

Systematic note taking means that you have a system for recording and storing your notes. McGee (2007) explains that teachers often write anecdotal notes on sticky notes with prewritten dates on them. Other teachers write anecdotal notes on mailing labels. You then tape the sticky notes or labels on pages (many recommend laminated pages so the sticky notes and labels adhere to the pages) in a folder or notebook for each child, along with dated writing samples. Periodic means that you plan or schedule the dates for when you will do the observations of particular children. After you have collected anecdotal notes across several observations for an individual child, you then reread your notes and write your inferences and next steps in a special section of the folder or notebook in which you have stored the anecdotal notes and writing samples. Figure 7.5 is a simulated example of

---

Sully   10-31-14

Sully took a long time to start writing. When I suggested that he draw something about Halloween and write about his drawing, he started drawing. He drew a pirate holding a bucket of candy. He did not use capital letters or periods in his writing (see writing sample).

FIGURE 7.5. Simulated example of anecdotal notes for a first grader's writing.

anecdotal notes for a first grader, Sully. The teacher's inferences (which should be written after reading several sets of anecdotal notes for the same student) were that Sully had a difficult time figuring out what to write about. He also did not appear to know how to begin and end sentences with initial capital letters and periods. The teacher's next steps were (1) to have Sully keep an idea notebook with drawings and/or writing ideas so that he could identify a topic to write about in the writing workshop; (2) to use a mini-lesson to remind the class of the importance of using initial capital letters and periods to separate sentences; and (3) after writing his selection, to have Sully work with another child, Robert, who was good at using initial capital letters and periods to separate sentences, to proof his writing.

Rubrics

Rubrics are a list of criteria that describe what students should include in their work and how you plan to evaluate the work (Bromley, 2007). Developing and sharing rubrics with your students is one way to improve and evaluate your students' written responses, writing, and work on projects. When you share the rubric with your students prior to their completing a written response, assignment, or project, you are showing them how to accomplish the work and what you value.

You can create your own rubrics, use those developed by other school district personnel, or adapt or use rubrics published in instructional texts or posted on the Internet. Writing rubrics usually include four to six evaluation levels and focus on ideas, organization, language, and mechanics. The 6 + 1 Trait® Rubrics are free, popular scoring guides that may be used instructionally with children or as assessment tools (*http://educationnorthwest.org/resource/464*). Form 7.1 (at the end of the chapter) is a writing rubric that can be used when students are writing their own stories. Form 7.2 (at the end of the chapter) is a rubric that could be used for an informational report written by second graders.

You also should provide opportunities for your students to use the rubric to evaluate their own performance and to compare their evaluation with your evaluation. When students compare their evaluation with that of the teacher, they usually become more self-regulated and improve their performance. Glazer (2007) describes how children as young as 7 and 8, with guidance from their teachers, were able to use simple composing, retelling, and writing rubrics to evaluate and reflect on their own performance. If you want your students to evaluate themselves or a partner, then we recommend that you use three sets of faces (a smiley face, a neutral face, and a frowny face; see Form 7.1), rather than "Yes, Okay, or No" (see Form 7.2) or a numerical scale (1–3).

Writing Conferences

An excellent way to monitor K–2 students' writing development, and to help them improve their written responses to texts, is through a teacher–student writing conference. During the writing conference, which may last between 5 and 15 minutes depending on the child's age and writing progress, you can review what the child is currently working on, or if the child has been writing independently since the last conference, have the child select a sample of his or her writing to bring to the conference to discuss.

Some teachers hold individual writing conferences with each of their students once per week, while others may hold individual writing conferences with each of their students twice or once per month. Teachers often hold the conferences while other students are working in centers or writing or reading in pairs or independently. Sometimes, teachers create a writing conference center or station.

If the student has selected a writing sample to share in the conference, then one of the first questions to ask is why he or she selected the specific sample to share with you. Then, most teachers have the students read aloud their writing because it is often difficult to comprehend young children's writing, especially when they use inventive spelling and are still learning how to put spaces between words and use appropriate capitalization and punctuation. To encourage students to like writing, Bromley (2007) recommends that you first respond to the content and message in their writing before you respond to the mechanics. One task that encourages students to write more is when you compliment them on the progress that they have made in their content, message, communication and/or spelling, grammar, and punctuation.

For students who are just starting to write, your conferences also may focus on how they are representing print and organizing their writing. For example, a teacher who held writing conferences in the fall of first grade reported that she spent some time in the writing conferences helping her students to space their words by using a finger and to stretch their pronunciation of words to get more accurate spelling.

Teachers often use anecdotal notes to record students' writing progress. You can also use rubrics and /or writing evaluation sheets. One of us (Georgia) observed a teacher who developed a writing evaluation sheet on which the student wrote his or her name, the date, and the title of the writing piece that was being discussed. Then, after discussing the writing sample presented in the conference, the teacher wrote a goal for the student's writing on the evaluation sheet, and the student wrote a goal, in addition to indicating what the teacher could do to help the student reach the goal. According to Bromley (2007), your assessment feedback needs to be "positive, specific, and helpful" (p. 221). She recommends that you first respond to the content and message in students' writing before you respond to the mechanics.

Conclusion

The relationship between reading and writing is reciprocal because the two processes are the flip side of each other. When students respond to text by drawing and writing about it, they not only demonstrate their text comprehension but they also facilitate it by making connections among what they read, understand, and think. Appropriate writing activities include response journals and logs, dialogue journals, and double-entry journals. Once students are accustomed to writing short responses to reading, they should be encouraged to participate in extended responses, the writer's workshop, disciplinary projects, themed disciplinary units, and multimedia projects. An excellent reading–writing activity for preschoolers through grade 2 is the Language Experience Approach.

English learners should be given the opportunity to think, respond, and write in their L1, English, and a combination of the two languages about texts read in English. However, we need to use ESL sheltering techniques so that English learners understand our instruction, and their thinking and writing are supported. When English learners participate in the writer's workshop, they will need our support to peer-edit or proof each other's English writing and may need explicit instruction on spelling and writing differences between their L1 and English.

Establishing a formative writing assessment system helps us to understand and evaluate students' written responses to texts, writing development, and use of writing to learn. A typical writing assessment system includes anecdotal notes, writing and project rubrics, and writing conferences. In evaluating students' written responses to text and writing, we need to emphasize the content and message conveyed in the writing rather than the mechanics. Chapter 8 provides ideas for how to assess and evaluate emergent readers' reading comprehension.

Story-Writing Rubric

Student Name	☺	😐	☹
1. The title tells what the story is about.			
2. The characters are introduced.			
3. The setting is described.			
4. The story begins with a problem.			
5. There is a beginning, middle, and end.			
6. There are repeated events.			
7. The problem is solved.			
8. The description is good.			
9. The story makes sense.			
10. The story is interesting to read.			
11. Illustrations are included.			
12. The spelling and punctuation are correct.			

Report-Writing Rubric

Student Name	Yes	Okay	No
1. The title tells what the report is about.			
2. The first sentence explains the content of the report.			
3. The first sentence makes someone want to read the report.			
4. The facts are written in the student's own words.			
5. The facts are interesting and complete.			
6. The facts are presented in sentences.			
7. The sentences are grouped in paragraphs that make sense.			
8. The report concludes with a good ending.			
9. A chart, diagram, or drawing is included to make the report clear.			
10. The report is interesting to read.			
11. The spelling and punctuation are correct.			

Based on Kletzien and Dreher (2004, p. 135).

CHAPTER 8
· · · · · · · · · · · ·

Assessing Reading Comprehension in the Early Grades

GUIDING QUESTIONS

- What do we need to know about young children to evaluate their current reading comprehension?
- What do we need to know about young children to predict their later reading comprehension?
- What literacy assessments can we use to evaluate and improve the comprehension instruction of *emergent readers*?
- What literacy assessments can we use to evaluate and improve the comprehension instruction of *novice readers*?
- What assessment considerations do we need to pay attention to when working with English learners and students from diverse linguistic and cultural backgrounds?

Overview of Research

Reading comprehension is difficult to assess. There is not a single assessment that can tell you or external stakeholders (e.g., parents; school, district, and state officials; community and state leaders) everything we need to know about a child's comprehension abilities. Because we are unable to see inside the reader's head to measure what is happening before, during, and after reading, we have to rely on verbal or written evidence. If readers are new to the assessment, anxious about it, or not fluent in English (such as English learners), then their oral and written performances may hide their ability to comprehend English text. We also know that a reader's comprehension varies according to the text, context, and task.

The assessment challenges are magnified in the early grades. Emergent readers in prekindergarten and kindergarten typically are characterized by their "pretend reading," use of pictures, and reliance on memory to "read" the story. However, this type of reading actually provides information on how young children approach reading and understand its purpose (Sulzby, 1985). As a result, a teacher can learn a lot about a young child's meaning making from the emergent reader's text "reading" because the child is creating meaning without knowledge of the alphabetic system. So at this stage both the text reading and the child's discussion of the text can provide indicators for measuring comprehension. For example, we want to document a child's knowledge of print concepts, how the child uses illustrations and memory to construct the telling of the story, and text-handling skills. In addition, we want to record the type of language the child uses to talk about the text: conversational language or contextualized language, such as "The tall man goes to a store," or book language or decontextualized language, such as "Once upon a time, there was a handsome prince who had to go to the market to find a gift. . . ."

Emergent readers become novice readers when they use the alphabetic system to support their reading of easy texts. Their ability to consistently use the first letter of a word to successfully achieve one-to-one finger-pointing, which indicates a voice–print match, is observable evidence of this shift. Novice readers deliberately attempt to make what they say match printed words in addition to conveying the text message. This is a difficult juggling act for the novice reader.

Recalling and spontaneously applying new knowledge about the alphabetic system is cognitively demanding. Automatically retrieving high-frequency words that cannot be decoded adds to this cognitive burden. During the primary-school years, children continue to acquire knowledge about how the alphabetic system works (Bear et al., 2011). Their increasing knowledge helps improve their efficiency and fluency as they accurately read increasingly difficult texts. The cognitive energy required for these developing processes results in less energy being available for comprehension processes. Consequently, in the primary grades there is a symbiotic relationship among word recognition, fluency, and comprehension. If a child cannot identify the words or misidentifies them, he or she typically has difficulty understanding the text. If reading is slow and labored, it compromises the ability to generate a cohesive mental representation of the text. Evidence indicates that the correlation between reading fluency and reading comprehension is high in the primary grades but diminishes as children proceed through the intermediate grades when word recognition becomes automatic (Paris & Hamilton, 2009). However, this means that as teachers of young children we need to document how young children are transitioning from orally retelling stories they have *heard* to creating oral (and written) representations of texts that they are *reading* independently.

In Chapter 1 we discuss the pressure points that contribute to comprehension. Among these were the reader contributions of prior knowledge, vocabulary, working memory, self-regulation of cognitive strategies, and motivation or engagement, along with language and decoding (Perfetti & Adlof, 2012). The ability to orchestrate multiple systems simultaneously is not intuitive or automatic for the novice reader. The ways that a child synchronizes these processes and how they result in the reading comprehension thresholds that were discussed in Chapter 1 must be assessed and documented in deliberate ways during the primary-school years.

McKenna and Stahl (2009) include foundational skills, language comprehension, and strategic knowledge in the cognitive model of reading assessment (see Figure 8.1). This model is based on the premise that reading comprehension is the primary purpose of reading and that skills along three different pathways

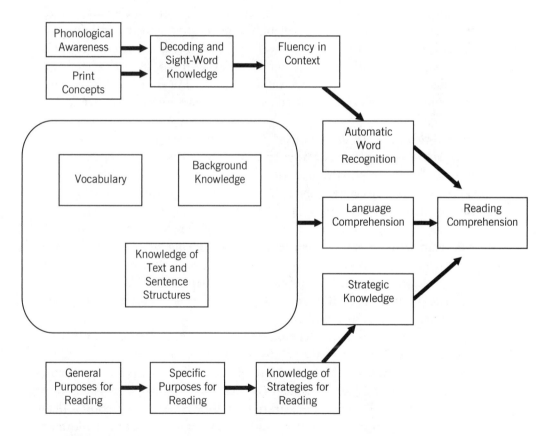

FIGURE 8.1. The modified cognitive model. From McKenna and Stahl (2009, p. 23). Copyright 2009 by The Guilford Press. Reprinted by permission.

contribute to it. During the assessment process we can use guiding questions along each pathway of the model to identify the ways that we can support the development of each child's comprehension thresholds. The top pathway is linear. It includes the foundational processes that contribute to automatic word recognition. This chapter does not include assessments that address the development of these skills; other books provide refined ways to trace this developmental pathway (Bear et al., 2011; Hayes & Flannigan, 2014; McKenna & Stahl, 2009; Walpole & McKenna, 2007).

The middle pathway includes the nonlinear pressure points that contribute to language comprehension: (1) background knowledge, (2) vocabulary, and (3) knowledge of language and text structures. Finally, the bottom pathway addresses strategic knowledge. Moving from most general to most specific conceptually, we consider a child's awareness and application of (1) general purposes for reading, (2) specific purposes for reading, and (3) knowledge of reading strategies. Although this knowledge is listed from general to specific, we are not suggesting that children develop it in a linear manner. For example, as children progress through school, they are likely to acquire increasingly sophisticated and varying purposes for reading. Sometimes familiar strategies will help them overcome meaning-making hurdles as they read for new purposes. At other times, they may need to be taught new disciplinary- or media-specific strategies. All of these reading comprehension pressure points must be assessed as children read a variety of increasingly difficult texts.

Prior knowledge, sense of narrative, strategic processing, memory, and self-regulation contribute in important ways to the creation of a mental representation based on text. These are portrayed in the bottom two pathways of the cognitive model. They may be documented long before conventional reading begins, and can be affected by instruction as reading and knowledge along the top pathway develops. It makes good sense to intervene early to correct misconceptions about the purpose of reading and to shape comprehension processing while it is more easily molded. For example, even as children begin learning about letter–sound relationships, we want to provide instruction that reminds them that making sense of the text is the primary purpose of all reading. Or similarly, fast reading is not better if you can't tell me what you just read.

The comprehension assessments that we are recommending are sensitive to developmental shifts. They also have positive consequential validity. That is to say, both instruction and reading achievement are likely to shift in a positive direction as a consequence of using the assessment activity. For example, if teachers know that children will be assessed using a narrative retelling rubric, instruction is likely to address the story grammar elements and include opportunities for children to retell the stories they read. The CCSS reform movement strongly encourages teachers to use formative assessments to evaluate student performance *and* inform their instruction.

Common Formative Assessments and Classroom-Based Assessments

With the CCSS reform movement, district and school personnel increasingly are working with teachers to develop common formative assessments, tied to the CCSS for language arts, which can be embedded in teachers' instruction. The purpose of formative assessments is to inform and differentiate teachers' instruction according to individual student progress in attaining the CCSS, and to guide student learning (Heritage, 2010; Osmundson, 2011). An advantage of formative assessment is that it is intended to be part of your instruction, so that it does not require you to dedicate additional time to the administration of a test or assessment. It is also based on the texts you are using and the instruction you are providing. Formative assessments may include student self-assessment to guide student learning and peer assessment to promote student collaboration. With the addition of systematic recording and periodic scheduling, so that you document students' individual progress, many of the assessment tasks that we described in Chapters 4–7 can be used as formative assessments or as part of a formative assessment system. Possible examples include the Knowledge Rating Scale, Vocabulary Recognition Task, or Vocabulary Assessment Magazine; strategy checklists, think-alouds, and interviews; writing and project rubrics; anecdotal notes; and reading and writing conferences.

One of us (Georgia) has been working with K–5 bilingual teachers to turn some of their language arts instructional activities into formative assessments tied to the CCSS for language arts. She has worked with a second-grade teacher who has embedded formative assessment into her guided reading lessons by periodically, and systematically, recording each student's reading progress on a chart that she keeps on a clipboard. On the chart, the teacher briefly indicates whether a child effectively applies a cognitive strategy (such as prediction, hypothesis testing or inferencing, visualization, and use of story structure or nonfiction text features and structures) to his or her reading and/or discussion of reading during the guided reading lesson. She also takes a brief running record (explained below) of the child's oral reading, notes any struggles/frustrations the child has with the text, and indicates whether the child needs help with specific vocabulary from the assigned text.

Common Formative Assessments

Below we describe several tasks—retellings, prompted recall, video recall, emergent storybook reading scale, and oral reading miscue analysis or running records—that you can use to evaluate your students' reading comprehension or emergent reading comprehension either as a formative assessment or as a *common formative assessment*. Common formative assessments are assessments that have been collaboratively designed by teams of teachers who teach the same grade level (Ainsworth & Viegut, 2006; Dufour, Dufour, Eakey, & Many, 2006). They might also be designed by a school or district literacy team. Common formative assessments are intentionally designed to align with learning standards or some other agreed-upon skills. The data from the common formative assessments is used to identify students who need more support, areas of need among those students having difficulties, and identify areas that call for instructional improvement among the teachers.

If you want to employ any of the tasks as common formative assessments, then you must use the set of materials that you develop for assessment purposes only. For common formative assessments, we also recommend that you create a script that can be used with each video or text and that you administer the activity consistently with each child every time. When you use common formative assessments, you will use consistent procedures and scoring protocols, although the texts and formats may vary according to the reading levels of your students. Common formative assessments, especially writing samples, are often scored collaboratively among a grade-level team of teachers. The results can be used to inform instruction, deliver a different kind of instruction, or develop instructional interventions such as those that are discussed in Chapter 9.

Retelling

Retelling tasks require the child to orally report the information that he or she saw, heard, or read. For children not yet reading conventionally (i.e., the emergent reader), a retelling may follow a teacher read-aloud or a video viewing. In addition to revealing a child's listening or visual comprehension, the retelling will reveal how well the child integrates prior knowledge with the information from the text or the video, knowledge of key vocabulary and use of decontextualized language, and knowledge of text or story structure. Novice readers can be asked to retell a text they heard read aloud or that they read orally through shared, paired, or independent reading or that they read on their own or silently. When children retell a text they read, the retelling can provide valuable information about how they comprehended the text. However, to make sure children focus on comprehension while reading the text, they should be told before they read the text that they will be asked to retell it afterward. We recommend using the procedures that are described in the text box on the next page.

The openness of the retelling task facilitates your observation of the child's thought processes, what the child values as important, and any sociocultural influences involved in the child's story interpretation (Narvaez, 2002). Story retellings have been used successfully with children as young as 4 years old (Lynch et al., 2008; Morrow, 1985). Studies have demonstrated that the practice of retelling narrative and expository texts, even without specific instruction, results in

ADMINISTERING A RETELLING ASSESSMENT

- Before the child reads the text, listens to the text, or views the video, tell the child: "Be sure to pay close attention to the meaning of the *story/informational text/video* because at the end I am going to ask you to tell me everything that you remember and ask you some questions about the *story/informational text/video*."
- After the child reads, listens, or views the video, tell the child: "Now I want you to tell me everything you remember about the *story, informational text, or video*. I want you to tell it to me as though you were telling it to your *brother/sister/friend* who has never *heard/seen* it."
- Use prompts as needed to encourage a comprehensive retelling. Allow the child to tell as much as he or she can recall unprompted. Then conclude with "Do you remember anything else?"
- For children who say they don't recall anything or only recall one or two ideas, you may want to choose some of the prompts below. Indicate the level of prompting on your record-keeping sheet. Also, be sure that the prompts you provide match the structure of the text or video.

Narrative	Informational
How did the story begin?	What was the book/video about?
What was the problem?	What were the big ideas? What was the most important information that you remember? Is there anything else that you remember?
What happened next?	What did the author want us to know about the topic?
How did the *character* solve the problem? How did the book end?	Was there anything that you read/saw that was interesting to you or that was new to you?

improvements in children's adherence to story grammar, selection of high-level idea units, and prompted recall (Gambrell, Pfieffer, & Wilson, 1985; Morrow, 1984, 1985).

There are some considerations in the use of retellings as an assessment measure. An oral retelling of a story places high cognitive demands on young children. "Especially for longer stories, the resource demands of producing an organized and sequentially and causally coherent story may exceed the resources available to children, especially young five- and six-year-olds" (Goldman et al., 1999, p. 139). Additionally, some children may think that because you know the story, it is not necessary for them to thoroughly report the events to you. Asking children to retell the story to a puppet not present when the story was read or to another adult or child who did not hear the story read often results in a more complete retelling.

However, to get a full representation of the child's understanding of a text, you always want to follow the retelling with some questions about the text. Many times, children can answer high-level questions about the text, revealing information and thinking that they do not express spontaneously.

Commercially produced informal reading inventories and assessment kits that call for children to perform retellings tend to use a rubric to quantify their retellings. Sometimes the rubric is a simple, holistic rating scale. For example, the retelling might be categorized as:

- *Excellent* (thorough, includes all important information and supporting information).
- *Satisfactory* (includes important information, omits or misunderstands other ideas).
- *Minimal* (mentions isolated details, omits or misunderstands important information).
- *Unsatisfactory* (no response, inaccurate, or lacks text information).

Other rubrics might score the retelling based on the number of story grammar elements (setting, main characters, secondary characters, problem, number of plot episodes, resolution). For informational texts, the retelling should analyze the number of superordinate and subordinate ideas by level of importance. Finally, some assessment systems count the number of idea units (single subject and verb phrases). Of the three scoring systems, an analysis of a child's recall of story grammar elements or main ideas and supporting details is useful for informing instruction. Certainly, consideration of the length of the retelling, the degree of text-based information, the number of inaccuracies, and the proportion of prior knowledge included should all be part of a thorough analysis of a child's retelling. It is also important to notice whether the child is using the appropriate text or story structure to support a paraphrased retelling of key ideas or whether he or she is relying on memory to construct a verbatim retelling that matches snippets of text.

For example, the two retellings in Figure 8.2 demonstrate how Diego (pseudonym) used the text structure to organize his retelling and it served as a scaffold to propel the retelling of many facts about spiders from the text. On the other hand, Eli (pseudonym) relied on pure memory to recall random facts from the text.

These data can be used to inform instruction. Rather than simply teaching children to identify the text features of informational text, Eli clearly needs instruction on how to use the headings as a signal to the text's organization of ideas. Then his teacher should help him use that organizational structure to support both the construction of knowledge and to organize his retelling.

We urge you to use caution in the use of the 1-minute retelling that is required by Dynamic Indicators of Basic Early Literacy Skills (DIBELS) Next during the Oral Reading Fluency test. Beginning mid–first grade, this test requires children

---

Diego's retelling

Spiders have two body parts. They have eight legs and around eight eyes and fangs. The boys are smaller than the girls. Sometimes the girls eat the boys after they lay the eggs. The eggs are in a silk sac. Then when they hatch they are spiderlings. They make webs with silk. Orb webs. Cobwebs. I can't remember the other ones. Orb spiders and cobweb spiders aren't poisonous. Black widows and tarantulas are poisonous.

Eli's retelling

Spiders spin webs. They only have two body parts. Babies are spiderlings. Some spiders can jump. Orb web. Some spiders swim.

FIGURE 8.2. Retelling comparison.

to retell as much as they can in the 1 minute following their timed reading of a grade-level passage. The retelling is evaluated based on the number of words and a general rating of the retelling. The DIBELS website justifies this measure by stating that a fluency score must be based on reading for meaning, not simply calling out words quickly. They also claim that there is statistical evidence of reliability and validity for their measures. We urge caution because there is no consideration of the content of the retelling. Additionally, the children are not likely to have read the entire passage and are not even required to read the title. Finally, issues of content, genre, prior knowledge, and the reading level of the student are neglected in the DIBELS Next retelling task. Unless you are using their data management system that requires the retelling, you may want to omit this 1-minute retelling.

Just as there is evidence that children create similar retellings whether based on a read-aloud or a video, there is also evidence that second graders produce similar oral, handwritten, and computer-written retellings (Cameron, Hunt, & Linton, 1985; Geva & Olson, 1983). As a teacher of young children, you can expect a standard story opening, elaborated actions, and less elaborated endings. Plots and character descriptions become more developed with age and instructional attention. Second graders exhibit increasing ease with verb tense decisions, appropriate pronouns, and story resolutions. By second grade, better readers tend to adapt their retelling to the audience, using gist statements to retell to a tester and verbatim statements from the text when reporting to a peer who has not heard the story. However, affective dimensions of the story, such as character development, emotion, character motives, and moral judgments, are typically absent from the retellings of children before the intermediate grades. Nevertheless, it is important to support children instructionally in their efforts to think along these lines.

Forms 8.1 and 8.2 (at the end of the chapter) can be used to document what your students include in their efforts to retell stories and informational texts. It is a good idea to document what they are including after listening to texts and compare that with what is included or omitted in their retelling of texts that they are reading. Keep in mind that easy-to-read texts may not include all of the story grammar elements.

Prompted Recall

Retellings provide teachers with insights about what children remember and perceive as important. They can reveal much about their ability to identify the levels of important information in a nonfiction text as well as their ability to put together a sequence of events in either a narrative or informational text. However, children understand and remember much more than they are likely to include in a retelling. When questioned about plot details, affective dimensions, and important conceptual information represented in a text or video, children can often

---

PROMPTED RECALL

General Questions

- What is the theme of this story? What lesson do you think the author wants us to learn from this story? (narrative)
- What is this (*passage/book/video*) mainly about? (informational)
- Describe the setting. Why is the setting of this story important?
- How would you describe *the character*? What does *the character* say or do to make you describe him or her that way?
- What does . . . tell us about . . . ?
- How are . . . and . . . alike (or different)?
- What is important about . . . ?
- How is . . . related to . . . ?
- Why is it important that . . . ?
- Explain. . . .

Questions for Prompting Critical Thinking

- Why did the author write this text?
- For whom did the author write this text?
- Why do you think the author used language or text features in particular ways? Specify the use of figurative language, regional dialects, incorporation of second languages, illustrations, diagrams, and other craft choices.
- How do other texts (or authors) that you have read convey this idea/theme?
- How might we rewrite this *story/essay* to convey a different point of view?

demonstrate knowledge and insights that were not presented in their retelling. Prompted recall (sometimes referred to as cued recall) is an opportunity for us to ask questions that force children to think about the text or video at higher levels than they would without prompting. Both literal and inferential questions should be included. After school entry, questions that address critical literacy should be incorporated during instruction and assessment. The text box on the previous page includes some examples of questions and question stems that can be used to gauge a child's understanding of the text or video. (Form 9.2 at the end of Chapter 9 also provides additional examples of questions.) The expectations in the assessment should mirror instructional expectations. Most informal reading inventories and assessment kits include literal, inferential, and vocabulary questions for each passage or leveled book. Additionally, the CCSS provide a clear road map for formulating questions that prompt high-level thinking and prepare children for future high-stakes assessments.

Question answering reduces the cognitive demands for young children and makes clear what ideas the teacher is seeking and finds important. Since different types of information are revealed to us about the young readers' comprehension processes, it is valuable to include both retelling and prompted recall opportunities during both assessment and instruction.

Assessing the Comprehension of Emergent Readers

Video Recall

We know that a preschooler's ability to retell and answer questions about a narrative presented as a video positively correlates with his or her ability to retell and answer questions about narrative texts 2 years later (Kendeou et al, 2006). Therefore, you might show a short video of a story and ask emergent or novice readers who have had challenges with texts (or with attention difficulties) to retell the events in the video. We recommend that you follow the retelling by asking the child to answer a few questions about the key ideas or themes of the story and record the child's retelling on Form 8.1 (at the end of the chapter). You should use the information obtained from the retelling to inform your instruction and to prompt more complete retellings during small-group or one-on-one instruction. See Chapter 9 for additional suggestions for comprehension interventions.

Emergent Storybook Reading

Sulzby's (1985) classification scheme allows teachers to assess the emergent reader's attempt to read a favorite storybook. Sulzby included features of story content, story structure, oral language, and decoding precision in the formation of a developmental continuum of emergent reading. Her classification scheme moves from early "picture-governed attempts" to more sophisticated "print-governed attempts" to a child's actual reading of a narrative storybook with pictures. The children in Sulzby's study were asked to read a favorite storybook to the researcher. You might use the same approach to assess an emergent reader by asking the child to "read" a favorite book or a familiar book that you or another adult recently read aloud to the child. If the child declares that he or she cannot read, tell him or her to "read as best you can" or "pretend to read the book" (McKenna & Stahl, 2009, p. 96). McKenna and Stahl (2009) devised an Emergent Storybook Reading Scale to assist you with consistent record keeping. Form 8.3 (at the end of the chapter) is a modification of that scale. The form serves as a useful guide to measure a progression of emergent reading ability before a child is capable of conventional reading. Therefore, this scale is likely to be most useful in preschool and kindergarten. Additionally, it provides clear indications of a child's ability to formulate a cohesive text-based narrative that might be useful with novice readers. However, when children begin conventional reading they should be assessed using a leveled reading system such as the Benchmark Assessment System 1 (F&PBAS1; Fountas & Pinnell, 2010).

Picture-Governed Attempts

At the beginning stage, *labeling and commenting*, the child uses a label, phrase, or sentence to describe the picture on each page, such as "moon," "kitty cat" or "She got boo boo." Often the child is pointing to the picture or using some hand motion. The oral language used is often less mature than the child typically uses in social interactions. Children may ask questions that replicate remnants of an adult read-aloud routine or provide a reaction such as "That's scary." In this and the next stage, each page is treated individually, and there is no way for you, the listener, to get a sense of the whole story.

In the *following the action* stage, the child's stories still are unformed, and the child treats the page as a discrete unit. The child's reading attempt portrays the action in the pictures as if it is currently occurring. Accordingly, the child uses verbs in the present tense. The child may use physical body movements and sound effects to describe the page.

The next stage is *dialogic storytelling*. Although the story may be disjointed, this is the first stage where you are likely to get a sense of the story from the child's oral expression. The child may create voices for dialogue or may direct dialogic comments to you. However, in this stage, rather than turning to you as an aside, the child's attention tends to stay more focused on the page than it did at earlier stages. As a result, it may be more difficult to determine if the child intends the speech as reading or conversation. During this stage, there is a mixture of present and past tense verb forms. Although there are some examples of "labeling and commenting" and "following the action," you are able to infer that the child is attempting to put together a story.

In *monologic storytelling*, the child performs a monologue that is clearly a story and delivered with storytelling intonation. The pictures are propelling the "reading," but the monologue has the flow of a story with plot connections across pages. Because the reading sounds like storytelling, the child might signal the conclusion of the reading by saying, "That's all" or "I'm done."

The next stage is *mixed storytelling and reading*. Although the child's reading is still governed by pictures, he or she uses speech that ranges between a conversational style and a written text style or register. The child's storytelling may hold the plot together by emphasizing some of the story map features, but he or she will occasionally insert verbatim or near-verbatim text from memory, recalling the story read. For example, a child might insert a repeated pattern or dialogue into his or her storytelling.

In *reading similar to original story*, the child's language selection and intonation sound more like an expressive oral reading than oral storytelling. Repetitive language or "fairytale patterns of three," characteristics of author's craft, may be evident in the reading even if the book the child is reading doesn't have these elements. The child's awareness of "book talk," or written register, strongly influences the way the child reads the story. Although the child's reading is not verbatim, it is a good match for the events on each page. Even without looking at the pictures, you know the gist of the story from the child's reading.

Last is *reading verbatim-like story*. In this stage, the child acts as though he or she is reading the pictures. The child tries to recite the story verbatim from memory using the formal language that represents the written register, narrative story structure, and other strategic mental clues. Even though the child is not attending to print, he or she may attempt to retrieve precise wording by asking the adult to read the bits that he or she cannot remember verbatim. Despite the child's awareness that the adult can read the text, he or she still treats his or her own reading as a solitary discourse unit driven by meaning and pictures.

Print-Governed Attempts

In the *print-awareness* stage, the child realizes that a conventional text reading involves reading the printed words, not the pictures. This transitional moment is a significant demarcation that teachers of young children need to document because it is a developmental indicator that calls for an instructional shift. At this point, the child decides that he or she needs to know more about print in order to read the book. As a result, many children at this juncture proclaim that they don't know how to read and may refuse to read books that they were previously able to "pretend read" with a comprehensive storyline and plot details. If you teach young children, you want to conduct ongoing assessments of this progression so that you are able to distinguish between a child who is newly aware of the print and a child who has minimal language skills and is unable to create a narrative from a storybook—that is, a child who is in the *labeling and commenting* or *following the action* stage. Children pursuing the latter approach, or still in the picture-governed stages, and those pursuing the print-governed approach require two distinctly different instructional supports.

Children in the picture-governed stages benefit from the dialogic reading protocol described in Chapter 3. Dialogic reading supports the development of oral language and increasingly sophisticated, spontaneous verbal expressions in response to texts. Dialogic reading will nudge the child from *labeling and commenting* or *following the action* toward the more fully developed reading depicted in the later picture-governed stages.

The child who has arrived at the print-awareness stage is ready to learn about the alphabetic system and how to begin to integrate that knowledge with what he or she already knows about the meaning of a story to arrive at a precise text match. Nonetheless, children at this stage should be encouraged to continue to apply their strong storytelling abilities (or retellings of informational texts) to books that have been read aloud to them. As teachers, we want to view the child's knowledge of narrative structure, written register, and text structures as the foundation or base for reading comprehension while we build on additional, new knowledge of high-frequency words, sound–letter associations, and orthographic patterns to help children arrive at precise, accurate reading of unfamiliar text. The print-awareness stage is the jumping-off point for the child to begin reading text on his or her own.

The next stage is *aspectual reading*. When you listen to children read at this stage, it may sound like they are regressing compared with earlier stages. Now that the child is tied to print, he or she is trying out repertoires of integrating the text on the page with the meaning of the story. The fluency suffers as the child attends to one or two aspects of the printed words. For example, the child may recognize the word *look* or *mom* logographically as a whole word unit and use it to anchor what he or she sees to what he or she says. The child may pay attention to a few known letters and attempt to sound out words. The cognitive burden of dealing with print causes many children at this stage to abandon their recall or memory of a familiar story. Diagnostically, this is a good developmental place to shift assessment to a leveled reading assessment package with a fine gradient of reading levels such as F&PBAS1 (Fountas & Pinnell, 2010).

The last two stages are *reading with imbalanced strategies* and *reading independently*. Sulzby (1985) distinguishes between the last two stages according to the degree to which a child self-regulates his or her use of reading strategies to arrive at a precise reading of printed text. This self-regulation may be evident through the child's self-correction of errors. Independent readers balance their use of word recognition strategies, syntax, and meaning to arrive at an accurate reading of the text. However, at this developmental stage, the F&PBAS1 or some other systematic benchmark assessment kit that employs a fine gradient of leveled texts provides a more precise evaluation.

Assessing the Comprehension of Novice Readers

Oral Reading Miscue Analysis or Running Records

A miscue analysis is an evaluation of oral reading errors that may be conducted as part of a running record of text reading or as a part of an informal reading inventory. For novice readers, error analysis can provide a lens for viewing comprehension processes during text reading (Clay, 2006; Goodman, Watson, & Burke, 1987). Particularly, how the child self-corrects reading errors to produce an accurate, syntactically correct, and sensible representation of the text allows the teacher to evaluate the child's ability to make sense of text while reading connected text at his or her instructional level.

Although miscue analysis gained popularity and validation through Goodman and colleagues' (1987) Reading Miscue Inventory process, today most teachers of novice readers use the less complicated running record. The Reading Miscue Inventory is time-consuming, requiring a text of at least 500 words and detailed levels of analysis of each error at the passage level, sentence level, partial-sentence level, and word level. Running records or the error analysis of the oral reading of a leveled passage in an informal reading inventory simply requires asking yourself two questions: "At the point of the error, what visual (alphabetic/decoding), syntactic or structural, and semantic information did the reader appear to use to read the word?" and, if the error was corrected, "What additional information did the reader appear to use to correct the error?" After tabulating the errors, an analysis of the error pattern can be used to inform instructional teaching points. The meaning–structure–visual (MSV) error analysis displays these processing patterns and is an important component of the running record. The MSV analysis informs instruction.

For example, an examination of Simon's and Mallory's running records (see Figures 8.3 and 8.4, respectively) indicates that they found several of the same words difficult as they were reading *Kitten Chased a Fly* (Randell, 1985/1992). However, the approaches they each used when they came to a hard word were distinctly different and tended to be consistent. Their errors provide a window into their mental processing.

In attending the visual cues, Simon made sure that his reading matched the correct number of words on the page and maintained one-to-one matching. He wasn't just telling the story without regard for attending the print. One-to-one matching is a developmental indicator that he is able to read some high-frequency words and is capable of employing the first letter of a word to confirm accuracy. Children reading Level C books tend to be in the late emergent–early letter name stage of word recognition. They are still learning to use consonants to read and spell words, but they have not yet become aware of vowel sound application (Bear et al., 2011). However, Simon is not consistently using the first letter as a tool to figure out an unfamiliar word or to self-monitor. When he comes to an unfamiliar word, meaning trumps. As long as his guess makes sense he keeps on reading,

Page	Text and Running Record of Oral Reading	Error: Information Used
2	✓ ✓ ✓ ✓ Kitten chased a fly,	
3	✓ ✓ ✓ ✓ but it got away	
4	✓ ✓ ✓ *butterfly* Kitten chased a moth,	Meaning, Structure
5	✓ ✓ ✓ ✓ but it got away	
6	✓ ✓ ✓ *rat* Kitten chased a mouse,	Meaning, Structure
7	✓ ✓ ✓ ✓ but it got away	
8	✓ ✓ ✓ ✓ Kitten chased a butterfly,	
9	✓ ✓ ✓ ✓ but it got away	
10	✓ ✓ ✓ ✓ Kitten chased a lizard,	
11	✓ ✓ ✓ ✓ but it got away	
12	✓ ✓ ✓ ✓ Kitten chased a bird,	
13	✓ ✓ ✓ ✓ but it got away	
14	✓ ✓ Kitten chased	
15	✓ ✓ ✓ *yarn* a ball of wool . . .	Meaning, Structure
16	*Then caught* And she got it.	Meaning, Structure Meaning, Structure

FIGURE 8.3. Simon's running record.

Page	Text and Running Record of Oral Reading	Error: Information Used
2	✓ ✓ ✓ ✓ Kitten chased a fly,	
3	✓ ✓ ✓ ✓ but it got away	
4	✓ ✓ ✓ *mouth* Kitten chased a moth,	Visual (letter/sound)
5	✓ ✓ ✓ ✓ but it got away	
6	✓ ✓ ✓ ✓ Kitten chased a mouse,	
7	✓ ✓ ✓ ✓ but it got away	
8	✓ ✓ ✓ ✓ Kitten chased a butterfly,	
9	✓ ✓ ✓ ✓ but it got away	
10	✓ ✓ ✓ *līzd . . . zero* Kitten chased a lizard,	Visual (letter/sound)
11	✓ ✓ ✓ ✓ but it got away	
12	✓ ✓ ✓ ✓ Kitten chased a bird,	
13	✓ ✓ ✓ ✓ but it got away	
14	✓ ✓ Kitten chased	
15	✓ ✓ ✓ *www . . . ōl* a ball of wool . . .	Visual (letter/sound)
16	*Anna gōt* And she got it.	Visual (letter/sound) Visual (letter/sound)

FIGURE 8.4. Mallory's running record.

satisfied with his word choice. Simon needs to focus more carefully on matching the first letter with his guesses that propel his reading.

Mallory's running record displays a different problem-solving process when she comes to an unfamiliar word. Like Simon, she has recently begun making a voice-to-print match indicating an awareness of using the first letter of a word and a small bank of high-frequency words. However, when she comes to the unknown word she focuses her attention on the first letter and says a word that has that sound. Often the words she retrieves are words that her teacher used during the phonics lesson to teach the sound. For Mallory, the visual system trumps meaning. She needs to learn to confirm her visual approximations with meaning.

Both children need instruction on self-monitoring and cross-checking that what they read makes sense, looks right (letter–sound), and sounds right (structurally). If Simon's pattern is not corrected, we end up with a child whose overreliance on pictures and meaning interferes with reading acquisition as the books become less predictable and lengthier. Relying on context to figure out hard words in the older grades has been demonstrated to actually compromise high-level comprehension processes (Stanovich, 1980). If Mallory's problem is not corrected, she is at risk for becoming a word caller whose letter-by-letter sounding out interferes with reading fluently and meaningfully.

When conducting an assessment for the purpose of establishing a benchmark, most teachers today use either an assessment kit such as the F&PBAS1 or the Developmental Reading Assessment, Kindergarten through Grade 3, Second Edition (DRA2, K–3; Beaver, 2006). Informal reading inventories also call for children in the early grades to read aloud a leveled passage as the teacher documents each word that the child reads aloud. This may be conducted manually using pencil and paper or using one of the new electronic record-keeping systems that make use of tablets for supporting score calculations and data management.

Informal reading inventories use passages of about 100–300 words that have been leveled using traditional readability formulas. However, the kits include leveled "little books" that consist of complete stories or informational books that have been leveled using a set of qualitative criteria. All of these systems provide a typescript of the text. However, one of the advantages of the running record is that for frequent progress monitoring, teachers can take a running record of oral reading using any text a child is reading for guided reading instruction as long as a consistent and uniform coding system is applied for recording the reading. Clay (2006) recommends that progress monitoring running records be administered using any texts that a child can read with 90–95% accuracy. Easier texts don't allow for enough errors to be analyzed and harder texts tend to reflect processing that is so disrupted by decoding errors that it doesn't provide a clear window into mental processing.

Although you may ask the student to provide a retelling and to answer a few key questions, the word recognition accuracy and error analysis should inform your guided reading instructional decision making about comprehension in Fountas and Pinnell (2006, 2010) text Levels A–G. Because children are at the beginning stages of the developmental word recognition process, any reading of these simple texts relies on deriving meaning from familiar content, pictures, and the predictability of the text's structure. Story grammar elements and the introduction of unfamiliar conceptual information are minimal. Within this text-level band, the texts and the leveling system are designed so that meaning and structure strongly support a developing knowledge of letter–sound relationships and orthographic patterns. It is likely that if children are achieving an accuracy level of 90–95%, they are using meaning to propel the reading because their word recognition abilities are limited to automatic recognition of a small bank of high-frequency words, and the ability to apply knowledge of beginning and ending sounds and preliminary short vowel discrimination (Bear et al., 2011, p. 49). However, it is important to point out that these texts are different from decodable texts. Decodable texts are written to provide children with intense opportunities to practice particular alphabetic or orthographic patterns and a specified set of identified high-frequency words. The readability of decodable texts is based entirely on a specified sequence of foundational skills instruction. The features that make both leveled texts and decodable texts accessible to novices are precisely why it is so important to have a strong read-aloud and shared reading curriculum that incorporates complex texts and sophisticated vocabulary for developing comprehension.

Children who are reading at Levels H–J should be held accountable for a retelling after a running record. Details about the thoroughness and elements of the retelling should be used to inform instruction. However, movement to the next level should be dictated by reading accuracy rates. If children between these levels are reading with high levels of accuracy and fluency (above 75 words correct per minute) with minimal comprehension, a targeted comprehension intervention should be applied during guided reading or during classroom differentiation activities using the texts at these levels.

For Levels J and K a miscue analysis of a child's oral reading of a 100- to 450-word passage is still useful. Even though students are beginning to read texts silently, we still want to assess and analyze oral reading. Children now must rely on their knowledge of the alphabetic system and automatic recognition of high-frequency words to successfully read texts at this level. An analysis of the oral reading still tells us how they are orchestrating the juggling act between word identification and meaning making. Fluency rates and prosodic indicators, like phrasing and expression, should both be noted as comprehension pressure points. Content may be unfamiliar, text can't be directly derived from looking at the pictures, and the compositional structure of the book is complex. Now, the length and complexity of these texts make it possible to gather more complete information about the child's comprehension processes when the child participates in a retelling and prompted recall following an oral reading of the text with 90–95% accuracy.

Commercial Kits and Informal Reading Inventories

It is essential to have an assessment system that includes a sensitive, reliable metric for measuring variations in the sophistication of retellings and prompted recall ability. In order to ensure reliability and validity of the assessment process, most schools find it necessary to purchase commercial kits or informal reading inventories that have been developed and tested over time with large samples of children. This increases the likelihood that the text passages are reliable benchmarks for particular readability levels. Both the kits and inventories will have teacher-friendly guides or rubrics for scoring what a child retells about each text sample after reading. Usually, the teacher's manual will provide information about how other children around the country scored on each passage. This information is useful for comparing your students with their age peers. For example, you might think that only retelling 30% of the ideas in a text is a poor performance. However, based on extensive field-testing, the retelling means for all of the kindergarten through second-grade passages in the Qualitative Reading Inventory–5 range from 19 to 38% of each story's idea units (Leslie & Caldwell, 2010). These figures are based on students who were actually able to read the passages within their instructional range. Therefore, a child who is retelling 25% of the story's ideas may not be doing poorly. It is important to compare your students with the test guide's data describing how other children performed on particular passages in the commercial kits or commercially produced reading inventory. Before purchasing a kit, you want to be sure that the publisher is providing these data!

Additionally, all inventories and some kits provide specific questions that should be used after reading to measure the reader's prompted recall. Literal, inferential, and vocabulary questions that have been tested with samples of children are included. Being able to identify the kinds of questions that children find challenging is useful for informing instruction. Some children have difficulty generating inferences, while other children may have difficulty finding explicit text evidence to support their answers. Other children may spout off information that sounds very interesting and may even be factual, without really answering the question. Having a standardized set of questions that tap into multiple comprehension processes helps us to know more about our students and how we can meet their instructional needs.

Kits such as the DRA (Beaver, 2006) and F&PBAS1 (Fountas & Pinnell, 2010) have a refined gradient of early text levels that is sensitive to the shifts that take place from kindergarten through early second grade. The readability gradient of these text levels is based on (1) print features, (2) familiar content, (3) text structure and predictability, and (4) language and literary elements. The gradient in most informal reading inventories tends to be less sensitive to the shifts in emergent and novice readers' orchestration of word recognition and comprehension. The passages in informal reading inventories tend to be governed by traditional notions of readability, word difficulty, and sentence length. However, they have a wider range of narrative and informational passages and more clearly defined, standardized ways of measuring comprehension. Additionally, informal reading inventories provide multiple forms allowing for opportunities to sample reading comprehension of narrative and informational texts and oral and silent reading and to determine listening comprehension. Therefore, we like using the reading kits with the fine gradient though mid–second grade and then transitioning to an informal reading inventory.

Becoming intimately familiar with the manual that accompanies the test materials provides a wealth of information for us about the nuances of test development, the test's strengths, possible limitations, and opens the door to a clearer understanding of administrative procedures. It is important to note that almost all of the English reading inventories and kits have been developed for and tested on native English speakers. Therefore, they are not appropriate to use with English learners or dialect speakers unless you can make informed decisions about how you score their oral reading, retellings, and cued retellings in English. To help you with the latter, read the section at the end of this chapter on assessment considerations for English learners and students from diverse cultural and linguistic backgrounds.

Using Lexiles

The Lexile Framework for Reading (*www.lexile.com*) is a developmental scale that is a means of matching native English-speaking readers with texts. Computer technology's influence on text analysis has contributed to the increasing popularity of Lexile usage. The Lexile scale is based on the frequency of usage of the text's words and length of the sentences in the text. The CCSS use Lexiles to describe the text-level expectations and reading recommendations for students. There is no kit or reading inventory for identifying a reader's Lexile reading level or text reading range. Instead, MetaMetrics® analyzes and publishes the Lexile measures for thousands of texts. Additionally, MetaMetrics has formed partnerships with test publishers that now have the capacity to translate scores on existing assessments into Lexile measures (e.g., TerraNova, Gates–MacGinitie). Typically, a reader's Lexile reading range is based on a statistical calculation derived from the success or difficulty that a reader has with texts that have particular Lexiles. The easiest and most accurate way to determine your students' Lexile reading levels is to look at your reading kits and inventory manuals to find out whether the reading levels of the text passages or books have been translated to Lexiles (e.g., AIM-Sweb, DIBELS Next, Qualitative Reading Inventory–5). Second, you could simply use a conversion chart to convert your child's text reading level to arrive at an approximate Lexile readability range. Originally, the Lexile Framework for Reading (Stenner, Burdick, Sanford, & Burdick, 2007) produced Lexiles that ranged from 0 to 370L for first grade and 340L to 500L for second grade. The CCSS recommends that teachers provide instructional support for children in second and third grades to allow for reading and comprehending texts that range from 420L to 820L. It is expected that children in second grade will participate in supported reading of the more difficult stretch texts within that reading band. We recommend that teachers use a qualitative leveling system like Fountas and Pinnell

(1996, 2006) for identifying reading levels and determining flexible guided reading groups through Level K. Beyond Level K, the Lexile Framework for Reading is likely to be more sensitive for determining text complexity for the sophisticated reader because it is a linear readability scale with fine gradations of difficulty that are based on quantitative criteria closely associated with comprehension.

In second grade, teachers need to be mindful of the Lexiles of books that they choose for read-alouds and shared reading (see Table 4.1 on page 66). Both teacher read-alouds and shared reading materials should be theme driven and range from approximately 420L to 820L. The level of instructional support provided should be dictated by your students' needs.

Standardized and Standards-Based Reading Comprehension Tests

When you want to compare a student's reading comprehension performance with those of other students, then a large-scale assessment, such as a standardized test or a standards-based reading comprehension test, is often used. Commercial testing companies typically develop and publish standardized reading comprehension tests, such as the Gates–MacGinitie Reading Test and Iowa Test of Basic Skills, published by Riverside Publishing, or the Stanford Diagnostic Test (SDRT), published by Pearson Assessment. Standardized tests are developed to differentiate students' reading performance, so that individual student performance can be compared with those of other students of the same age or grade. The tests have been pilot- and field-tested with a large sample of native English speakers so that they are considered valid (reflect the construct that they are supposed to measure) and reliable (if students take comparable versions of the test more than once under the same testing conditions, the majority of them will receive the same test score) for this population of students. The tests are considered "high-stakes" tests because they are typically used for accountability purposes to determine whether teachers and schools are actually teaching children to read.

Standardized tests are summative assessments because they are typically given once a year, provide a single score, but do not tell what the individual student can do well or not do well or the type of progress the student has made. So it is difficult to know why a student scored poorly or highly, and the test results cannot be used to improve your instruction.

Standards-based tests are summative assessments, but unlike standardized tests are not norm referenced or designed to produce scores along a normal curve. Rather, they are designed to match standards and are considered criteria-referenced tests. If everyone in the same class or at the same grade level attains the standards or criteria being assessed, then everyone will receive a common score that indicates proficiency. However, similar to standardized tests, they are summative assessments, and currently do not provide you with the type of information you need to improve your instruction or guide students' learning. Although administration of these high-stakes tests usually begins in third grade, teaching to the standards must be a schoolwide effort.

At this time, new large-scale standards-based assessments tied to the CCSS for language arts are being developed by testing consortia of specific states, such as the Smarter Balanced Assessment Consortia and Partnership for Assessment of Readiness for College and Careers (PARCC). Although both consortia plan to use computer technology to administer the assessments and say that they will be able to provide progress information that teachers can use to inform their instruction, it is too soon to evaluate these efforts.

We typically do not recommend that you use standardized or standards-based test scores to inform your reading comprehension instruction or to guide student learning. The RAND Reading Study Group (2002) pointed out that both types of tests do not represent the complexity of reading comprehension because they are not based on an "articulated theory of comprehension" (p. 53) and do not evaluate the various facets of reading comprehension. Sometimes, it is helpful to know how students' reading comprehension performance compares with those of other students (see the discussion of English learners below), but we do not think that the information you currently receive for students younger than second grade from either type of assessment is particularly valid or reliable. Both types of tests are group administered, timed, and usually include a set of relatively short reading passages with multiple-choice items. Sometimes, there are a few constructed responses or short fill-in items.

The formats and administration of the two types of tests typically present an unusual and anxious assessment context for most young children, as illustrated by Miriam Cohen's (2006) fictionalized picture book on how first graders take a standardized test. In one of the examples in the book, the children are asked to complete the following: "Rabbits eat ( ) lettuce, ( ) dog food, ( ) sandwiches." One of the story characters, George, knows a lot about rabbits, but he doesn't know which item to select for his answer because none of the answer choices match his knowledge of rabbits. For example, he knows that if rabbits don't eat carrots, their teeth will grow too long and hurt them, but "carrots" is not one of the answer choices. However, he has not learned how to choose the "best" answer, a testwise characteristic of high performers on standardized and standards-based texts.

A complete discussion of standardized and standards-based reading comprehension tests is beyond the scope of this book. To learn more about standardized and standards-based reading comprehension tests, we recommend that you read specific books on this topic, such as McKenna and Stahl (2009); Paratore and McCormack (2007); Sabatini, Albro, and O'Reilly (2012); and Sweet and Snow (2003).

Assessment Considerations for English Learners and Students from Diverse Cultural and Linguistic Backgrounds

A number of professional associations have warned educators and researchers about the bias problems involved in using English assessments developed for and normed on native English speakers with English learners and dialect speakers (American Educational Research Association, American Psychological Association, & National Council on Measurement in Education, 1999):

> [When a test is] administered in the same language to all examinees in a linguistically diverse population, the test user should investigate the validity of the score interpretations for test takers believed to have limited proficiency in the language of the test because the achievement, abilities, and traits of examinees who do not speak the language of the test as their primary language may be seriously mismeasured by the test. (p. 118)

As pointed out earlier in this book, due to their developing oral English proficiency, English learners often demonstrated increased comprehension of an English text when they were encouraged to discuss or write about the English text or answer questions about it by using their L1, code mixing, and/or code switching (García, 1991, 2003). Similarly, we need to make sure not to discriminate against dialect speakers when they use their dialect to discuss, write about, or answer questions about texts written in school English. These issues apply to many of the assessments that we reviewed in this chapter: retellings, prompted recall, video recall, emergent storybook reading scale, standardized tests, and standards-based tests.

When using oral miscue analysis and running records, it is important to take into account the varied English pronunciation patterns of English learners and dialect speakers. You cannot really know whether a student's accented pronunciation or varied decoding of an English word reflects a problem unless you know their L1 or dialect and conduct a retelling to see if the student understands what he or she orally read. Sometimes, English learners and dialect speakers will skip syntactic features in English that are not characteristic of their L1 or dialect (such as "she" and "he" for speakers of Chinese and possession ['s] for AAVE speakers; García, 2003). To know whether they actually understood what they read, you need to ask them related comprehension questions. Because many English learners and dialect speakers often are interrupted when they orally read in English, it is also important to evaluate their reading comprehension by having them read silently and provide a retelling and/or answer comprehension questions (García, 2003).

When English assessments developed for native English speakers in the United States are used with English learners, dialect speakers, and other students from diverse cultural backgrounds, it is often difficult to know what actually is being measured: their reading, writing, language, and vocabulary development or their English proficiency and U.S. cultural assimilation. Miramontes (1987) reported that 50% of the Spanish-speaking students who participated in an oral miscue analysis of their English reading might have been misclassified as learning disabled due to their limited oral English proficiency.

Even English and Spanish versions of the Peabody Picture Vocabulary Test (PPVT) have been critiqued because their administration may discriminate against English- and Spanish-speaking students who are from different English- and Spanish-speaking populations. In a review of assessment issues for language-minority students, García, McKoon, and August (2006) reported that the administration procedures for the English and Spanish versions of the PPVT might discriminate against students from culturally diverse backgrounds because the test stops "after a student has missed a certain number of words in a row [which] may constitute a bias when the order of the words is not based on a word frequency measure from the student's first language or cultural group" (p. 606).

To prevent some of the bias issues noted above and the overclassification of English learners in special education, Public Law 94-142, the Education for All Handicapped Children Act, requires that English learners' academic performance be assessed in their home language and compared with their performance in English before they can receive special education services. If English learners can perform at grade level in their L1, then a low performance in English is probably due to their developing English proficiency and not to any cognitive or linguistic difficulty.

Still, it is sometimes difficult to know why English learners do not perform well on assessment measures in their L1 *and* English. For example, one of us (Georgia) was consulted about the slow and laborious decoding performance of a bilingual third grader in both English and Spanish. The reading specialist and bilingual speech and language specialist thought that the child might have a learning disability. In this case, administering a standardized reading comprehension test in Spanish, the L1, was helpful because it indicated that the child could comprehend Spanish text at grade level, much higher than his oral reading had indicated.

The best way to offset bias problems is to use multiple assessment methods in both the L1 and English, and to consult with cultural and linguistic insiders who are knowledgeable about the students' cultural and linguistic backgrounds and reading comprehension assessment issues related to students from diverse populations. For more information on biases in the reading comprehension assessment of English learners and students from diverse cultural and linguistic backgrounds, we recommend that you read Herrera, Murry, and Cabral (2007); García and Bauer (2009); García, Bray, et al. (2008); García and DeNicolo (2009); and García and Pearson (1994).

Conclusion

Although there is no single test that we can use to learn about our students' reading comprehension, there is a collection of tools that we can apply to inform instruction and support the meaning-making process. Building clear bridges among listening comprehension, transitional or novice reading comprehension, and the comprehension of the sophisticated reader will ensure that the primary purpose of all reading is to make sense of text. Documenting these processes in the early years enables us to provide the instruction that strengthens children's ability to understand text and express that understanding effectively through their own spoken and written language. The assessments in this chapter can serve as formative assessments, separate classroom-based assessments, and as a preliminary screener to identify children who may need additional support in the areas of listening and reading comprehension.

FORM 8.1

Retelling Record (Narrative)

Reading _____ **Listening** _____ **Video** _____

Spontaneous, Unprompted (U), or Prompted (P)	Does the Child Include . . .	Yes/No
	Setting and its role	
	Characters	
	A goal or initiating event	
	A problem faced by a character; episodes involving the character and efforts to solve the problem	
	A solution to the problem	
	A clear ending	

Retelling Record (Informational)

Reading _____ Listening _____ Video _____

Spontaneous, Unprompted (U), or Prompted (P)	Does the Child Include . . .	Yes/No
	Key ideas	
	Supporting subordinate ideas	
	Application of text structure to organize retelling	
	Importations and inferences	
	Erroneous information	
	Inclusion of conceptual vocabulary	

Modified Emergent Storybook Reading Scale

Stage	Characteristics	Notes
Picture Governed		
Labeling and commenting	1. Each page is treated as a separate unit. 2. Child either names or describes person/animal on each page or comments on it.	
Following the action	1. Each page is treated as a separate unit. 2. Child describes the action on each page.	
Storytelling in dialogue format	1. Child begins to make links between pages. 2. Overall, the listener can perceive a story, although it is disjointed. 3. Storytelling is in dialogue form, propelled by prompts from adult.	
Storytelling in monologue format	1. Child bridges plot between pages. 2. Tends to take the form of a monologue.	
Reading and storytelling mixed	Speech varies from storytelling to written register.	
Reading similar to original story and reading verbatim-like	1. Intonation sounds like reading. 2. Reading matches story events. 3. Attempt to recreate verbatim reading from pictures and memory.	

(continued)

After Sulzby (1985). From McKenna and Stahl (2009, p. 96). Copyright 2009 by The Guilford Press. Adapted by permission.

Stage	Characteristics	Notes
Print Governed		
Print awareness	1. New awareness that we read printed words. 2. Child may refuse to read based on lack of print knowledge.	
Aspectual reading	1. Child attends one or two aspects of printed words. 2. Beginning efforts to balance letter sounds and meaning. *Shift to leveled-text reading assessment.*	
Reading with strategies imbalanced	1. Developing balance in use of word recognition, syntax, and meaning. 2. May recognize errors, but unsure how to fix.	
Reading independently	1. Effective balance of word recognition, syntax, and meaning to arrive at accurate reading of print. 2. Self-corrections provide cues to processing.	

CHAPTER 9

Beyond the Classroom

INTERVENING TO PROVIDE ADDITIONAL COMPREHENSION SUPPORT

GUIDING QUESTIONS
• •

- How do we determine whether a young child needs an early comprehension intervention?
- Who should provide the interventions?
- What types of interventions are developmentally appropriate and effective with young children?
- How do we determine if the intervention is effective?

SETTING THE STAGE

One of us (Kay) is conducting a read-aloud with her second graders during her November unit on Native Americans. She is reading Paul Goble's stunningly beautiful 1978 Caldecott Award–winning book *The Girl Who Loved Wild Horses*. It is the story of a girl who leaves her family to live with a herd of wild horses. Kay reads the page, midstory, that describes time passing and the girl's physical and emotional withdrawal symptoms that arise when members of her tribe remove her from the horses and return her to live with her family. Then Kay asks the children the initiating question, "What is happening at this point of our story?" Her student Jessica responds: "They are going to eat that big tomato." Jessica is apparently referencing the illustration that depicts a reddish sun setting over the canyon.

The memory of this episode has stayed with Kay because, despite being an experienced teacher, she felt lost and powerless in figuring out where to begin to help Jessica. What can a teacher do to help a student whose comprehension is consistently so far off the mark?

Figuring Out How to Help: Using Assessment to Dig More Deeply

It makes sense to identify and remediate comprehension problems that show up in young children before they become confounded with decoding issues. In fact, there is evidence that inferential comprehension emerges from the time that children are as young as 2 years old. Young children make inferences, or fill in unspecified information, when they listen to adults talk, watch a video, or hear a text read aloud. Therefore, by the time children are 4 years old, a sensitive observer is likely to be able to identify children who may not be generating developmentally appropriate inferences during storybook reading, while listening to others or while watching a video. If we wait until third grade to identify comprehension problems, it can be complicated to determine the root of the child's difficulty and even harder to successfully intervene.

Among older students, it might be that the child has word recognition and fluency problems that are preventing him or her from being able to read a grade-level text with understanding. In third grade, a great deal of text reading is in service to the acquisition of new disciplinary knowledge. Therefore, prior knowledge, vocabulary, and text structure obstacles may hinder comprehension processes even if word recognition is automatic. As a result, it is important for teachers of young children to provide opportunities for them to demonstrate high levels of comprehension after viewing videos or hearing texts read aloud and to document these abilities. Using the assessments that are described in Chapter 8 is a good starting place. These might be considered screening assessments that enable you to determine if students are on track and to identify the instruction that is called for in order to meet the needs of the students in your classroom. Unlike decoding and high-frequency word recognition, comprehension is not an all-or-nothing skill. Children's comprehension is observable along a continuum that ranges from inadequate to fully adequate, or expansive. Therefore, there is neither a single test nor a "cutoff" score that can be used to determine whether a child needs a comprehension intervention. Data from the assessments described in Chapter 8 should be collected and used diagnostically before moving to the assessments and interventions described in this chapter.

For students like Jessica something more is needed, both diagnostically and instructionally. The assessments described in this chapter are resource intensive. They call for knowledgeable teachers, multistep individualized administration, and time. Therefore, they need to be reserved for a small percentage of children whom you suspect need a more intense and targeted intervention. In a response-to-intervention (RTI) model, these assessments and interventions are reserved for supplementary support beyond the Tier 1 instruction, which is supposed to be differentiated for all children. Ideally, the specialized assessments and interventions in this chapter might be employed by the Tier 2 or 3 interventionist, the speech–language specialist, the Title I ESL or bilingual teacher, or a special educator. However, we have also provided ideas for how classroom teachers might incorporate some of these interventions within their classrooms if resources are limited. From our perspective, the teacher's label doesn't matter as much as ensuring that an expert provides the child with the support needed to meet his or her identified learning needs. In the words of a well-known sports motto, "Just do it." Everything in this chapter may be considered appropriate for children who range from PreK through second grade, depending on the children's performance on a range of reading and listening comprehension tasks.

Narrative Comprehension of a Wordless Picture Book Task

For children with comprehension difficulties, an investigation of their narrative abilities is a good starting point. Extensive research has been conducted in this area. Narratives are important communication devices that are demonstrated in children as young as 2–3 years old. Whether a narrative is used to express a need or to recount daily events, the basic narrative structure of characters within settings engaged in goal-driven activities permeates all kinds of stories in Western cultures. Narratives are the means by which the youngest children make sense of the world. As a result, narrative abilities have a tremendous influence on reading comprehension, and it is one of the major areas that needs a systematic and thorough examination. The Narrative Comprehension of a Wordless Picture Book Task (NCWPBT; Paris & Paris, 2003) is a useful assessment for collecting quantitative diagnostic evidence about a child's sense of narrative story structure, as well as explicit and inferential comprehension without the interference of decoding. Importantly, the task has been demonstrated to have concurrent and predictive validity with more traditional standardized reading comprehension measures.

Administering the NCWPBT

The NCWPBT uses a wordless picture book to evaluate how a child approaches a story that is told in pictures, not words. Paris and Paris (2003) used *Robot-Bot-Bot* (Krahn, 1979), but any wordless picture book of moderate length with a clear story line, explicit sequence of events, and key story elements can be used. The assessment consists of three subtests: a picture walk, story retelling, and cued recall or prompted comprehension. As with most comprehension assessments, it is a good idea to audio-record what the child says to ensure scoring accuracy.

If the NCWPBT is being used with English learners, dialect speakers, or with children from cultural backgrounds different from native English speakers in the United States, then you need to make sure that the person who is assessing the children understands how stories are told in the children's particular L1, dialect, and home culture, and adapt the scoring forms accordingly (see Chapter 2). It is also important to evaluate the storytelling of English learners in the language the children know best, usually the L1. If a child can tell a story appropriately in the L1 but not in English, then the child does not have difficulty with narratives or comprehension. Once the child has developed sufficient English proficiency, he or she will be able to transfer what he or she knows about narratives in the L1 to English. With ESL support, the child will also be able to learn the narrative structure characteristic of English speech and texts.

PICTURE WALK

First, give the child the book and invite him or her to look through it. Next, encourage the child to go through the book page by page saying what he or she is thinking while looking at the pictures. Use Form 9.1 (at the end of the chapter) to score the picture walk. You will note that the first four categories of scoring bear similarity to the Modified Emergent Storybook Reading Scale (see Form 8.3 at the end of Chapter 8). It is important to remember that during the picture walk the child needs to generate a story, whereas during the Storybook Reading Scale task the child is using pictures to prompt a retelling of a familiar story that has been previously read. Book-handling skills, level of engagement, fullness of description, use of storybook or conversational register, and whether the child describes an illustration in isolation or as an episode within a connected story are common to both assessments. However, in scoring the picture walk we also look for evidence of comprehension strategy application such as prediction, self-monitoring, and question generation. In the next two tasks, we gather additional specific evidence of narrative comprehension and awareness of story elements.

STORY RETELLING

Immediately following the picture walk, remove the book from the child and ask him or her to retell as much of the story as possible. When the child finishes, ask if he or she remembers anything else. The child scores a point for including each of the main story elements: setting, characters, character's goal or initiating event, problem or plot episodes, problem solution, and clear ending. Use Form 9.2 (at the end of the chapter) to score the retelling.

PROMPTED RECALL.

The cued recall task of NCWPBT is designed to assess the child's comprehension of the story as a coherent, connected whole. This task is consistent with the theory presented in Chapter 8. There are specific explicit and implicit understandings that are essential to narrative comprehension: story elements, themes, causal relations, role of setting, and characters' feelings and motivations. Children may not spontaneously express their awareness of all of these elements during a retelling. If we hope to be able to design an intervention that is targeted to a student's needs, we need to have a clear sense of the student's level of awareness and how we can use that knowledge to build a bridge to what is beyond the child's current level of awareness. We can follow the Paris and Paris (2003) protocol by asking questions about the text during a teacher-led second pass through the picture book. You may give a child credit for the item without asking the question if they included detailed information in their retelling. Form 9.2 is a means of documenting what story elements and inferences the child generated spontaneously during a retelling or in response to your prompts.

During the second pass, you will guide the child through the book, stopping to ask explicit questions that relate to story elements, including the identification of characters, setting, initiating event, problem, important episodes, and resolution. You might ask for elaborations on problem identification or resolution by adding, "What makes you think that?" or "How do you know that?"

Throughout this second guided walk through the book, you will also ask implicit questions that call for children to generate inferences. These questions prompt children to elaborate on themes, characters' feelings, dialogues, causal relationships between episodes, and predictions with justifications. These questions should be followed by "why" probes to distinguish between levels of shallow and deep thinking. The questions on Form 9.2 are examples for each category, but we recommend that you generate a script with specific questions for the wordless picture books that you are using.

ANALYZING THE RESULTS

The NCWPBT is not a criterion test. There is not a particular cutoff score that will clearly identify whether a child needs additional comprehension support or not. Rather, it is an assessment that is designed to gauge narrative comprehension in a way that minimizes the impact of decoding, vocabulary, listening, and memory—factors that typically muddle the interpretation of early reading assessment measures. It can provide you with insights into the specific aspects of narrative comprehension that are either in place or not in place for a young child. Those aspects can then be the target of explicit instruction during an intervention period of 6–8 weeks. After a period of intervention, the NCWPBT protocol can be used again with a different wordless picture book to determine whether or not quantitative progress has been made based on the total score of the pretest and posttest.

If you wish to implement this approach, it is a good idea to identify two or three wordless picture books that are similar in length and plot complexity. Create a set of scripts to establish standardized test administration and scoring analysis procedures for each book. That way you will be able to gauge student progress across a marking period or school year. Because children who are not native English speakers or who are from diverse cultural backgrounds may respond to wordless picture books according to their own cultural knowledge and experiences, it is important to choose wordless picture books appropriate for this particular population.

Vocabulary Tests

The Peabody Picture Vocabulary Test, Fourth Edition (PPVT-4; Dunn & Dunn, 2007) is a norm-referenced, individually administered test that focuses solely on receptive vocabulary. It is co-normed with the Expressive Vocabulary Test, Second Edition (EVT-2; Williams, 2007), a norm-referenced, individually administered test that focuses on expressive vocabulary. Both tests can be administered to children as young as 2½ years old. However, the tests have been normed on native English-speaking children, so they are not appropriate for English learners or children from other cultural and linguistic backgrounds.

In administering the PPVT-4, the examiner says a word and the child selects one of four pictures that best portrays the word. In the EVT-2, the examiner asks a question about a picture and the examinee must respond with a label, synonym, or phrase to describe the picture. No reading is required on either test. In addition to the age and grade-level norms, growth-scale value scores are now available. These increase the instruments' sensitivity to detecting smaller changes over time. Using both tests allows the examiner to compare an individual's abilities in both receptive and expressive vocabulary in formats that are not confounded by reading and writing abilities. These tests require 15–20 minutes for each administration. They also require knowledge of baselines and ceilings. As a result, classroom teachers and general education interventionists do not usually administer them. They are more frequently given as part of a battery of tests used to determine special education eligibility. However, a reading specialist or a speech–language therapist would also be qualified to administer the test.

These tests are norm referenced. As a result, they enable a quick and clean comparison of how a particular child's receptive and expressive vocabularies compare with other students of the same age, grade cohort, and cultural and linguistic background. These tests are not appropriate for English learners.

The items on these tests are selected from a large corpus of words in the English language. As a result, even with explicit attention to vocabulary in an intervention setting, it is hard to get a child's score on these tests to shift very much over a brief interval. However, that does not diminish their value. *We would never deliberately teach the vocabulary assessed on these tests. That would invalidate them.*

The PPVT-4 and the EVT-2 can be used in a general way to diagnose whether a child's receptive and expressive vocabulary are about equal or if one is stronger than the other. They can also be used to give you a clear picture of the role that a child's vocabulary knowledge may be playing within the more general comprehension profile. If receptive vocabulary is within a range that is typical for other children in his or her age cohort, then other factors may be greater contributors to the child's comprehension challenges. However, if vocabulary is weak, then you will want to be deliberate in providing elaborated vocabulary instruction by using the techniques described later in this chapter and those described in Chapter 3 (e.g., for native English speakers, you can use Text Talk by Beck & McKeown, 2001). For all students, including English learners, you want to be sure to situate reading activities within theme-embedded instruction that supports repeated exposures to vocabulary and ongoing development of target vocabulary. You will want to develop your own assessments of the target vocabulary that you select for instruction. Chapter 4 provides a few examples.

The Preschool Language Assessment Instrument, Second Edition (PLAI-2; Blank, Rose, & Berlin, 2003) is a useful tool for determining the language processing abilities of native English-speaking children between the ages of 3 years and 5 years, 11 months. It includes both receptive and expressive items. Its format enables the evaluation of two levels of children's literal language abilities and two increasingly sophisticated levels of inferential language abilities. For example, the examiner would ask the child to respond to pictures in a test booklet by answering the questions "What is this?" or "What is happening in this picture?" The inferential questions are considered more difficult because they call for the children to provide information about decontextualized objects or events; for example, "What will happen if . . . ?" and "How do you know?" Some schools may give this test as an entrance-level screener, or your speech–language specialist may be familiar with it and be able to administer it for you to ensure appropriate administration procedures. Several of the researchers who worked on storybook reading interventions used this as a pretest and posttest to assess student progress.

We do not recommend using the PPVT-4, the EVT-2, or the PLAI-2 more than twice a year. The administration and scoring require assessment expertise and strict adherence to the manuals! They should be used as sophisticated assessment tools for a very small number of students.

We also advise you not to use these standardized tests with English learners. If you suspect that a young English learner has a language delay, then it is essential to evaluate the child in his or her L1. If the PLAI is used with dialect speakers of English or children from diverse cultural backgrounds, then you need to make sure that the evaluator knows the cultures of the children, their familiarity with the pictures, and how they would answer the inferential questions so that the scoring of their answers is culturally appropriate.

Who, When, and Where?

The school day is very full. Finding time in the day to provide additional instruction that supplements, but does not replace, the general curriculum is always a challenge. Often preschool and kindergarten classrooms have fewer instructional hours than other primary grades, cut short by nap times or half-day schedules. In the primary grades, intervention programs abound for high-priority foundational skills, leaving few resources for one more area of intervention. You might be asking yourself, "How in the world could we ever fit this into our day? I don't know if anyone in our school has the time, expertise, or materials to provide this level of support for something that has never been a priority at this stage of student development. I just can't see my school principal buying into this."

You are right. This is a novel concept. However, if we want children in third grade to read complex texts with high levels of comprehension and to express that comprehension eloquently in speech and writing, it is going to take years to get there. More than 80% of children who have been identified with language-related disorders now spend most of their time in general education settings. English learners also need differentiation and additional scaffolding in the L1, ESL, and/or all-English classroom settings to make the most of language-dependent tasks. Therefore, early education classroom teachers must find ways to incorporate language-specific instruction within the general education setting.

There is increasing evidence that young children with language difficulties are often the same children who display reading comprehension difficulties in the intermediate grades (Catts, Fey, Tomblin, & Zhang, 2002; Justice, Mashburn, & Petscher, 2013). Additionally, comprehension of narrative storybooks and videos in preschool correlates with general reading comprehension at age 8 (Kendeou, Bohn-Gettler, White, & van den Broek, 2008). Reading comprehension dominates the CCSS, even in the kindergarten standards. Understanding stories and other texts is a lifelong pursuit, while learning to decode occurs within a very narrow slice of the learning trajectory. Comprehension is always the purpose of reading. As a result, it should always be at the forefront of instruction.

Who?

Paired Teacher Classrooms

In many of the classrooms we visit, there are two teachers present. Often one of the two teachers has special education certification, but not always. Whenever there are two teachers in a classroom, it opens the door to differentiation and meeting individual needs. One of the two teachers could assume responsibility for a comprehension intervention for one to three children who are demonstrating a need for additional comprehension or language support. Some of the interventions described later in this chapter only require 15 minutes a few times a week and would fit neatly into this instructional model.

Speech–Language Specialist

The speech–language specialist is likely to have the most training in assessing and intervening early to address comprehension challenges. Make friends with this jewel! He or she can help in any number of ways. First, this specialist is a source of knowledge and materials for those of you who are likely to end up providing interventions by yourselves. Second, some of the children who are having comprehension problems may already be receiving special education speech services for language issues. How can the two of you work together to support the students that you both teach in ways that benefit everyone, especially the children you share? Is inclusion a possibility?

When one of us (Kay) was teaching first grade, she and the speech teacher decided to collaborate to bolster the support for children with comprehension and language processing problems. Kay asked that all children in the grade-level cohort with language-based speech problems be assigned to her class. That resulted in the speech teacher coming to her classroom for three 30-minute blocks each week. The speech teacher arranged to come on Monday, Wednesday, and Friday during guided reading/center time. On Monday, the speech teacher worked with her identified children and from one to three additional children to provide intense language–vocabulary development for the shared reading of the stretch text being taught that week. On Wednesday, she conducted a small comprehension-driven conversation group for the same small group of children to reinforce the comprehension of the shared reading story. On Friday, she typically worked only with the children who had speech individualized education plans (IEPs) to work with them on specific IEP goals that might or might not be related to the classroom activities. The classroom curriculum supported the speech teacher's goals, and her expertise related to language development techniques and intervention created a cohesive learning setting for children with and without IEPs.

If inclusion is not a possibility, consult with the speech–language specialist for resources to meet the needs of children who are struggling with comprehension. He or she may be able to provide you with diagnostic suggestions, instructional techniques, instructional support materials, and helpful journal articles. If your children are already working with the speech–language therapist, show your interest in working collaboratively and intentionally to build bridges between the classroom curriculum and the resource room.

School Reading Specialist

Unfortunately, school reading specialists are becoming less common in many school settings. Schools may receive additional financial resources for hiring special education teachers, but typically schools must use general funds to pay for specialized reading support. As a result, if schools have the luxury of a knowledgeable reading teacher, he or she is often spread very thin. This individual is needed to teach students with the most severe reading difficulties, often in the intermediate grades where the high-stakes tests are administered. In the primary grades, building easily measured foundational skills or increasing students' text levels often becomes the instructional priority for the reading interventionist. Additionally, if your school relies heavily on packaged intervention programs, you are unlikely to find one that targets comprehension in the primary grades.

You may want to advocate for the establishment of a single comprehension group for one to three of the neediest children in your grade-level cohort. Often administrators and teachers need to see the evidence that something works before becoming receptive to a change. Conducting an action research project to demonstrate the impact of a primary grade–level comprehension intervention on achievement results later in grade 3 is a good way to make a convincing case for using the highly valued reading teacher to improve comprehension in the early grades.

Volunteers and Parents

Training classroom volunteers and parents to conduct dialogic read-alouds using specific protocols is a powerful way to increase the intensity and frequency of effective read-aloud interactions and, over time, to improve comprehension. Evidence indicates that read-alouds have the most impact on language development and comprehension when they are conducted in one-on-one settings. However, most teachers are unable to use their time in this way. Therefore, by training classroom volunteers and parents to conduct dialogic reading you are increasing (1) the effectiveness of read-aloud procedures used by parents and volunteers, (2) the number of read-alouds that children will be likely to hear, and (3) the one-on-one opportunities for responding to a read-aloud. This intensity and accountability for response are imperative for children who may be having difficulties comprehending a storybook and using language to reflect what they are comprehending.

Simply asking parents to come for a read-aloud training may not be the most welcoming invitation. Finding a time that is convenient to parents is important. As a classroom teacher, Kay found that combining the training session with a brief classroom performance of some kind by the children, so that child care is not an obstacle to attendance, worked well. After you demonstrate the dialogic reading techniques discussed in Chapter 3 and perhaps the questioning prompts that you are using in the classroom, it is a good idea to present the parents with a DVD of the procedure and a cheat sheet in their language. When talking to parents of English learners, reinforce the value of reading and discussing books in the L1. Today, videotaping is extremely easy and most families have some means of playing DVDs. It is nice to introduce these techniques to *all* parents and then reiterate their importance to the parents of children who may be experiencing difficulties.

Bilingual (L1) and ESL Teachers

We often see English learners in the primary grades who are doing well learning the foundational skills in English, but whose teachers express concern about their overall English reading. In fact, the National Literacy Panel on Language-Minority Children and Youth (August & Shanahan, 2006) reported that English learners decode in English as well as native English speakers but have more problems with English text comprehension.

If you are working with English learners who also attend L1 and/or ESL classes, then it is important to collaborate with those teachers to create a cohesive, supportive language comprehension curriculum that transfers across settings. Providing students with new information, vocabulary, or literacy experiences or assignments in the L1, followed by ESL support so that they understand what is being taught in English before presenting them with comparable information, vocabulary, or literacy experiences or assignments in the all-English classroom usually works best. If English learners do not receive L1 instruction, then doing the above with the ESL teacher is also very helpful. Communicating regularly with the L1 and/or ESL teacher to ensure that themed disciplinary instruction is consistent across settings and that book discussions are happening in ways that make meaning connections clear to the students should be a priority.

A number of picture books are now available in multiple languages. It is helpful when an L1 speaker reads and discusses the L1 version of a book to English learners before you or the ESL teacher later reads and discusses the English version, especially when you remind the children that they have heard the story read before in their L1. Even when you don't have the same exact versions in the two languages, it is helpful to read books on similar topics to English learners, with the L1 version being read and discussed prior to the English version because the L1 book reading and discussion helps to build the students' prior knowledge and conceptual knowledge, which they can use to help them understand the English version.

Also, be sure to call on the L1 and ESL teacher for resource tips on how to make your read-aloud experiences and disciplinary instruction comprehensible for English learners. As with the speech–language specialist, the bilingual and ESL teacher may have materials, instructional tips, and other professional resources that should help to enhance the comprehension of the English learners in your classroom. Additionally, work with the bilingual and/or ESL teacher in the creation of training sessions and materials for parents of English learners.

When and Where?

Determining when and where additional comprehension instruction occurs depends on the resources available in your school. Much like the general practitioner in a medical model, the classroom teacher is the best person to serve as the gatekeeper and overseer of the support services that his or her students are receiving. You might decide to assign an America Reads volunteer to do a one-to-one dialogic storybook read-aloud with an English learner twice a week in addition to the bilingual or ESL pullout services that the student is receiving. If you teach in a second-grade classroom, your grade-level team might decide to have one small homogeneous comprehension group taught by the reading interventionist. You might decide that the interventionist will support the children in having small-group discussions about text and creating written responses to text since the children need a high degree of support to consolidate meaning, verbalize their understandings, and reflect their comprehension in written formats. The writing will be done in response to texts that were read as part of themed disciplinary units in the classroom.

The way that you structure support will depend on the resources available at your school and whether you are implementing the ideas in this chapter as a member of a school team or independently. However, even if you are reading this book independently, there are some ideas in this chapter that you can use to support your students who need something extra to strengthen their comprehension.

Interventions

The recommendations that we are making come from the research being conducted in multiple fields: cognitive psychology, special education, speech and language, and bilingual and ESL education. However, despite the differences in background, there are some common findings that should serve as the foundation for planning an early intervention for comprehension:

- One-to-one intervention is best and group size should not exceed three children (Linan-Thompson, Vaughn, Hickman-Davis, & Kouzekanani, 2003; Wanzek & Vaughn, 2010; Whitehurst et al., 1994).
- Interventions with younger children (K–1) tend to yield larger effects than interventions in grades 2–3 (Wanzek & Vaughn, 2010).
- Incorporate retelling and prompted recall (teacher questioning) to ensure

the most accurate approximation of student comprehension (Goldman et al., 1999; Morrow, 1984, 1985; Paris & Paris, 2003; Swanson et al., 2011).

- Include multiple readings of the same text (Desmarais, Nadeau, Trudeau, Filiatrault-Veilleux, & Maxes-Fournier, 2013; Swanson et al., 2011).
- Attend to the needs of English learners sooner rather than later (Linan-Thompson et al., 2003), but in collaboration with the bilingual and/or ESL teacher.

The interventions we discuss in the rest of this chapter can be used with all children, including English learners, as long as you adapt them according to the children's diverse linguistic and cultural backgrounds (see the recommendations provided throughout this chapter and in Chapter 2). For example, if you are working with an English learner, providing the intervention in the child's L1 is the best approach. If that isn't possible, then using sheltered ESL techniques to provide the intervention in English is the next approach. The child's limited English proficiency may limit his or her oral and written responses to questions asked in English. If you think the latter is likely to occur, we recommend that you invite an informed or trained L1 speaker to be present during the intervention, so that he or she can help the child understand the questions you are asking and translate the child's L1 answers for you. We say informed or trained because it is important for you to spend some time making sure that the L1 speaker knows what you want him or her to do.

Dialogic Reading Intensive with Inference Training (Narratives)

Even in preschool, teacher storybook read-alouds are often conducted in a whole-class format. For the child who appears to be developing a little more slowly than the others, seems to be having difficulty spontaneously responding to the storybook read-aloud, or is language reticent, shifting to a one-to-one or small-group setting is called for. There is evidence that employing a small-group dialogic reading intervention will increase performance in comprehension, general language abilities, vocabulary, and phonological awareness for young children with specific language impairment and children who are showing signs of literacy difficulties (Desmarais et al., 2013; Swanson et al., 2011; van Kleeck, Vander Woude, & Hammett, 2006; Whitehurst et al., 1994; Zevenbergen & Whitehurst, 2003).

Time and Frequency

This intervention procedure should take approximately 15 minutes and be conducted between 2 and 4 days a week. It might be half of a 30-minute intervention block that includes attention to other early literacy needs or be offered in isolation.

It could be combined with the integrated theme intervention that we describe later in this chapter or with student reading interventions in late first grade and early second grade. The teacher should reread each storybook between two and eight times. Student engagement, enjoyment, and comprehension should serve as the guide for determining how many times the book should be reread.

Procedures

For the youngest children or for children who need more experience responding to the literal information in texts, you may wish to begin by using the PEER (prompt, evaluate, expand, and repeat) protocol for dialogic reading described in Chapter 3. These procedures work best for easy picture books that may not contain a majority of story grammar elements or a complete causal sequence of events. Use questioning and elaboration prompts to get the children to talk about what is being portrayed in the book. Use the children's engagement as a guide to incorporate more extended responses using the CROWD (completion, recall, open-ended prompts, Wh- questions, and distancing prompts) interaction techniques.

For children who can use language to form literal responses to simple picture books, dialogic reading should incorporate storybooks with a comprehensive narrative story structure. As in NCWPBT (Paris & Paris, 2003), the teacher should stop intermittently to ask the child literal and inferential questions that address the story grammar elements that make important contributions to the causal sequence of the story (see Form 9.2 at the end of the chapter).

These interactive reading procedures can be viewed as the developmental precursor to strategy instruction. Instead of explicitly teaching these young children strategies, the embedded prompts during reading engage the children in an apprenticeship model of strategic reading.

Even if you are an experienced teacher, it is a good idea to script the questions that will target the thinking that you want to foster. Craft questions purposefully in order to ask children to identify the important explicitly stated story grammar elements and to prompt the generation of inferences that enable the children to link the causal chain of events. Comprehension requires not only remembering what the text says but also the ability to think beyond the words to generate inferences. Making inferences that identify characters' goals, internal intentions, feelings, and states of mind and tracing actions that enable the accomplishment of goals are among the most important thinking abilities that we want to foster during the teacher read-aloud (Kendeou et al., 2008). These inferences might not be generated spontaneously by young children, but using dialogic reading to model and prompt them can move children closer to the bull's-eye of high-level thinking in response to texts. If we consider a dartboard, we want to use instructional prompting to move children's thinking from their unassisted responses in the outer rings closer to the comprehension bull's-eye. There is evidence to indicate that the ability to generate inferences distinguishes high from low performers on comprehension tests (Bowyer-Crane & Snowling, 2005; Cain & Oakhill, 1999). When children have difficulty answering questions, you should provide prompts that move from least supportive to most supportive and that include questioning, expanding what children say, providing cloze tasks with sentence frames ("Jim drives a _____.") , and modeling answers or thinking aloud.

Making It Happen

Dialogic read-alouds can be conducted with individual students or small groups in short 15-minute sessions. Yet, dialogic reading interventions have the potential to yield powerful and long-lasting effects. Creating a set of books with scripted sets of questions that can be embedded in naturalistic ways during read-alouds is a worthwhile goal for a grade-level team or a professional development series. For example, each teacher in a team of four kindergarten teachers might agree to write a script of questions for just three books. That would give the team 12 books that could be used in a small-group intervention four to six times each. If the dialogic reading is conducted within an intervention setting twice a week, the kindergarten team would have enough lesson scripts for 24–36 weeks.

Using Multimedia

The ability to comprehend a narrative and to generate inferences transfers across media. In Chapter 4, we discuss a variety of ways to incorporate video in the classroom to increase comprehension and vocabulary development. These techniques can be modified in intervention settings. Using short, but fully developed stories in video formats is an excellent way to bootstrap comprehension instruction and to provide variety in an instructional routine while keeping goals consistent. Presenting information in both verbal and visual channels enhances cognitive processing and engagement. This allows for attention to be sustained for high-level questioning and discussion after the viewing. Multimedia is especially useful for English learners when written captions are presented or when text accompanies the oral narration and video. The same embedded questioning procedures that were described in the previous section can be applied during video viewing. The text box on the next page provides an example of how one might implement effective questioning to develop comprehension while using a video.

Additionally, there is evidence that computer-assisted interventions (read-alouds conducted through a computer) have the potential to yield high effects on reading comprehension and vocabulary growth (Swanson et al., 2011). Computer-assisted read-alouds generally include interactive features that allow children to actively engage in the story line or in character manipulation. While we don't recommend using this resource as a primary component of an intervention, using

SAMPLE KINDERGARTEN LESSON FOR *THE FROG PRINCE*

Video Lesson: *The Frog Prince (www.youtube.com/watch?v=P6KzfK35ufU)*

Day 1	Students watch video of *The Frog Prince* in a small-group context. Stop video and discuss at each time-marker indication.
00:35	Why is the princess crying? What is the princess's problem?
02:16	Why did the frog agree to help the princess? Do you think the princess will keep her promise? What makes you think that? Explain what Princess means when she says, "The frog is talking nonsense. Life in a castle is not for him."
03:16	What just happened? What is the frog thinking? Why is the king telling Princess that she must let the frog inside? What will happen next?
04:55	What caused the princess to change her mind about the frog? What will happen next? What makes you think that?
05:16	What lessons do you think the storyteller wanted us to learn from the story?
Day 2	In a small group, children watch the story uninterrupted. Partner 1 retells the story to Partner 2. Then each child draws a "quick pic" of five story scenes on a story frame worksheet. Finally, Partner 2 shares pictures and retells the story to Partner 1.
Day 3	*Optional.* Students watch the video. Follow-up discussion with the teacher focuses on the frog's point of view.

Note. Based on Stahl (2014).

computer-assisted reading to provide repeated readings of a text that has been discussed with the teacher can provide variety and increase home involvement. The ability to read the book repeatedly with immediate assistance and in ways that children view as fun makes it an additional option that holds promise for supporting English learners.

Informational Content Intensive

Have you ever thought or said, "Josh comes from a low-income family. As a 6-year-old, his exposure to the world is quite limited. He often has trouble comprehending because he has no connection to the experiences or the vocabulary that is essential for making sense of many texts that he encounters in school. I have no way of providing the experiences that contribute to essential background knowledge and vocabulary that is provided by many parents outside of the school day"?

Two intervention programs that have been implemented successfully in preschool and kindergarten classrooms provide insights into the necessary components of an effective early comprehension intervention designed to support children's concept development, disciplinary vocabulary, and early reading skills. World of Words (WOW; Neuman, Newman, & Dwyer, 2011; Neuman & Wright, 2013) and PAVEd for Success (Schwanenflugel et al., 2010; SERVE Center, 2010) share several common features:

- Units are built around a 5- to 10-day disciplinary content theme.
- Lists of target vocabulary are established for each theme.
- A comprehensive approach to vocabulary instruction includes multiple exposures to semantic clusters of words in multiple related and repeated read-alouds; isolated, explicit vocabulary work; and small-group conversations about the thematic concepts incorporating embedded vocabulary application.
- Picture cards depicting target words support learning.
- Building bridges between what is known about a topic to what is unknown occurs as the topic is explored across a series of days using varied activities that engage the children in employing the target words in multiple contexts across varied forms of media.
- Extension activities include writing/drawing to represent vocabulary concepts, categorizing activities, and other active forms of conceptual development around the semantic cluster of words.
- Phonological awareness is addressed as part of the intervention through songs, poems, videos, and other, more explicit techniques.

The informational content intensive is based on the studies of WOW and PAVEd for Success that were conducted in PreK and kindergarten. WOW was a supplementary 15-minute intervention that was administered in addition to the core literacy program. PAVEd for Success was administered to all of the children in each classroom, and each component contributed a piece to the comprehensive literacy program. Therefore, suggestions in this chapter may be effectively implemented as a pullout intervention or in a classroom as a teacher-led station.

Unique Features of WOW

Each study had unique features that we believe could be combined to make a powerful early intervention. For example, the extensive use of video was an important component of WOW. Children viewed several short videos each week because there is evidence that when information is introduced through multiple pathways, children learn more and retention is increased. Instruction also included an emphasis on characteristics of words that belonged to the semantic cluster and *why* members of a category belonged together. This ability to categorize is extremely important in refining understandings of the target vocabulary (Stahl & Nagy, 2006). However, it also aids comprehension development. It is the foundation for generating inferences and determining whether students will be able to transfer learning about the category to novel words that are not being taught or what is frequently referred to as becoming a self-extending learner. In addition, Baumann (1986) observes that categorizing should be the first step in teaching children to infer main ideas.

As language develops, clusters of words tend to be learned together and reflect broader conceptual knowledge links or networks of mental representations. By targeting these networks instructionally, we are teaching not just the words; we are working in deliberate ways to expand the entire representational system about a topic. Two young children may both know the word *apple*, but have very different networks of knowledge surrounding the same word (see Figure 9.1). These networks have important implications for broader understanding, inference generation, and general comprehension. The WOW discussions around category and relatedness are designed to expand and solidify these representational networks of knowledge. Neuman and Wright (2013) translate these theories into classroom practices that are aligned with the CCSS.

Unique Features of PAVEd for Success

PAVEd for Success emphasizes the role of small-group conversation. In studies of the program, children responded to three levels of questions about texts that were read aloud to them multiple times, and they participated in 15 minutes of teacher-facilitated small-group conversations about the topic each week. Hamilton and Schwanenflugel (2011) recommend that children participate in three 5-minute conversations each week. Their guidebook contains activities and materials for 24 vocabulary mini-units, including a selection of "Start 'em Up Topics" for each unit. They also suggest that teachers follow the children's interests when generating conversations. Although theme-related conversations are an ideal way to get children to apply the target vocabulary and express their knowledge and interest in the disciplinary theme, a teacher who is aligning small-group conversations with the principles established by PAVEd for Success can be confident that young students' oral language skills are growing (see Form 9.3 at the end of the chapter).

Pulling It All Together

You can create a powerful intervention for young students by combining the features of these two research-validated interventions. We recommend that you create a set of lessons for 2 weeks that are built around the same disciplinary unit

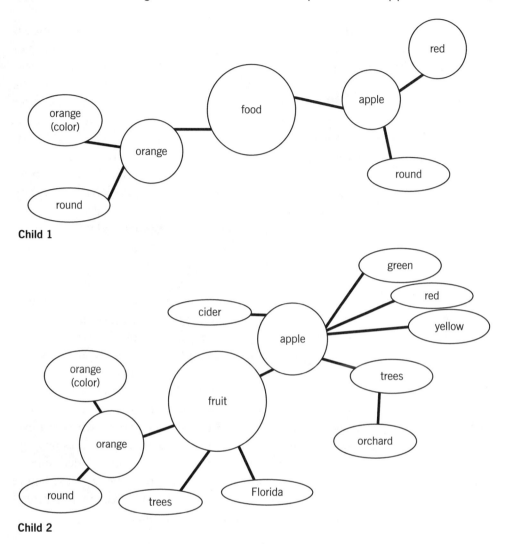

FIGURE 9.1. Mental representations for the word *apple*.

that is being taught by the classroom teacher. Identify 12–20 target vocabulary words that are related to the theme or use the words that have been selected as target vocabulary by the grade-level team. The number of words selected should be based on the language skills of the students, the relatedness of the words, and their difficulty. It is a good idea to create a list that is a deliberate assortment by level of difficulty and expectation of frequency of encounter. Each lesson should be conducted for 15 minutes a day with a small group of three to four children. Start each lesson with a song or poem related to the theme. This beginning will create engagement and enhance phonological awareness and print concepts.

Next, show a short informational video related to the topic. For example, if the topic is transportation, show a short video clip each day about a member of the category. These videos should focus whenever possible on a prototype to serve as a mental model to support the key properties of the category. After showing the video, lead a discussion on the characteristics of the prototype. For example, after a video on boats a teacher would ask *Wh-* questions such as "What is the same about cars and boats?" "What makes boats a special way to travel?" and "What are some different kinds of boats that we saw in the video?" If you have never made much use of videos and wonder where to find the videos for this instruction, simply Google your topic and select "Video" when your search results appear. You will be shocked and pleasantly surprised by the number of short videos (2–5 minutes) that are available for every topic imaginable. For instance, videos now available for boats help children experience what it is like to be bumping along at high speeds on a noisy speedboat, rafting between canyons in the white waters of the Colorado River, or peacefully sailing on the vast ocean amid the unique music of rushing water and halyards clanging in the wind. The instructional application of videos during vocabulary development holds the potential for expanding a child's mental representational network in a way that was not possible 5 years ago.

Follow the video activity with a read-aloud and discussion about boats. On the following days, picture cards should be introduced to review the members of the category and to sort by features as more members of the category are introduced. As more knowledge is learned about the category, children can be presented with "time for a challenge" prompts that require them to analyze whether novel items possess the characteristics that would constitute category membership (e.g., "Is a fish a type of transportation?"). Journal writing/drawing is included once or twice in each unit and includes 5-minute conversations three times a week. Figure 9.2 is a menu of typical activities that would be included in a 2-week informational content intensive. Figure 9.3 is a sample 2-week lesson frame.

Activity	Days	Minutes
Poems, rhymes, and songs	All	1–2
Video about the topic with discussion	4–5	5–8
Teacher read-aloud about the topic with discussion	All	5–8
Use picture cards to review vocabulary, sort vocabulary, or play "time for a challenge"	5–8	1–2
Conversation group (different from teacher-led discussion about a video or book)	6	5
Journal writing/drawing	1–2	3–5

FIGURE 9.2. Informational content intervention menu.

Monday	Tuesday	Wednesday	Thursday	Friday
Week 1				
Introduction: poem or song Video and discussion Read-aloud	Poem or song Video and discussion Read-aloud Conversation group	Poem or song Picture cards Read-aloud Conversation group	Poem or song Video and discussion Read-aloud Picture cards Time for a challenge	Poem or song Read-aloud Journal writing/drawing Conversation group
Week 2				
Poem or song Video and discussion Read-aloud Picture cards	Poem or song Picture cards Read-aloud Conversation group	Poem or song Video and discussion Read-aloud Picture cards	Poem or song Picture cards Read-aloud Conversation group	Assessment Picture cards Time for a challenge Journal writing/drawing Conversation group

FIGURE 9.3. Informational content-intensive lesson frame.

195

Comprehension Strategy Intensive

There is evidence that explicit strategy instruction is effective for children beginning in about second grade. Before that time, strategy use by children might be prompted through teacher questioning during interactive teacher–child read-alouds. However, once children begin reading longer, more complex texts themselves, the application of strategies will be needed for them to be able to overcome meaning-making hurdles during their own reading. Strategies should be taught explicitly to all children, with guided practice, using the techniques described in Chapter 5. However, some children may need more intense work in a small group to support reading comprehension. Before drawing conclusions about children having poor comprehension, it is important to survey the general education classroom to ensure that explicit comprehension instruction is occurring. The Teacher Self-Assessment and Goal Setting form (see Form 1.1 at the end of Chapter 1) can be used to gauge the comprehensiveness of classroom practices.

Before second grade, most high-level comprehension instruction will be conducted as listening/speaking activities. However, in second grade students will need to engage in an increasing amount of reading and writing activities. Teachers of children at this level will need to be mindful of the balance. It is likely that work in the comprehension intervention setting will be supporting second graders in making this transition. At this stage it is a good idea for children to directly transfer what they do collaboratively in listening–speaking to reading–writing. Their listening–speaking activities should actually be viewed as a rehearsal for their writing. Teachers of children at this stage must be mindful that if the writing gets in the way of the thinking, it is a signal to back up and provide more supportive scaffolding. In the intervention setting, this scaffolding can take a variety of forms. It should not mean that you always move the child to an easier text. Scaffolding might involve the teacher playing a more active role or it might mean that children work in partners to complete a writing task. It might mean changing the medium. Perhaps children watch a video or read a shorter text to allow greater time for writing. For second graders in an intervention setting, it is likely that conversation will always occur before any writing in response to text.

Collaborative Strategic Reading

Collaborative strategic reading (CSR) is a reading comprehension intervention that is based on reciprocal teaching (RT; Palincsar & Brown, 1984). Klingner and Vaughn (1996; Klingner, Vaughn, Arguelles, Hughes, & Leftwich, 2004) have conducted a number of studies that investigated the impact of CSR on children with reading difficulties, children with identified reading disabilities, and English learners. Their studies were typically conducted in grades 3–5 during instructional sessions that ranged from 25 to 45 minutes. CSR is a small-group intervention that is conducted using informational text. Like RT, the four comprehension strategies are each taught individually, explicitly, and thoroughly before the children use them collectively in a small student-led discussion group. Children read (silently or aloud) a text selection that has been divided into sensible sections. The four CSR strategies are:

1. *Preview.* Activate prior knowledge, brainstorm, and predict.
2. *Click and clunk.* Self-monitor to determine whether reading is fluent and making sense or whether there are clunks that hinder the reading process. Use "clunk cards" that describe specific fix-up strategies such as *reread* and *chunk long words.*
3. *Get the gist.* After reading each section of text, generate a sentence that summarizes the text in 10 words or fewer.

After all sections of reading are completed:

4. *Wrap-up.* Discuss the key ideas and generate important questions about the reading. Keep a record in a learning log that documents clunks, gist statements, and the wrap-up questions.

We have included CSR is this chapter because it has a strong track record of effectiveness with English learners and children who have reading disabilities. In studies with third graders, it yielded improvement in both fluency and comprehension (Vaughn et al., 2000). In an intervention setting with second graders, the teacher should play an active role in facilitating the discussion around the four strategies and gradually releasing the responsibility to group members. The incorporation of writing the gist statements and wrap-up questions would likely occur over time and in a way that provides variety to the routine. Another variation might be to have the children do the "during" reading activities with a partner, with the whole intervention group discussing only the preview and wrap-up collectively. In order to yield results while avoiding boredom, CSR can be used 3 days a week in combination with other comprehension intervention activities. As with other strategy routines, it is essential to remember that the goal of CSR is for the children to comprehend the text that they read, not to perfect the application of a rigid protocol or uttering strategy-related clichés in rote ways.

Compare–Contrast Text Structure Protocol

Williams, Stafford, Lauer, Hall, and Pollini (2009) demonstrated that explicit instruction of compare–contrast text structures can support second-grade children's comprehension and their ability to create written compositions that reflect this structure. This intervention might be used for 30–45 minutes, 2 or 3 days a week in conjunction with CSR or with other interventions. This form of instruction must be incorporated into a themed disciplinary unit that lends itself to studying category members that can be compared and contrasted, such as animals or plants. This protocol forces interventionists and classroom teachers to work together to provide a cohesive comprehension intervention for students. Lessons involve reading texts that compare members of a category, providing explicit instruction in clue words (*alike, both, compare, but, however, contrast*), discussing ideas and vocabulary, identifying explicit ways that the targets are alike and different, completing a feature analysis to compare the group members on shared and unique features, and using a paragraph frame to create a simple summary that compares and contrasts two items (Armbruster, Anderson, & Ostertag, 1987; Williams et al., 2009).

The use of writing frames to support student writing has a firmly established research base and is particularly recommended for children who have difficulty organizing their thoughts or generating ideas (Graham & Harris, 2005; Williams et al., 2009). A frame that young children might use to write about two plants of their choice that they just read about might look like the paragraph frame in Figure 9.4.

Theme Identification Instruction

One of the most important inferences that children need to be able to make is the overarching theme of a story. Generating the theme of a story goes beyond putting together episodes in a plot. It calls for connection to other stories and the human experience. Research indicates that young children have sensitivity to themes, but they may have difficulty putting the theme into words or expressing the theme spontaneously without explicit instruction (Morrow, 1992). Common themes of texts found in the primary grades are universal truths such as "Be honest," "Never give up," "Be accepting of those who are different," or "Don't be greedy." Williams and colleagues (2002) demonstrated that explicit instruction can help second graders, including those with reading disabilities and those children from high-poverty

---

Two plants that live in the rain forest are _____ and _____ . They are alike in some ways. They both _____ .
Also they both _____ . In other ways they are different: _____
_____
_____ .

FIGURE 9.4. Example of a writing frame paragraph.

QUESTIONS TO SUPPORT THEME GENERATION

Theme-Based Questions

- Was what happened in the story good or bad?
- Why was it good or bad?
- What do you think was the main lesson that the character(s) learned?
- What should we learn from the characters' experiences in this story?

Transfer Questions

- When is it important to _____? (personal transfer)
- When is it easy/hard to _____? (personal transfer)
- Can you think of other stories or movies that you know that were written to teach the reader/audience the same lesson?

homes, to identify instructed themes when they are encountered in new stories. The instructional protocol calls for the incorporation of the same high-level questions during and after reading that were included in Form 9.2 (at the end of the chapter). However, Williams and colleagues recommend a rich and thorough discussion that adds the questions in the text box above. Adjust the questioning to be specific to the shared story that you read together.

In some cases, this discussion may simply be a small-group follow-up to the whole-class shared reading activities that are being conducted around a complex text in the classroom. When rich, complex stories are being introduced in the classroom, extensive discussion by the children is needed. Often there is not time during the literacy block to make sure that all children have really understood the unwritten ideas expressed in the texts or made the connections to the broader, abstract literary themes about the human experience. A comprehension intervention should ensure that children come away from the instructed text capable of recognizing universal themes and should provide them with the tools and confidence to transfer this ability to novel texts during independent reading.

Conclusion

Most early reading interventions conducted in school settings focus on foundational skills or they provide the support needed to help children fluently read texts of increasing difficulty. However, since comprehension develops across a lifetime, it is a good idea to provide comprehension interventions for children whose difficulties show up even before they begin reading. By providing small-group opportunities to develop narrative comprehension, engage in conversations in response to texts, and expand language development and conceptual networks, we increase the likelihood that children will be able to make sense of the texts they read independently as they grow as readers. Formative assessment measures that provide details in documenting children's ability to express in speaking and writing their growing awareness of plot episodes, causal sequences, the internal states of characters, and themes provide good gauges of their development and instructional needs in comprehending narratives. Formative assessments that document children's ability to express the logically organized networks of knowledge expressed in informational texts serve similar purposes.

Picture Walk for Narrative Comprehension
of a Wordless Picture Book

"This book is called _____ . In this book, the pictures tell the story. There are not any words written. I'd like you to look at the pictures in the book and use your own words to tell me the story."

Picture Walk Element	Score Description	Score
Book-Handling Skills Orients book correctly, has sense of appropriate viewing speed and order. (Viewing errors may include skipping pages or speeding through pages.)	Incorrectly handles book and makes more than two viewing errors.	0
	Makes one or two viewing errors (i.e., skips pages).	1
	Handles book appropriately and makes no viewing errors.	2
Engagement Is behaviorally and emotionally involved during picture walk, as judged by attention, interest in book, affect, and comfort.	Displays off-task behavior or negative comments.	0
	Displays quiet, sustained behavior.	1
	Shows several examples of attention, affect, interest, or effort (e.g., spontaneous comments).	2
Picture Comments Makes discrete comments about a picture, which can include describing objects, characters, emotions, actions, and opinions as well as character vocalizations.	Makes no picture comments.	0
	Makes one picture comment or verbalization.	1
	Makes two or more comments or verbalizations about specific pictures.	2
Storytelling Comments Makes comments that go across pictures and demonstrate an understanding that the pictures tell a coherent story. Can include narration, dialogue, using book language, and storytelling voice.	Makes no storytelling comments.	0
	Provides storytelling elements, but not consistently.	1
	Through narration or dialogue connects story events and presents a coherent storytelling line.	2
Comprehension Strategies Displays vocalization or behaviors that show attempts at comprehension such as self-corrections, looking back and ahead in book, asking questions for understanding, and making predictions about story.	Demonstrates no comprehension strategies.	0
	Elicits one instance of comprehension strategies.	1
	Demonstrates comprehension strategies at least two or more times.	2

Based on Paris and Paris (2003). Administration instructions are from McKenna and Stahl (2009, p. 94). Copyright 2009 by The Guilford Press. Adapted by permission.

Elements of a Narrative Retelling
(Spontaneous and Prompted)

Elements		Spontaneous Retelling	Prompted Recall
Explicit			
Setting	Where/when did the story take place?		
Characters	Who is the story about?		
Episodes	What is happening here?		
Elaborations	What do you know about _____?		
Language	What does *word* mean? What does the author mean by *phrase*?		
Causal Sequence/Inferential			
Initiating event/problem	What is the story about? What is the character's problem? Why is this an important part of the story?		
Internal response	How does the character feel? What is the character thinking? What makes you think that?		
Goal	What does the character want to happen/to get?		
Attempts/episodes	What will happen next? What makes you think that? Why? What will the character do to solve the problem/achieve the goal?		
Consequences of each attempt and internal response	Did what the character tried work? Why or why not? What caused the change? What does (*literal*) tell you about (*inference*)?		
Outcome/resolution	Did the character achieve the goal?		
Value/Theme			
Evaluation	Did the character do the right thing? What life lesson can we learn from this story?		

Based on Stahl (2014a); van Kleeck (2008); and Warren, Nicholas, and Trabasso (1979).

Teacher Self-Inventory of Conversations

	Week of . . .		
Use an audio recording of the small-group conversations to self-monitor your conversational moves.			
I conducted three conversations lasting at least 5 minutes with each child individually or in a small group.			
Conversation was child-centered. Children's interests were the focus of the conversation. I did not dominate the conversation or use it as a chance to reteach. I listened.			
I allowed adequate wait time for children to formulate their responses, especially English learners.			
I used sophisticated vocabulary (Tier Two words and content words) during our conversation.			
I used questioning to prompt a discussion of feelings, goals, motivations, and values. (Children often do not spontaneously include these in their own stories.)			
I encouraged elaborations through questioning.			
I used language expansions to respectfully (without correcting) clarify, add missing grammatical elements, or elaborate children's speech (e.g., Child: "We was fixin' to go to the park by the river." Teacher: "You and your brother got ready to go to the park? What did you plan to do when you got to the park?").			
I used open-ended questioning to elicit hypothesizing, clarifying, interpreting, and evaluating.			
I accommodated my English learners by interjecting some of their first language in the conversation, allowing extra wait time, and adapting the complexity of the conversation to match their needs.			

From Hamilton and Schwanenflugel (2011). Copyright 2011 by Brookes Publishing. Adapted by permission.

References

Adger, C. T., Wolfram, W., & Christian, D. (2007). *Dialects in schools and communities* (2nd ed.). New York: Routledge.

Ainsworth, L., & Viegut, D. (2006). *Common formative assessments: How to connect standards-based instruction and assessment.* Thousand Oaks, CA: Corwin Press.

Almasi, J. F. (2003). *Teaching strategic processes in reading.* New York: Guilford Press.

American Educational Research Association, American Pyschological Association, & National Council on Measurement in Education. (1999). *Standards for educational and psychological testing 1999.* Washington, DC: American Educational Research Association.

Armbruster, B. B., Anderson, T. H., & Ostertag, J. (1987). Does text structure/summarization instruction facilitate learning from informational text? *Reading Research Quarterly, 22,* 331–346.

Ashton-Warner, S. (1965). *The teacher.* New York: Simon & Schuster.

Au, K. H., & Jordan, C. (1981). Teaching reading to Hawaiian children: Finding a culturally appropriate solution. In H. T. Trueba, C. P. Guthrie, & K. H. Au (Eds.), *Culture and the bilingual classroom: Studies in classroom ethnography* (pp. 139–152). Rowley, MA: Newbury House.

Aud, S., Wilkinson-Flicker, S., Kristapovich, P., Rathbun, A., Wang, X., & Zhang, J. (2013). *The condition of education 2013* (NCES 2013-037). Washington, DC: U.S. Department of Education, National Center for Education Statistics. Retrieved September 5, 2013, from *http://nces.ed.gov/pubsearch.*

August, D., & Shanahan, T. (Eds.). (2006). *Developing literacy in second-language learners: A report of the National Literacy Panel on Language-Minority Children and Youth.* Mahwah, NJ: Erlbaum.

Bacon, R. (1988). *Our dog Sam.* Adelaide, Australia: Rigby Limited.

Baker, L., & Brown, A. L. (1984). Metacognitive skills and reading. In P. D. Pearson, R. Barr, M. L. Kamil, & P. B. Mosenthal (Eds.), *Handbook of reading research* (Vol. 1, pp. 353–394). New York: Longman.

Barracca, D., & Barracca, S. (1990). *The adventures of taxi dog.* New York: Dial.

Baumann, J. F. (1986). The direct instruction of main idea comprehension ability. In J. F. Baumann (Ed.), *Teaching main idea comprehension* (pp. 133–178). Newark, DE: International Reading Association.

Bear, D. R., Invernizzi, M., Templeton, S., & Johnston, F. (2011). *Words their way: Word study for phonics, vocabulary, and spelling instruction* (5th ed.). Upper Saddle River, NJ: Pearson Education.

Beaver, J. M. (2006). *Developmental reading assessment, kindergarten through grade 3* (2nd ed). Parsippany, NJ: Pearson Education.

Beck, I. L., & McKeown, M. G. (2001). Text talk: Capturing the benefits of read aloud experiences for young children. *The Reading Teacher, 55,* 10–35.

Beck, I., McKeown, M. G., & Kucan, L. (2002). *Bringing words to life: Robust vocabulary instruction.* New York: Guilford Press.

Bergman, J. L. (1992). SAIL—A way to success and independence for low-achieving readers. *The Reading Teacher, 45*(8), 598–602.

Betts, E. A. (1946). *Foundations of reading instruction.* New York: American Books.

Bezdicek, J., & García, G. E. (2012). Working with preschool English language learners: A sociocultural approach. In B. Yoon & H.-K. Kim (Eds.), *Teachers' roles in second language learning: Classroom applications of sociocultural theory* (pp. 171–188). Charlotte, NC: Information Age.

Bishop, R. S. (1997). Selecting literature for a multicultural classroom. In V. J. Harris (Ed.), *Using multiethnic literature in the K–8 classroom* (pp. 1–19). Norwood, MA: Christopher-Gordon.

Blank, M., Rose, S. A., & Berlin, L. J. (2003). *Pre-school language assessment instrument* (2nd ed.). Austin, TX: PRO-ED.

Bloom B. S. (1956). *Taxonomy of educational objectives: Handbook I. The cognitive domain.* New York: McKay.

Boushey, G., & Moser, J. (2009). *The daily 5: Fostering literacy independence in the elementary grades.* Portland, ME: Stenhouse.

Bowyer-Crane, C., & Snowling, M. J. (2005). Assessing children's inference generation: What do tests of reading comprehension measure? *British Journal of Educational Psychology, 75,* 189–201.

Bravo, M. A., Cervetti, G. N., Hiebert, E. H., & Pearson, P. D. (2008). From passive to active control of science vocabulary. In *Fifty-sixth yearbook of the National Reading Conference* (pp. 122–135). Chicago: National Reading Conference.

Bromley, K. (2007). Assessing student writing. In J. R. Paratore & R. L. McCormack (Eds.), *Classroom literacy assessment: Making sense of what students know and do* (pp. 210–224). New York: Guilford Press.

Brown, R., & Coy-Ogan, L. (1993). The evolution of transactional strategies in one teacher's classroom. *Elementary School Journal, 94*(2), 221–233.

Cain, K., & Oakhill, J. V. (1999). Inference making and its relation to comprehension failure. *Reading and Writing, 11,* 489–503.

Calkins, L. (1991). *Living between the lines.* Portsmouth, NH: Heinemann.

Cameron, C. A., Hunt, A. K., & Linton, M. J. (1985). Medium effects on children's story rewriting and story retelling. *First Language, 8,* 3–18.

Carle, E. (1989). *The very hungry caterpillar.* Jefferson City, MO: Scholastic.

Carmichael, C. (1998). *Used-up bear.* New York: NorthSouth.

Catts, H. W., Fey, M. E., Tomblin, J. B., & Zhang, X. (2002). A longitudinal investigation of reading outcomes in children with language impairment. *Journal of Speech, Language and Hearing Research, 45*(6), 1142–1157.

Cazden, C. B. (1988). *Classroom discourse: The language of teaching and learning.* Portsmouth, NH: Heinemann.

Chall, J. S. (1996). *Stages of reading development* (2nd ed.). Fort Worth, TX: Harcourt-Brace.

Chall, J. S., & Jacobs, V. A. (1983). Writing and reading in the elementary grades: Developmental trends among low-SES children. *Language Arts, 60*(5), 617–626.

Clark, J. M., & Paivio, A. (1991). Dual coding theory and education. *Educational Psychology Review, 3*(3), 149–210.

Clay, M. M. (2006). *An observation survey of early literacy achievement.* Portsmouth, NH: Heinemann.

Cohen, M. (2006). *First grade takes a test.* Long Island City, NY: Star Bright Books.

Coley, J. D., DePinto, T., Craig, S., & Gardner, R. (1993). From college to classroom: Three accounts of their adaptations of reciprocal teaching. *Elementary School Journal, 94*(2), 255–266.

Comeau, L., Cormier, P., Grandmaison, E., & Lacroix, D. (1999). A longitudinal study of phonological processing skills in children learning to read in a second language. *Journal of Educational Psychology, 91*, 29–43.

Coughlan, C. (1999). *Beetles.* Mankato, MN: Pebble Books.

Cummins, J. (1981). The role of primary language development in promoting educational success for language minority students. In California State Department of Education (Ed.), *Schooling and language minority students: A theoretical framework* (pp. 3–49). Los Angeles: Evaluation, Dissemination and Assessment Center, California State University, Los Angeles.

Cummins, J. (1986). Empowering minority students: A framework for intervention. *Harvard Educational Review, 56*, 18–36.

Daniels, H. (2002). *Literature circles: Voice and choice in book clubs and reading groups.* Portland, ME: Stenhouse.

DePaola, T. (1979). *Oliver Button is a sissy.* New York: Harcourt Brace Jovanovich.

Desmarais, C., Nadeau, L., Trudeau, N., Filiatrault-Veilleux, P., & Maxes-Fournier, C. (2013). Intervention for improving comprehension in 4–6 year old children with specific language impairment: Practicing inferencing is a good thing. *Clinical Linguistics and Phonetics, 27*(6–7), 540–552.

Diaz-Rico, L. T., & Weed, K. Z. (2010). *The crosscultural, language, and academic development handbook: A complete K–12 reference guide* (4th ed.). Boston: Allyn & Bacon.

Dickinson, D. K., McCabe, A., & Anastasopoulos, L. (2003). A framework for examining book reading in early childhood classrooms. In A. van Kleeck, S. Stahl, & E. B. Bauer (Eds.), *On reading books to children* (pp. 95–113). Mahwah, NJ: Erlbaum.

Dillon, L., & Dillon, D. (2002). *Rap a tap tap: Here's Bojangles—Think of that!* New York: Blue Sky Press.

DuFour, R., DuFour, R., Eakey, R., & Many, T. (2006). *Learning by doing: A handbook for professional learning communities*. Bloomington, IN: Solution Tree USA.

Duke, N. K. (2000). 3.6 minutes per day: The scarcity of informational texts in first grade. *Reading Research Quarterly, 35*, 202–224.

Duke, N. K., & Pearson, P. D. (2002). Effective practices for developing reading comprehension. In A. E. Farstrup & S. Jay Samuels (Eds.), *What research has to say about reading instruction* (3rd ed., pp. 205–242). Newark, DE: International Reading Association.

Duke, N. K., Purcell-Gates, V., Hall, L. A., & Tower, C. (2006). Authentic literacy activities for developing comprehension and writing. *The Reading Teacher, 60*, 344–355.

Dunn, L., & Dunn, D. (2007). *Peabody Picture Vocabulary Test* (4th ed.). San Antonio, TX: Pearson.

Durgunoğlu, A. Y., Nagy, W. E., & Hancin-Bhatt, B. J. (1993). Cross-language transfer of phonological awareness. *Journal of Educational Pyschology, 85*(3), 453–465.

Durkin, D. (1978–1979). What classroom observations reveal about reading comprehension instruction. *Reading Research Quarterly, 14*(4), 481–533.

Echevarría, J., Vogt, M., & Short, D. (2010). *Making content comprehensible for elementary English learners: The SIOP model*. Boston: Allyn & Bacon.

Elbow, P. (1998). *Writing without teachers* (2nd ed.). New York: Oxford University Press.

Fitzgerald, J., & Shanahan, T. (2000). Reading and writing relations and their development. *Educational Psychologist, 35*, 39–51.

Fountas, I. C., & Pinnell, G. S. (1996). *Guided reading: Good first teaching for all children*. Portsmouth, NH: Heinemann.

Fountas, I. C., & Pinnell, G. S. (2006). *Leveled book list K–8*. Portsmouth, NH: Heinemann.

Fountas, I. C., & Pinnell, G. S. (2010). *Benchmark Assessment System* (2nd ed.). Portsmouth, NH: Heinemann.

Fountas, I., & Pinnell, G. S. (2011). *Assessment guide: A guide to Benchmark Assessment System 1* (2nd ed.). Portsmouth, NH: Heinemann.

Francis, D. J., Lesaux, N., & August, D. (2006). Language of instruction. In D. August & T. Shanahan (Eds.), *Developing literacy in second-language learners: Report of the National Literacy Panel on Language-Minority Children and Youth* (pp. 365–413). Mahwah, NJ: Erlbaum.

Gambrell, L. B., Pfieffer, W. R., & Wilson, R. M. (1985). The effects of retelling upon reading comprehension and recall of text information. *Journal of Educational Research, 78*, 216–220.

Gammill, D. M. (2006). Learning the write way. *The Reading Teacher, 59*, 754–762.

Garas-York, K., Shanahan, L. E., & Almasi, J. F. (2013). Comprehension: High-level talk and writing about texts. In B. M. Taylor & N. K. Duke (Eds.), *Handbook of effective literacy instruction: Research-based practice K–8* (pp. 246–278). New York: Guilford Press.

García, G. E. (1991). Factors influencing the English reading test performance of Spanish-speaking Hispanic children. *Reading Research Quarterly, 26*(4), 371–392.

García, G. E. (1998). Mexican-American bilingual students' metacognitive reading strategies: What's transferred, unique, problematic? *National Reading Conference Yearbook, 47,* 253–263.

García, G. E. (2000). Bilingual children's reading. In M. Kamil, P. Mosenthal, P. D. Pearson, & R. Barr (Eds.), *Handbook of reading research* (Vol. 3, pp. 813–834). Mahwah, NJ: Erlbaum.

García, G. E. (2003). The reading comprehension development and instruction of English language learners. In A. P. Sweet & C. E. Snow (Eds.), *Rethinking reading comprehension* (pp. 31–50). New York: Guilford Press.

García, G. E. (Chair). (2006, December). *Synthesizing three elements of reading comprehension instruction.* Symposium conducted at the National Reading Conference, Los Angeles, CA.

García, G. E., & Bauer, E. B. (2009). Assessing student progress in the time of No Child Left Behind. In L. M. Morrow, R. Rueda, & D. Lapp (Eds.), *Handbook of research on literacy and diversity* (pp. 233–253). New York: Guilford Press.

García, G. E., Bray, T. M., Mora, R. A., Carr, S., & Rinehart, N. (2008, April). *Examining the relationship between changes in teachers' reading comprehension instruction and the reading test performance of Spanish-speaking Hispanic students.* Paper presented at the annual conference of the American Educational Research Association, New York.

García, G. E., Bray, T. M., Mora, R. A., Primeaux, J., Ricklefs, M. A., Engel, L. C., et al. (2006). Working with teachers to change the literacy instruction of Latino students in urban schools. *National Reading Conference Yearbook, 55,* 155–170.

García, G. E., & DeNicolo, C. P. (2009). Making informed decisions about the language and literacy assessment of English language learners. In L. Helman (Ed.), *Literacy development with English learners: Research-based instruction in grades K–6* (pp. 64–86). New York: Guilford Press.

García, G. E., McKoon, G., & August, D. (2006). Synthesis: Language and literacy assessment. In D. August & T. Shanahan (Eds.), *Developing literacy in second-language learners: A report of the National Literacy Panel on Language-Minority Children and Youth* (pp. 583–596). Mahwah, NJ: Erlbaum.

García, G. E., McKoon, G., & August, D. (2008). Language and literacy assessment. In D. August & T. Shanahan (Eds.), *Developing reading and writing in second-language learners: Lessons from the report of the National Literacy Panel on Language-Minority Children and Youth* (pp. 251–274). New York: Routledge.

García, G. E., & Pearson, P. D. (1994). Assessment and diversity. *Review of Research in Education, 20,* 337–391.

García, G. E., Pearson, P. D., Taylor, B. A., Stahl, K. A. D., & Bauer, E. B. (2007). *Instruction of reading comprehension: Cognitive strategies or responsive engagement?* Unpublished grant materials, University of Illinois, Champaign, and Institute of Education Sciences, Washington, DC.

García, G. E., Pearson, P. D., Taylor, B. M., Bauer, E. B., & Stahl, K. A. D. (2011). Socioconstructivist and political views on teachers' implementation of two types of reading comprehension approaches in low-income schools. *Theory Into Practice, 50*(2), 149–156.

Gee, J. P. (1990). *Social linguistics and literacies: Ideology in discourses. Critical perspectives on literacy and education.* London: Falmer Press.

Geva, E., & Olson, D. (1983). Children's story retelling. *First Language, 4,* 85–109.

Ginsburg, M. (1997). *Mushroom in the rain: Adapted from the Russian of V. Suteyev.* Westport, CT: Aladdin Books.

Glazer, S. M. (2007). A classroom portfolio system: Assessment is instruction. In J. R. Paratore & R. L. McCormack (Eds.), *Classroom literacy assessment: Making sense of what students know and do* (pp. 227–245). New York: Guilford Press.

Goldenberg, C. (1992/1993). Instructional conversations: Promoting comprehension through discussion. *The Reading Teacher, 46*(4), 316–326.

Goldman, S. R., Reyes, M., & Varnhagen, C. K. (1984). Understanding fables in first and second languages. *NABE Journal, 8,* 835–866.

Goldman, S. R., Varma, K. O., Sharp, D., & Cognition and Technology Group at Vanderbilt. (1999). Children's understanding of complex stories: Issues of representation and assessment. In S. R. Goldman, A. C. Graesser, & P. van den Broek (Eds.), *Narrative comprehension, causality, and coherence: Essays in honor of Tom Trabaso* (pp. 135–159). Mahwah, NJ: Erlbaum.

Goodman, Y. M., Watson, D. J., & Burke, C. L. (1987). *Reading miscue inventory: Alternative procedures.* New York: Owen.

Graham, S., & Harris, K. R. (2005). *Writing better: Effective strategies for teaching students with learning difficulties.* Baltimore: Brookes.

Graham, S., & Hebert, H. (2010). *Writing to read: Evidence for how writing can improve reading* (report from the Carnegie Corporation of New York). Washington, DC: Alliance for Excellent Education.

Graves, D. H. (1994). *A fresh look at writing.* Portsmouth, NH: Heinemann.

Grattan, K. W. (1997). They can do it too!: Book club with first and second graders. In S. McMahon & T. Raphael (Eds.), *The book club connection: Literacy, learning and classroom talk* (pp. 267–283). New York: Teachers College Press.

Gregory, N., & Lightburn, R. (1995). *How Smudge came.* Red Deer, Alberta, Canada: Red Deer College Press.

Guthrie, J. T., Van Meter, P., McCann, A. D., Wigfield, A., Bennett, L., Poundstone, C., et al. (1996). Growth of literacy engagement: Changes in motivations and strategies during concept-oriented reading instruction. *Reading Research Quarterly, 31,* 306–332.

Guthrie, J. T., Wigfield, A., Barbosa, P., Perencevich, K. C., Taboada, A., Davis, M. H., et al. (2004). Increasing reading comprehension and engagement through concept-oriented reading instruction. *Journal of Educational Psychology, 96,* 403–423.

Hacker, D., & Tenent, A. (2002). Implementing reciprocal teaching in the classroom: Overcoming obstacles and making modifications. *Journal of Educational Psychology, 94*(4), 699–718.

Hadithi, M. (1990). *The lazy lion.* London: Hodder & Stoughton.

Hall, M., & Stahl, K. A. D. (2012). Devillainizing video in support of comprehension instruction. *The Reading Teacher, 65,* 403–406.

Hamilton, C. E., & Schwanenflugel, P. J. (2011). *PAVEd for Success: Building vocabulary and language development.* Baltimore: Brookes.

Harris, V. J. (2003). The complexity of debates about multicultural literature and cultural authenticity. In D. Fox & K. Short (Eds.), *Cultural authenticity in children's literature* (pp. 116–134). Urbana, IL: National Council of Teachers of English.

Hart, B., & Risley, T. R. (1995). *Meaningful differences in the everyday experiences of young American children: The everyday experience of one and two year old American children*. Baltimore: Brookes.

Hayes, D. P., & Ahrens, M. G. (1988). Vocabulary simplification for children: A special case of "motherese." *Journal of Child Language, 15*, 395–410.

Hayes, L., & Flannigan, K. (2014). *Developing word recognition*. New York: Guilford Press.

Heath, S. B. (1982). Questioning at home and at school: A comparative study. In G. Spindler (Ed.), *Doing the ethnography of schooling: Educational anthropology in action* (pp. 102–131). New York: Holt, Rinehart & Winston.

Hebert, M., Gillespie, A., & Graham, S. (2013). Comparing effects of different writing activities on reading comprehension: A meta-analysis. *Reading and Writing, 26*, 111–138.

Heritage, M. (2010). *Formative assessment and next-generation assessment systems: Are we losing an opportunity?* Washington, DC: Council of Chief State School Officers.

Hernández, H. (1989). *Multicultural education: A teacher's guide to content and process*. New York: Macmillan.

Herrera, S. G., Perez, D. R., & Escamilla, K. (2010). *Teaching reading to English language learners: Differentiated literacies*. Boston: Allyn & Bacon.

Himmelman, J. (1998). *A ladybug's life*. New York: Children's Press.

Holdaway, D. (1982). Shared book experience: Teaching reading using favorite books. *Theory Into Practice, 21*, 293–300.

Hubbard, R. S.,Winerbourne, N., & Ostrow, J. (1996). Visual responses to literature: Imagination through literature. *The New Advocate, 9*, 309–323.

Jiménez, R. T., García, G. E., & Pearson, P. D. (1996). The reading strategies of bilingual Latina/o students who are successful English readers: Opportunities and obstacles. *Reading Research Quarterly, 31*(1), 90–112.

Johnston, P. H. (2004). *Choice words: How our language affects children's learning*. Portland, ME: Stenhouse.

Justice, L. M., Mashburn, A., & Petscher, Y. (2013). Very early language skills of fifth-grade poor comprehenders. *Journal of Research in Reading, 2*, 172–185.

Kendeou, P., Bohn-Gettler, C., White, M. J., & van den Broek, P. (2008). Children's inference generation across different media. *Journal of Research in Reading, 31*(3), 259–272.

Kendeou, P., Lynch, J. S., van den Broek, P., Espin, C. A., White, M. J., & Kremer, K. E. (2006). Developing successful readers: Building early comprehension skills through television viewing and listening. *Early Childhood Education Journal, 33*(2), 91–98.

Kintsch, W. (1998). *Comprehension: A paradigm for cognition*. Cambridge, UK: Cambridge University Press.

Klassen, C. (1993). Exploring "the color of peace." Content-area literature discussions. In K. M. Pierce, C. Gilles, D. R. Barnes (Eds.), *Cycles of meaning: Exploring the potential of talk in learning communities* (pp. 237–259). Portsmouth, NH: Heinemann.

Kletzien, S. B., & Dreher, M. J. (2004). *Informational text in K–3 classrooms: Helping children read and write*. Newark, DE: International Reading Association.

Klingner, J. K., & Vaughn, S. (1996). Reciprocal teaching of reading comprehension strategies for students with learning disabilities who use English as a second language. *Elementary School Journal, 96,* 275–293.

Klingner, J. K., Vaughn, S., Arguelles, M. E., Hughes, T. J., & Leftwich, S. A. (2004). Collaborative strategic reading: "Real-world" lessons from classroom teachers. *Remedial and Special Education, 25,* 291–302.

Krahn, F. (1979). *Robot-bot-bot.* New York: Dutton Children's Books.

Kuhn, M. R., Schwanenflugel, P. J., & Meisinger, E. B. (2010). Aligning theory and assessment of reading fluency: Automaticity, prosody, and definitions of fluency. *Reading Research Quarterly, 45,* 230–251.

Lesaux, N., & Geva, E. (2006). Synthesis: Development of literacy in language minority students. In D. August & T. Shanahan (Eds.), *Developing literacy in second-language learners: Report of the National Literacy Panel on Language-Minority Children and Youth* (pp. 53–74). Mahwah, NJ: Erlbaum.

Leslie, L., & Caldwell, J. S. (2010). *Qualitative reading inventory* (5th ed.). Boston: Allyn & Bacon.

Lester, H. (1988). *Tacky the penguin.* Boston: Houghton Mifflin.

Leu, D. J., Coiro, J., Castek, J., Hartman, D. K., Henry, L. A., & Reinking, D. (2008). Research on instruction and assessment in the new literacies of online reading comprehension. In C. C. Block & S. R. Parris (Eds.), *Comprehension instruction: Research-based best practices* (2nd ed., pp. 321–346). New York: Guilford Press.

Linan-Thompson, S., Vaughn, S., Hickman-Davis, P., & Kouzekanani, K. (2003) Effectiveness of supplemental reading instruction for second-grade English language learners with reading difficulties. *Elementary School Journal, 103*(3), 221–238.

Lindfors, J. W. (1987). *Children's language and learning* (2nd ed.). Englewood Cliffs, NJ: Prentice-Hall.

Lobel, A. (1977). *Mouse soup.* New York: Harper & Row.

Lynch, J. S., van den Broek, P., Kremer, K. E., Kendeou, P., White, M. J., & Lorch, E. P. (2008). The development of narrative comprehension and its relation to other early reading skills. *Reading Psychology, 29*(4), 327–365.

Martin, B., & Carle, E. (1992). *Brown bear, brown bear, what do you see?* New York: Holt.

Martínez-Roldán, C. M. (2005). The inquiry acts of bilingual children in literature discussions. *Language Arts, 83*(1), 22–32.

Martínez-Roldán, C. M., & López-Robertson, J. M. (2000). Initiating literature circles in a first-grade bilingual classroom. *The Reading Teacher 53*(4), 270–281.

McGee, L. M. (2007). Language and literacy assessment in preschool. In J. R. Paratore & R. L. McCormack (Eds.), *Classroom literacy assessment: Making sense of what students know and do* (pp. 65–84). New York: Guilford Press.

McIntyre, E., & Turner, J. D. (2013). Culturally responsive literacy instruction. In B. M. Taylor & N. K. Duke (Eds.), *The handbook of effective literacy instruction: Research-based practice K–8* (pp. 137–161). New York: Guilford Press.

McKenna, M. C., Conradi, K., Young, C. A., & Gee Jang, B. (2013). Technology and the common core standards. In L. M. Morrow, T. Shanahan, & K. K. Wixson (Eds.), *Teaching with the common core standards for English language arts: PreK–2.* New York: Guilford Press.

McKenna, M. C., & Stahl, K. A. D. (2009). *Assessment for reading instruction* (2nd ed.). New York: Guilford Press.

McMahon, S. I., & Raphael, T. E. (1997). *The book club connection: Literacy learning and classoom talk*. New York: Teachers College Press.

Mellonie, B., & Ingpen, R. R. (1983). *Lifetimes: A beautiful way to explain death to children*. New York: Bantam Books.

Miramontes, O. B. (1987). Oral reading miscues of Hispanic students: Implications for assessment of learning disabilities. *Journal of Learning Disabilities, 20*(10), 627–632.

Moll, L. C. (2001). The diversity of schooling: A cultural-historical approach. In M. de La Luz Reyes & J. J. Halcón (Eds.), *The best for our children: Critical perspectives on literacy for Latino students* (pp. 13–28). New York: Teachers College Press.

Morrow, L. M. (1984). Reading stories to young children: Effects of story structure and traditional questioning strategies on comprehension. *Journal of Reading Behavior, 16*, 273–288.

Morrow, L. M. (1985). Retelling stories: A strategy for improving young children's comprehension concept of story structure, and oral language complexity. *Elementary School Journal, 85*, 646–660.

Morrow, L. M. (1992). The impact of a literature-based program on literacy achievement, use of literature, and attitudes of children from minority backgrounds. *Reading Research Quarterly, 27*, 251–275.

Munsch, R. N., & Martchenko, M. (1980). *The paper bag princess*. Toronto: Annick Press.

Murphy, P. K., Wilkinson, I. A. G., Soter, A. O., Hennessey, M N., & Alexander, J. F. (2009). Examining the effects of classroom discussion on students' comprehension of text: A meta-analysis. *Journal of Educational Psychology, 101*(3), 740–764.

Muspratt, S., Luke, A., & Freebody, P. (1997). *Constructing critical literacies*. Cresskill, NJ: Hampton.

Narvaez, D. (2002). Individual differences that influence reading comprehension. In C. C. Block & M. Pressley (Eds.), *Comprehension instruction: Research-based practices* (pp. 158–175). New York: Guilford Press

National Governors Association Center for Best Practices & Council of Chief State School Officers. (2010). *Common core state standards for English language arts and literacy in history/social studies, science, and technical subjects*. Washington, DC: Authors.

National Institute of Child Health and Human Development. (2000). *Teaching children to read: An evidence-based assessment of the scientific research literature on reading and its implications for reading instruction*. Washington, DC: National Institute of Child Health and Development.

Nelson, K. (1996). *Language in cognitive development: Emergence of the mediated mind*. New York: Cambridge University Press.

Neuman, S. B. (1996). Children engaging in storybook reading: The influence of access to print resources, opportunity, and parental interaction. *Early Childhood Research Quarterly, 11*, 495–513.

Neuman, S. B., Newman, E. H., & Dwyer, J. (2011). Educational effects of a vocabulary intervention on preschoolers' word knowledge and conceptual development: A cluster-randomized trial. *Reading Research Quarterly, 46*(3), 249–272.

Neuman, S. B., & Wright, T. S. (2013). *All about words: Increase vocabulary in the common core classroom, Pre-k–2*. New York: Teachers College Press.

Numeroff, L. (1985). *If you give a mouse a cookie*. New York: HarperCollins.

O'Flahavan, J. F. (1994/1995). Teacher role options in peer discussions about literature. *The Reading Teacher, 48*(4), 354–356.

Olness, R. (2007). *Using literature to enhance content area instruction: A guide for K–5 teachers*. Newark, DE: International Reading Association.

Osmundson, E. (2011, February 8). Effective use of classroom formative assessments for the CCSS. In the *Common Core State Standards: Planning for effective implementation*. Symposium conducted at the Northwest Comprehensive Center of Education, Portland, OR.

Palincsar, A. S. (1988, April). *Collaborating in the interest of collaborative learning*. Paper presented at the annual meeting of the American Educational Research Association, New Orleans, LA.

Palincsar, A. S. (1991). Scaffolded instruction of listening comprehension with first graders at risk for academic difficulty. In A. M. McKeough & J. L. Lupart (Eds.), *Toward the practice of theory-based instruction* (pp. 50–65). Mahwah, NJ: Erlbaum.

Palincsar, A. S., & Brown, A. L. (1984). Reciprocal teaching of comprehension-fostering and comprehension-monitoring activities. *Cognition and Instruction, 2*, 117–175.

Palincsar, A. S., & Brown, A. (1986). Interactive teaching to promote independent learning from texts. *The Reading Teacher, 39*, 771–777.

Palincsar, A. S., David, Y., & Brown, A. L. (1989). *Using reciprocal teaching in the classroom: A guide for teachers*. Unpublished manual, University of Michigan, Ann Arbor.

Paratore, J. R., & McCormack, R. L. (Eds.). (2007). *Classroom literacy assessment: Making sense of what students know and do*. New York: Guilford Press.

Paris, A. H., & Paris, S. G. (2003). Assessing narrative comprehension in young children. *Reading Research Quarterly, 38*(1), 33–76.

Paris, S. G. (2005). Re-interpreting the development of reading skills. *Reading Research Quarterly, 40*, 184–202.

Paris, S. G., & Hamilton, E. E. (2009). The development of children's reading comprehension. In S. E. Israel & G. G. Duffy (Eds.), *Handbook of research on reading comprehension* (pp. 32–53). New York: Routledge.

Pearson, P. D., & Gallagher, M. C. (1983). The instruction of reading comprehension. *Contemporary Educational Psychology, 8*, 317–344.

Perfetti, C., & Adlof, S. (2012). Reading comprehension: A conceptual framework from word meaning to text meaning. In J. P. Sabatini, E. R. Albro, & T. Reilly (Eds.), *Measuring up: Advances in how to assess reading ability* (pp. 3–20). New York: Rowman & Littlefield Education.

Perry, D., & Delpit, L. (Eds.). (1998). *The real e[stet]bonics debate: Power, language, and the education of African-American children*. Boston: Beacon Press.

Peterson, B. (1991). Selecting books for beginning readers. In D. E. DeFord, C. A. Lyons, & G. S. Pinnell (Eds.), *Bridges to literacy: Learning from reading recovery* (pp. 119–147). Portsmouth, NH: Heinemann.

Peterson, D. S., & Taylor, B. M. (2012). Using higher order questioning to accelerate students' growth in reading. *The Reading Teacher, 65*(5), 295–304.

Pressley, M., & Afflerbach, P. (1995). *Verbal protocols of reading: The nature of constructively responsive reading.* Mahwah, NJ: Erlbaum.

Pressley, M., El-Dinary, P. B., Gaskins, I., Scuder, T., Bergman, J., Almasi, J., et al. (1992). Beyond direct explanation: Transactional instruction of reading comprehension strategies. *Elementary School Journal, 92,* 511–554.

RAND Reading Study Group. (2002). *Reading for understanding: Toward an R&D program in reading comprehension.* Santa Monica, CA: RAND Corporation.

Randell, B. (1985/1992). *Kitten chased a fly.* Bothell, WA: Wright Group.

Raphael, T. E., & Boyd, F. B. (1997). When readers write: The book club writing component. In S. I. McMahon & T. E. Raphael (Eds), *The book club connection: Literacy learning and classroom talk* (pp. 69–88). New York: Teachers College Press.

Raphael, T. E., Pardo, L. S., Highfield, K., & McMahon, S. I. (1997). *Book club: A literature-based curriculum.* Andover, MA: Small Planet Communication.

Richek, M. A. (1987). DRTA: 5 variations that facilitate independence in reading narratives. *Journal of Reading, 3,* 632–642.

Rolstad, K., Mahoney, K., & Glass, G. (2005). The big picture: A meta-analysis of program effectiveness research on English language learners. *Educational Policy, 19*(4), 572–594.

Rosenblatt, L. M. (1995). *Literature as exploration.* New York: Modern Language Association of America.

Rosenshine, B., & Meister, C. E. (1994). Reciprocal teaching: A review of the research. *Review of Educational Research, 64,* 479–530.

Rylant, C. (2000). *In November.* Boston: Houghton Mifflin.

Sabatini, J. P., Albro, E. R., & Reilly, T. (Eds.). (2012). *Measuring up: Advances in how to assess reading ability* (pp. 3–20). New York: Rowman & Littlefield Education.

Saunders, W. M., & Goldenberg, C. (1999). Effects of instructional conversations and literature logs on limited- and fluent-English-proficient students' story comprehension and thematic understanding. *Elementary School Journal, 99,* 279–301.

Scherer, P. (1997). Book club through a fishbowl: Extensions to early elementary classrooms. In S. McMahon & T. Raphael (Eds.), *The book club connection: Literacy, learning and classroom talk* (pp. 250–266). New York: Teachers College Press.

Schisler, R., Laurice, J. M., Konrad, M., & Alber-Morgan, S. (2009). Comparison of the effectiveness and efficiency of oral and written retellings and passage reviews as strategies for comprehending text. *Psychology in the Schools, 47*(2), 135–152.

Schwanenflugel, P. J., Hamilton, C. E., Neuharth-Pritchett, S., Restrepo, M. A., Bradley, B. A., & Webb, M. Y. (2010). PAVEd for success: An evaluation of a comprehensive literacy program for 4-year-old children. *Journal of Literacy Research, 29,* 531–553.

Schwanenflugel, P. J., Kuhn, M. R., Morris, R. D., Morrow, L. M., Meisinger, E. B., Woo, D. G., et al. (2009). Insights into fluency instruction: Short- and long-term effects of two reading programs. *Literacy Research and Instruction, 48*(4), 318–336.

SERVE Center. (2010). The effectiveness of a program to accelerate vocabulary development in kindergarten (K-PAVE). Retrieved from *www.serve.org/KPAVEd.aspx*.

Shanahan, T., Callison, K., Carriere, C., Duke, N. K., Pearson, P. D., Schatschneider, C., et al. (2010). *Improving reading comprehension in kindergarten through third grade: A practice guide* (NCEE 2010-4038). Washington, DC: National Center for Education

Evaluation and Regional Assistance, Institute of Education Sciences, U.S. Department of Education. Retrieved from *whatworks.ed.gov/publications/practiceguides*.

Sharp, D. L. M., Bransford, J. D., Goldman, S. R., Risko, V. J., Kinzer, C. K., & Vye, N. J. (1995). Dynamic visual support for story comprehension and mental model building by young, at-risk children. *Educational Technology Research and Development, 43*(4), 25–42.

Silverman, R. (2013). Investigating video as a means to promote vocabulary for at-risk children. *Contemporary Educational Psychology, 38*(3), 170–179.

6 + 1 Writing Trait® Rubric. Portland, OR: Education Northwest. Available at *http://educationnorthwest.org/resource/464*.

Smitherman, G. (1986). *Talkin and testifyin: The language of black America*. Detroit, MI: Wayne State Press.

Smolkin, L. B., & Donovan, C. (2001). The contexts of comprehension: The information book read-aloud, comprehension acquisition, and comprehension instruction in a first-grade classroom. *Elementary School Journal, 102*, 97–122.

Snow, C. (2006). Cross-cutting themes and future research directions. In D. August & T. Shanahan (Eds.), *Developing literacy in second-language learners: Report of the National Literacy Panel on Language-Minority Children and Youth* (pp. 631–651). Mahwah, NJ: Erlbaum.

Snow, C. E., & Sweet, A. P. (2003). Reading for comprehension. In A. P. Sweet & C. E. Snow (Eds.), *Rethinking reading comprehension* (pp. 1–11). New York: Guilford Press.

Stahl, K. A. D. (2004). Proof, practice and promise: Comprehension strategy instruction in the primary grades. *The Reading Teacher, 57,* 598–609.

Stahl, K. A. D. (2008). The effects of three instructional methods on the reading comprehension and content acquisition of novice readers. *Journal of Literacy Research, 40,* 359–393.

Stahl, K. A. D. (2009). Comprehensive synthesized comprehension instruction in primary classrooms: A story of successes and challenges. *Reading and Writing Quarterly, 25,* 334–355.

Stahl, K. A. D. (2011). Applying new visions of reading development in today's classrooms. *The Reading Teacher, 65,* 52–56.

Stahl, K. A. D. (2012). Complex text or frustration level text: Using shared reading to bridge the difference. *The Reading Teacher, 66,* 47–51.

Stahl, K. A. D. (2013). Today's comprehension strategy instruction: "Not your father's Oldsmobile." In B. M. Taylor & N. K. Duke (Eds.), *Handbook of effective literacy instruction: Research-based practice K–8* (pp. 223–245). New York: Guilford Press.

Stahl, K. A. D. (2014a). Fostering inference generation with emergent and novice readers. *The Reading Teacher, 67*(5), 384–388.

Stahl, K. A. D. (2014b). What counts as evidence? *The Reading Teacher, 68*(2), 103–106.

Stahl, K. A. D., & Bravo, M. (2010). Contemporary classroom vocabulary assessment for content areas. *The Reading Teacher, 63,* 566–578.

Stahl, S., Hynd, C., Britton, B., McNish, M., & Bosquet, D. (1996). What happens when students read multiple source documents in history? *Reading Research Quarterly, 31,* 430–457.

Stahl, S. A., & Heubach, K. (2005). Fluency-oriented reading instruction. *Journal of Literacy Research, 37,* 25–60.

Stahl, S. A., & Nagy, W. E. (2006). *Teaching word meanings.* Mahwah, NJ: Erlbaum.

Stanovich, K. E. (1980). Toward an interactive–compensatory model of individual differences in the development of reading fluency. *Reading Research Quarterly, 16,* 32–71.

Stauffer, R. G. (1969). *Directing reading maturity as a cognitive process.* New York: Harper & Row.

Stauffer, R. G. (1970). *The language-experience approach to the teaching of reading.* New York: Harper & Row.

Stenner, A. J., Burdick, H., Sanford, E. E., & Burdick, D. S. (2007). *The Lexile framework for reading* (technical report). Durham, NC: Metametrics.

Sulzby, E. (1985). Children's emergent reading of favorite storybooks: A developmental study. *Reading Research Quarterly, 20,* 458–481.

Swanson, E., Vaughn, S., Wanzek, J., Petscher, Y., Heckert, J., Cavanaugh, C., et al. (2011). A synthesis of read-aloud interventions on early reading outcomes among preschool through third graders at risk for reading disability. *Journal of Learning Disabilities, 44*(3), 258–275.

Sweet, A. P., & Snow, C. E. (2003). *Rethinking reading comprehension.* New York: Guilford Press.

Tabors, P. O., Snow, C. E., & Dickinson, D. K. (2001). Homes and schools together: Supporting language and literacy development. In D. K. Dickinson & P. O. Tabors (Eds.), *Beginning literacy with language: Young children learning at home and at school* (pp. 313–334). Baltimore: Brookes.

Taffe, S. W., & Bauer, L. B. (2013). Digital literacy. In B. M. Taylor & N. K. Duke (Eds.), *Handbook of effective literacy instruction: Research-based practice K–8* (pp. 162–188). New York: Guilford Press.

Taylor, B. M., Pearson, P. D., Clark, K. F., & Walpole, S. (1999). Effective schools/accomplished teachers. *The Reading Teacher, 53*(2), 2–6.

Taylor, B. M., Pearson, P. D., Clark, K., & Walpole, S. (2000). Effective schools and accomplished teachers. Lesson about primary-grade reading instruction in low-income schools. *Elementary School Journal, 101,* 121–166.

Taylor, B. M., Pearson, P. D., García, G. E., Stahl, K. A. D., & Bauer, E. B. (2006). Improving students' reading comprehension. In K. A. D. Stahl & M. C. McKenna (Eds.), *Reading research at work: Foundations of effective practice* (pp. 303–315). New York: Guilford Press.

Taylor, B. M., Pearson, P. D., Peterson, D. S., & Rodriguez, M. C. (2003). Reading growth in high-poverty classrooms: The influence of teacher practices that encourage cognitive engagement in literacy learning. *Elementary School Journal, 104,* 3–28.

Tierney, R. J., & Readence, J. E. (2000). *Reading strategies and practices: A compendium* (5th ed.). Boston: Allyn & Bacon.

Tompkins, G. E. (2009). *Literacy for the 21st century: A balanced approach* (5th ed.). Boston: Allyn & Bacon.

Underwood, D. M. (2013). *Part-time princess.* New York: Disney-Hyperion.

Van Allsburg, C. (1985). *The polar express.* Boston: Houghton Mifflin.

van Kleeck, A. (2008). Providing preschool foundations for later reading comprehension:

The importance of and ideas for targeting inferencing in storybook-sharing interventions. *Psychology in the Schools, 45*(7), 627–643.

van Kleeck, A., Vander Woude, J., & Hammett, L. (2006). Fostering literal and inferential comprehension in Head Start preschoolers with language impairment using scripted book discussions. *American Journal of Speech–Language Pathology, 15*, 85–95.

Vaughn, S., Chard, D., Bryant, D., Coleman, M., Tyler, B., Linan-Thompson, S., et al. (2000). *Fluency and comprehension interventions for third-grade students. Remedial and Special Education, 21*(6), 325–335.

Vygotsky, L. (1978). *Mind in society: The development of higher psychological processes* (M. Cole, Ed.). Cambridge, MA: Harvard University Press.

Walpole, S., & McKenna, M. C. (2007). *Differentiated reading instruction: Strategies for the primary grades.* New York: Guilford Press.

Wanzek, J., & Vaughn, S. (2010). Research-based implications from extensive early reading interventions. *School Psychology Review, 36*(4), 541–561.

Warren, W. H., Nicholas, D. W., & Trabasso, T. (1979). Event chains and inferences in understanding narratives. In R. O. Freedle (Ed.), *New directions in discourse processing* (Vol. 2, pp. 23–52). Norwood, NJ: Ablex.

Werderich, D. E. (2006). The teacher's response process in dialogue journals. *Reading Horizons, 47*(1), 47–73.

Whitehurst, G. J., Epstein, J. N., Angell, A. L., Payne, A. C., Crone, D. A., & Fischel, J. E. (1994). Outcomes of an emergent literacy intervention in Head Start. *Journal of Educational Psychology, 86*, 542–555.

Williams, J. P., Lauer, K. D., Hall, K. M., Lord, K. M., Gugga, S. S., Bak, S. J., et al. (2002). Teaching elementary school students to identify story themes. *Journal of Educational Psychology, 94*, 235–248.

Williams, J. P., Stafford, K. B., Lauer, K. D., Hall, K. M., & Pollini S. (2009). Embedding reading comprehension training in content area instruction. *Journal of Educational Psychology, 101*(1), 1–20.

Williams, K. T. (2007). *Expressive vocabulary test* (2nd ed.). San Antonio, TX: Pearson.

Zevenbergen, A. A., & Whitehurst, G. J. (2003). Dialogic reading: A shared picture book reading intervention for preschoolers. In A. van Kleeck, S. A. Stahl, & E. B. Bauer (Eds.), *On reading books to children: Parents and teachers.* Mahwah, NJ: Erlbaum.

Index